SIAM AND CAMBODIA

PORCELAIN PRACHEDI AT WAT BOH.

Frontispiece.

SIAM AND CAMBODIA

In Pen and Pastel

WITH EXCURSIONS IN
CHINA AND BURMAH

BY
RACHEL WHEATCROFT

Gian Publishing House

29/6 SHAKTI NAGAR • DELHI-110007 • INDIA

GIAN PUBLISHING HOUSE
PUBLISHERS OF BOOKS ON HUMAN CIVILIZATION
29/6 SHAKTI NAGAR, DELHI-110007

First Reprint in India, 1986

Printed at Goyal Offset Printers, Delhi-110035
and published by Smt. Gayatri Garg
for Gian Publishing House, Delhi-110007

INTRODUCTORY NOTE

In some slight degree sketches replace a common tongue, and the fact that I went forth to paint, occasionally brought me contacts that for lack of speech I should not otherwise have been able to make in the East.

Sir Walter Raleigh's hard saying, ' The real question to be considered . . . is . . . why should you write at all ? " here has answer : insidious suggestion. Friends and acquaintances urged me to put pen to paper, and I add the book to the sketches rather than the sketches to the book. They supplement each other and need little introductory comment.

The enjoyment of sketching was great, though the fact that I was unhampered by any idea of reproduction has added to the difficulty of making the reproductions.

I offer warmest thanks to those friends both Eastern and Western who made my ways plain for sketching and to others who threw light on facts and customs easy of misinterpretation by foreign eyes.

I tender special homage of gratitude to that friend who has saved me—almost by force on occasion—from many of the snares and pitfalls of our mother tongue.

R. W.

January 1928.

CONTENTS

ERRATA.

P. 8, l. 4, *for* "Stern paddlejunks" *read* "Sternpaddle junks."

P. 9, l. 25, *for* "Without walls" *read* "Within walls."

P. 28. The illustration corresponds *with* p. 21 *not* p. 28.

P. 206, l. 17, *for* "that scorn the" *read* "the scorn that."

LIST OF ILLUSTRATIONS

LIST OF ILLUSTRATIONS

CHINA

CHAPTER I

HONG-KONG, CANTON AND PEKING

FOR years the East had called, and called in vain, then, at last, the 'Adventure of the Coffee Pot' (my Magic Carpet), by way of Messrs. Christie's sale rooms, wafted me to Ceylon. And there I determined to stay and earn the money to go much further.

So for two years and more the hospitable Y.W.C.A. at Colombo gave me a home. I had a studio where to paint the hundred new subjects, enjoy the warmth, see my friends, and teach those adventurous spirits who trusted themselves to my artistic guidance.

Truth to tell, to give drawing and painting lessons is far from lucrative, but in time (and before I had by any means exhausted Ceylon) it made further journeying possible, and with real regret I left that beautiful island under the spell of an urge towards the sunrise.

Eastwards, the three things on which my heart was set, before reaching Siam on my return journey, were geographically not very easy to combine. They were: First, in Java, the Great Buddhist *Stupa* of Borobudur. Second, from Peking, the Great Wall of China. On reading the later adventures of Robinson Crusoe in very early youth, I had vowed a pilgrimage there, probably as being both more accessible and more comfortable an adventure than the Desert Island. Anyhow the desire to go there survived. Third, the wonderful Khmer remains at Angkor in Cambodia.

Other places and countries were to group themselves round these three, and each stage was to furnish the wherewithal for the next. And so it happened.

On the way to Java there was just one incident. When we were crossing the equator some bolts in the piston valve got loose, so that for the six hours it took to repair them we were anchored, I like to think, to that imaginary line, and moreover, in so improbable a region, we were glad to wrap up against a bitterly cold seeming squall which overtook us and tested the ship's steadiness.

I found that boats compelling my stay in Java must be either longer or shorter than I had wished, and it will be a lifelong regret that prudence and foresight—disguising the primitive instinct of fear—prompted me to take the earlier boat, and allowed only ten days to spend on the island. On getting to Ceylon the rupee at 1s. 4d., and with the purchasing power of only 1s., had alarmed my thrifty soul, and now the guilder, as unit, worth 2s., seemed to lead straight to ruin, so I felt I must get to China and find some work, but little realised what my feelings would be there, when I had to change my hard-earned rupees into the Mexican dollar, worth approximately 2s. 6d., a terribly large unit to one accustomed to the shilling !

From Java the voyage was excellent, but the arrival at Hong-Kong was a sad contrast to the day of oily calm on which we had sailed from Tandjoeng Priok, the seaport of Batavia. Then it had been hot, the sky slightly overcast, and the water so smooth that shoals of fish showed black through the green. By force of contrast visions of hurricane had passed before my mind, but I am glad to say we met nothing worse than a rather choppy sea as we neared Hong-Kong. South China junks with mothwing sails and high sterns loomed through a cold sea mist which completely hid the beautiful harbour.

My arrival at Hong-Kong was chilly in every possible way. It was not only foggy but getting dark. Hong-Kong hotels are prohibitive to a working traveller, and I knew of nowhere else to go. So to avoid a double move, and that daylight might cheer me in my search for a lodging, I took advantage of the captain's permission to spend the night on board. The ship berthed at the sugar refinery some miles away, and, by ill-luck, the company's launch did not come out next day as expected, so it was only by the courtesy of Messrs. Butterfield & Swire and the use of their telephone and their launch, that I found a lodging in Hong-Kong the second night !

I had hoped to get a room at the Helena May Institute. The rooms for passing guests, however, are few, and they had none for me, but recommended a boarding-house. It was really quite a comfortable boarding-house, only it smelled exactly like the same type of place in a 'seaside resort' in England !

To find that smell of mutton at the ends of the earth seemed an insult, the beginning of the rainy season abominable, and I was generally disgruntled. Moreover, of the people I had hoped to meet at Hong-Kong only one was available, and, in spite of his hospitality, I prefer to dwell on my return in lovely October weather when my impressions of the beautiful island harbour were very different. Other than an interesting trip to Canton, the one amusing incident of my stay happened when, on my way to embark on the Blue Funnel boat for Shanghai, I was lost by a ricksha coolie in Kowloon.

The ship was clearly visible from the ferry and close by. But with odds and ends to carry I took a ricksha, pointing out the ship to the coolie, and saying 'Blue Funnel.' The 'boy' nodded emphatically and started rapidly in the opposite direction, which did not surprise me, as though the wharf was near by the way to reach it was not clear. After a while I drew his attention with my umbrella and repeated my directions, but he still pointed ahead and went his own way. Presently a great sign across the street reassured me: 'Passage to Wharf No. 1'—until I found it opened in the wrong direction. Not a soul in the street who looked as though able to understand a question in English, but Fate had thoughtfully sent a European couple in front of me into the passage. Hurrying to overtake them I came within speaking distance when they were halfway up a flight of steps, and asked if they could direct me, but my question was cut short by the unexpected sight of a most lover-like embrace! Happily their absorption was not too great for them to have heard me. Possibly, too, they were startled at finding that though out of sight of the street, they were not alone; anyhow they turned and explained the coolie's mistake and my way. The coolie had insisted on bringing me to the P. & O. Wharf, and the lovers must have been delighted that my boat was not theirs. I only hope that kiss brightened their way as it had cheered me on mine!

Times had long been troublous at Canton, and though

incomparably less so than now, the beginnings of Bolshevism were already fermenting under Sun Yat Sen. He was a demi-god to the Cantonese, and injudicious as demi-gods are apt to be when suffering from old age aggravated by over-adulation. Fortunately for me just then no obstacles were put in the way of intending travellers. Although there was a railway there was no train service, nor was there telegraphic communication with Hong-Kong, but boats carried mails and passengers. The passengers were delivered punctually, pirates permitting, but of letters the same could not be said. The fault probably lay with the Canton Post Office. Pirates were a sufficiently real danger for us to carry a guard of armed Sikh Police, also the first class was divided from the second and third classes by a strong grille.

With more time to spare than the average tourist who ' does ' Canton in a day, going up one night and coming down the next, I decided to go up by day and see the river. A French missionary father who knew the country well was glad to talk, and gave me interesting information. In a pirate-infested country it was no surprise to see what looked like fortifications with villages clustered round them, but astonishing to learn that the enormous buildings towering above the dwelling houses were pawnshops, which play a pivotal part in Chinese life, family fortunes turning on them. Strangeness and interest culminated in Canton itself, although even in 1924 little was left there but the abomination of desolation and destruction. In his anxiety to cut all connection with the past, Sun Yat Sen was billeting his soldiers in the temples and the houses of the rich —presumably those of the *ancien régime*—and they were breaking up beautiful hardwood altars and furniture for fuel to cook their rice. Except in one small section the walls and gates of the city had been pulled down. Great spaces of the town were mere heaps of rubble where houses had been razed and left. Broad roads had been run through these heaps, but not metalled, so that they consisted of little more than a series of small craters half full of water, for here too it was wet. Whether the cause of this state of things was the craze for Westernisation or else ideas of imperative sanitary reform matters little. The desire for money was probably as ever at the root of the evil, for along the river front were stores and hotels rising many-storied in imitation of the west.

I was to see the famous five-storied pagoda, so we climbed up on to the wall over heaps of débris where temples had once stood. On the site of one of them, under a small *T'ingze* was a Chinese coffin awaiting burial. Very surprising to a newcomer was its size and strength, built, as Chinese coffins are, out of young trees instead of being made with boards.

The ruins were the result of several years' fighting round the city, partly also of deliberate destruction. Of the pagoda itself, standing on an angle of the city wall, nothing remained but a shell; still I was glad to have climbed there for the view and for my first near sight of Chinese graves with which the hillsides below were covered. Obviously this was a propitious site for burial, one favoured by the Geomancers, without whose advice no Chinaman would undertake so serious a thing as the choice of his last resting-place, or more especially that of his parents. Graves in China are set everywhere and anywhere, and often become a source of great difficulty when buying land for building. It was Ching Ming, the festival of honour to the dead, so they were being enriched with gifts of paper money burnt by the gravesides that its essence might accompany the spirits of the deceased. The graves were decorated with red papers, and crackers were let off—crackers enliven every imaginable event in China !

All this on one side of the pagoda. On the other a resurrection day to order was in process. Sun Yat Sen had decreed that that particular valley was to be put under cultivation for the people's food, and that each family must remove its dead ! Even to our eyes it was gruesome enough to see the poor remains dug out and spread on other graves. In any Chinese but the most hardened kind of anarchist it must have awakened ghastly fears of cruel haunting by the spirits of their insulted dead.

In extraordinary contrast to this enforced modernising were the few untouched streets of old Canton. Here it was difficult to believe that any change could ever come. In streets so narrow that two could hardly walk abreast, carved shop fronts, coloured signboards, lanterns, goods, and the always curious crowd made pictures at every step. Bankers, jewellers, ivory workers, embroiderers, sellers of porcelain, food merchants, merchants of every unexpected thing, novelty for every sense, not least for that of smell ! Canton streets are among the most picturesque I have seen, and Ess : bouquet Canton undoubtedly the most powerful, so the nose may gain what the eye will most certainly lose by the destruction of old Canton. The Foreign Concession, Shameen, trim and treeful, I only saw from the river, as I was the guest of American missionaries downstream at Christian College. I fancy the life on the river remains pretty much what it has always been, crafts of recent type do not oust the old. We even saw a large stern paddlejunk, the paddle wheel worked by two men on a treadmill, and a large part of the immense population has its home in a junk or even a sampan. The wharves were so crowded that to reach one's boat meant a scramble over barges, launches, sampans—all or any as it might chance.

At Christian College it was a real joy to be in the country, and no longer looking at it from train or boat. The College is on an island, fruit trees, at that season in full flowering, fringe the shore, and as we approached successive waves of scent brought information of land under intensive cultivation as practised in China and with Chinese thrift to which nothing comes amiss. The perfume of orange blossom was overtaken by pig manure ! Lichee flower of great sweetness was closely followed by potent smells unnameable ; contrast after contrast, the sweet generally strange and its complementary vileness but too familiar ! A fine place the College, and it is run on principles of inclusion by a fine body of men from various free churches. Mainly an American undertaking, there are British on the staff too—the vice-president at that time was a Scotsman, and Christian Chinese professors take the Chinese studies. All are united in their aim of elevation through education, and wisely, though they hope for the conversion of their pupils to Christianity, they do not urge it.

Besides the usual instruction a great deal of practical work is done for the betterment of conditions among the surrounding population. Also, as for instance in agriculture and industrial entomology, research work is undertaken. In 1924, when I was there, the silk trade had been devastated by disease in the eggs, and in the Christian College laboratories the bad were eliminated by means of microscopic examination, and only the sound put on the market—a great help to hard-hit growers. At that time the College was in a flourishing condition and doing excellent work both social and educational. Probably since then, together with the rest of the Western institutions in Canton, it has seen hard times. It would be interesting to know how the definitely anti-Christian spirit shown by Canton to-day on the Yangtse is affecting the work of the College.

The greater part of my short six months in China was spent at Peking, the very ugly northern capital, its many scattered beauties set in dust and desolation. Yet it is endowed with a charm that to most of its visitors is irresistible. I arrived when most of the residents were preparing their summer exodus. Appalling dust was the most obvious of Peking's drawbacks, but it was some time before I realised that the head and front of offending was in its shape. Nowhere any relief from right angles. The city's centre, the Forbidden City, as the foreigners call it, is an oblong without walls. Worse than a contradiction in terms an oblong centre is a contradiction in spirit! The walls of the Imperial City form a square outside the Forbidden City, though these are being rapidly destroyed, and soon only their memory will be left to prove my point. The Imperial City is a small square within a large one formed by the Tartar City, enclosed in its turn by the Tartar Wall, so-called, built chiefly in the Ming period. Among the many fine things in this uncompromisingly ugly town are the gates and towers which break and crown the Tartar Wall.

Against the Tartar City on its south side and projecting beyond it at either end is another oblong which completes the game of bricks ; this is the Chinese City.

As the general shape so is the inner plan. Endless dusty roads run through the city's length and breadth. One series pointing due north and south is cut by another that lies straight east and west. The orientation is always exact. The grand streets are desolate, the rest squalid, and dust is everywhere. On the Chang-an-Chieh, at the hour of the return home of the student class, it was always amusing to see elegantly dressed Chinese in handsome silks and brocades sitting back in their rickshas with a white handkerchief concealing the face.

Connecting the streets are *Hutungs*, lanes which turn constantly but always in angles. Perfect orientation is a fetish. Every house must face due north, south, east and west, and all that can do so turn their backs squarely on the street. And to the street, but for the entrance door, most houses show only blank walls. Private houses, that is ; for shops must of necessity display their wares, and the shopping streets are consequently the picturesque ones. The houses to Western ideas lack comfort and convenience. In summer this is compensated by their charm, then the screen windows are covered with gauze to keep out flies and give air, but in winter when they are closely papered and the rooms heated with stoves or a *kong*, the choice must be between baking and freezing. In Peking few houses have an upper story, and the small buildings of which they are composed are set round courtyards. In the larger houses there are several courtyards, one beyond the other or at right angles to each other. The reception rooms face north and south and the less important apartments and sleeping rooms east and west. So essential are the points of the compass that inside the rooms, if anything is to be moved, it must move north, south, east or west—never in so indefinite a fashion as right or left! And in the face of all this rigidity the root of my dissatisfaction discovered itself. What possibility of organic growth can there be in a series of squares? The principle of growth is from within, ex-centric, so that, the New Jerusalem notwithstanding, the living city must be circular! This conclusion caused me great satisfaction, especially the thought of the eccentricities, always endearing things!

I was to stay at the Chinese house of an English doctor, and arrived in the last days of May. Situated in the Imperial City, its central courtyard was gay with flowers and comforted with a weeping willow, a soothing contrast to the dust and glare without. At the end of the south court shade was given by an erection of scaffolding much taller than the roofs with a wonderful ceiling of rolling mats, so arranged as to be drawn back for air when the sun was off. *Pengs* they are called, and every house has one in summer. The wonder is the way in which they are made to stand quite firmly tiptoe on the surface of the paved court. The poles are not dug into it as with scaffolding at home, nor yet, like the crazy-looking bamboo scaffolding of the tropics, do they stand in tubs. Their whole strength depends on the way in which they are lashed together. It was a pleasant place to find at the end of the dusty two nights and a day from Hankow.

If sounds can be said to have a setting that was the perfect one in which to make acquaintance with the friendliest thing of beauty in Peking, flights of tame pigeons making as they wheel queer and thrilling chords, growing louder overhead, then fading into dim distance. Pigeons with aeolian whistles under their tails ! Eerie, pleasant, absurd and most fascinating ! The Chinaman loves birds and has an amusing way of 'airing' them much as we exercise dogs. He carries his bird abroad in his cage with an awning to protect it from the sun or wind. The cages are gorgeous, no fitting can be too fine for the rich man's bird, its seed boxes are of porcelain or carved ivory ! The poor coolie has to dispense with the cage, but he too has a bird, some poor common little captive, which he takes out tethered by the leg to a crossbar tied to an upright stick. Some English people in China told me that, after a bad fright from a cat, their canary, a beautiful songster, quite stopped singing. On the advice of a Chinaman he was taken out and the change gave him back his voice. Not humanity alone suffers from monotony.

In Peking the wish to possess a songster in a cage seems universal. In many small shops the singers, more shrill than pleasant, were crickets, as in Florence on Ascension morning. Unexpected surroundings in which to be reminded of the *Festa del grillo*.

Mandarins in full dress are hardly to be met with since the revolution, while to catch sight of Manchu ladies in wonderful head-dress and close shuttered carriage is an event—the ladies are to be seen at the cinema now. Mule litters, too, are very rare, but Peking street scenes still have a character all their own.

Funerals are always with us, and in Peking happily they are among the most attractive and cheering things to be seen; rich funerals, that is, the poor are, as everywhere, pathetic. Paradoxically weddings come second to funerals in charm, and both are attractive, largely owing to the beggars. There is a beggars' guild in Peking, and among the privileges they claim is that of carrying corpses and brides! For these purposes indifferently they are dressed up by the undertakers according to the riches of their employers in wonderful three-quarter length coats of green, under which the inevitable Chinese blue trousers appear pleasingly, except where bare leg shows through. Sometimes they are furnished with imposing buff top-boots, and always with grey felt limpet hats each stuck with a scarlet knife feather. Bearers from thirty-two to a hundred in number, or for the really great even more, carrying an enormous scarlet catafalque, make a picture extraordinarily brilliant in itself, apart from the rest of the straggling procession. Many decorative beggars carry prized belongings of the defunct to grace his official departure from this life. Others again carry full-sized paper images of cherished possessions, also of servants and animals, to be burned at the graveside, that their spirits may travel with his spirit and serve him in the new life. There is music from gorgeous lacquer drums of gold over red, and outrageous trumpets sometimes so large that two men must carry them. One holds the mouthpiece and blows a lugubrious hoo hoo hoo-hoo, which is all of its thoughts the poor monster can utter, while, with a hand behind him, the man in front supports the other end. In very rich funerals there are priests too with other musical instruments, pleasant little tinkling gongs. And, alas ! especially in military funerals there is frequently a brass band, a custom borrowed from the West, together with funeral marches which fail to add solemnity to the occasion. Many unlighted lanterns are always carried, and honorific umbrellas with flapping flounces in many shapes, sizes and colours, the prevailing tint generally red. There are dozens of other things too, banners, tablets, symbols, and except for the catafalque-bearers, who are kept in time by a man who beats two sticks together for the purpose, the procession straggles along at its sweet will, mingling with the traffic. Occasionally they are stopped by the gongman dressed all in red, and reassembled.

Often a funeral does not take place for months after the decease, as it is necessary that the Geomancers should find the most propitious day, and the greater the delay the better are their chances of making money. The night of the death, however, there is an interesting little ceremony, and traveller's luck gave me the chance of seeing it.

At dark friends of the family, holding bunches of lighted joss sticks, head a little procession. After them life-sized images of the cherished possessions of the defunct in paper, then the nearest male relations in white mourning garments, sobbing and staggering along in blind grief, and lastly, if the family be rich, grey-clad priests. At the nearest piece of open ground the paper models are burnt and the mourners kow-tow, and when all is over ceremonial grief is put aside, and all walk home like sane men.

At the burial the men of the family walk in front of the catafalque clad in coarse white cotton

THE EVENING AFTER THE DECEASE.

To face page 14.

with white shoes and white head-pieces, which are neither caps nor yet bandages. The women follow at the tail of the procession in mule-drawn Peking carts, their hoods covered with white calico. On each cart is a sign conveying the exact degree of relationship of the occupant to the defunct. At departure, and from time to time on the route, there are great bursts of realistic weeping, and every now and then a pause for well-earned refreshment at a temporary mat teahouse. Burial is always outside the city and the way is long.

A really fine Peking funeral is a wonderful pageant, with the endless colourful accessories and hangings both round the catafalque and scattered throughout its length. The priests add much colour, especially if there be Lamas in red and yellow robes.

There are no priests in wedding processions, however rich, but though they have not the largeness and grandeur of funerals there is the same charm of colour. The bride, completely shut into her scarlet sedan chair, needs but four men to carry her, as do each of her two duennas seated in green and blue chairs. It is possible to catch a glimpse of them through windows, but the bride's chair has none. Beggars are bearers in weddings as well as in funerals, but in weddings they only carry lanterns and drums and trumpets—the same old hoo hoo hoo-hoo, apparently as appropriate an utterance to herald a bride as a corpse.

The wedding chests have gone before in a separate procession. Ultra-modern Chinese dispense with all these jollities and merely hide the poor little bride behind a red curtain in a motor car. It is dull for the onlooker, but less of a long-drawn agony for the chief actress perhaps. Dreadful tales are told of how sometimes weddings have imitated funerals too closely, and a corpse has been lifted out instead of the awaited bride, suffocated on the long journey from a distant part of Peking, being completely boxed in as custom compelled.

There are lucky days on which to be married as also on which to be buried, so if one procession is seen there may very likely be more. Unless very urgent, my business was always set aside if there was a wedding, or more especially a funeral to be followed and sketched.

During my stay there was a disappointing absence of dromedaries in the streets. They do not come much into the town in the summer, and those that did come were changing their coats and very shabby looking. In the autumn the poor beasts had all been requisitioned to carry ammunition or rations to the armies. Twice endless trains of the fine creatures passed on their way through the city, the string reaching up and down the straight street as far as the eye could see. Splendid they were now in their new coats, with thick woolly ruffs all down the flat under-edge of the long neck, and wearing wonderful 'shorts' of thick wool on the legs.

Queer things and interesting things to be seen in the streets of Peking are legion. But Peking has been so often described that its glories are best left to writers who do not suffer from the curious sense of inimity that Peking always provoked in me. I only felt really at peace with it on the Tartar Wall. There one was above it, the part between Hatamen and the Observatory being specially attractive. A sad loss that, as I hear it is now closed to the public. Now the only place for one to exercise above the dust is the strip bounding the

WEDDING PROCESSION.

To face page 16.

Legation Quarter. From here, besides the two great gates—Hatamen and Chienmen—the Temple of Heaven may be seen in the distance, and even realised as being circular—the only circular space to be seen in an aeroplane flight over Peking ! For the groundling the only relief from straight lines is on the roofs of the houses. To baffle the malignity of evil spirits ridges and eaves dip slightly. It is a happy dispensation that, though malign, the spirits are creatures of one idea and stupid. So the wily Chinaman, knowing that they only move in straight lines, cunningly dips his roof, sets a screen in front of his door, and leaves them hopelessly puzzled.

A pleasant thing connected with my stay in Peking was a change of name. The drawbacks of matrimony did not attend it, nor, to be fair, did its benefits, and it was not necessary to pay a heavy poll tax either. More exactly, the change was to a new view of my own name. Chinese servants had quickly docked me of a syllable, but their version of ' Wheat ' as a Chinese name to be carved on my seal was not pleasing. So it having been expounded to them that *Wheatcroft* literally meant *Cornfield*, some Chinese teachers sat in conclave and decided that the name was best represented in Chinese by the characters *Tien shin gun*, which signifies literally *heart—field—plough*, and, by allusion, ' One who loves the land.' Completely ignorant of Chinese literature the allusion is to me obscure, but the name entirely satisfactory !

CHAPTER II

THE WESTERN HILLS

During my months in Peking, of the many things I enjoyed those that stand in my memory for delight are excursions outside the city. I had been prepared by photographs for the beauty of the Great Wall, but it was exciting beyond expectation. Besides the power that belongs to all great walls, the sense of fortitude and stability, there is an impression of active energy, as though soldiers were hardly needed to defend it, and its many watch-towers were for its own use only. It is an inspiration to stand on a Tower and see the Wall travelling determinedly as far as the eye can reach in either direction, up hill and down dale, discovering even in the valleys ridges on which to perch itself, a breathless impetus carrying it to the top of the highest hills.

Puffing up the pass by train the Wall had impressed me merely as a magnificent enclosure. The first hint of its livingness was at the station where we stopped. Here it fled from the mechanical monster which had cut it through, a headlong flight up precipitous hillsides leaving its stairway wrecked behind it. We joined it by a gentler slope, and found it broad as a lane, and generally in wonderful preservation.

The beginnings of the present civil war unfortunately prevented another visit, the railway being given up to carrying soldiers. My visit was in July, and the hills, obviously never very green, were completely bare. In the crannies of the Wall itself were hints of what wild flowers there might be, strange varieties generally of things well known at home: salvia, campanula, morning glory, etc. There were also Mongolians lying in wait for the innocent sightseers, with stalls of lemonade and other refreshments and plenty of faked antiques. I bought one which, after filling me with hope, to my joy nearly took in a European expert and his Chinese adviser! And after much climbing we were glad to succumb to the refreshments—but wished the sellers away for all that!

The Wall's look of primeval energy is deceptive, for it was not built when the world was young. Its beginnings were in the third century B.C., and according to Colonel Wingate, who made a study of it in 1907, it was probably built by degrees and in sections, not of hewn stone but of round boulders and earth. Its composition was of brickwork and masonry only in valley bottoms or passes. In the fifteenth century it was repaired, and reached its astonishing length of 1500 miles in the sixteenth, when 300 miles were added to it.

To look down from the Wall's broad summit only a paltry thirty or forty feet to its base is something of a surprise. The watch-towers, at intervals of approximately 200 yards, are about forty feet high, but in some places they are 4000 feet above sea-level. The part seen by most travellers and all the sections barring roads which invading Tartars were likely to follow were rebuilt of solid masonry by the Mings, as were also those places where it could be seen at a distance from the skyline.

Together with the Great Wall to me the most fascinating things in North China are the mountain temples. Many of those in the Western Hills have been described, and some are known to every traveller who stays any time in Peking. I had the good fortune to take two camping trips with experts in the art right off the beaten track, going from temple to temple, camping in them, and spending a few days at each—precious opportunities for sketching.

The rest of the party were great walkers, but my feet, softened by three years of town life in the tropics, were undone by the first day's march up a stony river bed. The winding stream had to be crossed six times, and four of the bridges had been carried off by recent floods and not replaced. To ford a fairly wide rapid stream running over a bed of big stones was quite a new experience for me. Moreover, the water was often waist deep, and had it not been for the strong arm of my host, it would certainly have been necessary to swim !

The Black Dragon Temple on its shelf of rock above the deep dark pool where the dragon dwelt (he did not appear to mind the intrusion of bathers) was small and falling into ruin, but well worth the journey for its lovely situation, though without special intrinsic beauty. The priest in charge had gone to Peking, and we had the place to ourselves. I slept (in a camp bed) on the *Kong* of a barn-like building possibly meant for a guest house. The *Kong* is a raised platform with space underneath for heating in the bitter North China winters. This was mid-September and not cold yet.

On our next lap, two days later, a donkey was procured for me, and that was also something of an ad-

KWANYIN, GODDESS OF MERCY.

To face page 20.

venture—my first ride astride, seldom having been on a beast before. Moreover, the paths were not such as to inspire confidence on foot, much less mounted. So at the end of the day's march I nearly fell off with stiffness. It may have been by the pity of the entrancing little Goddess of Mercy, at whose feet I spent the night, that the next day saw me comparatively fresh, and she arranged a wet morning to give me time to sketch her. But can I forget the carelessly committed sacrilege! Base ingratitude, though by her mercy it goes yet unpunished or perchance undiscovered. Among the vessels kept for the offerings of food to the deity at festival time was a pile of little earthenware plates, valueless but charming. My hostess and I agreed that to the owner a small coin found in exchange for a plate would seem a treasure trove, so I carried one off . . . and several days later it came over me that no coin had been left in exchange. . . .

The temple was quite insignificant, with no special charms except the goddess, and a courtyard gay with cockscombs and a loofah vine, where we had dinner. The mountains round are honeycombed with coal mines, primitive as to machinery, and at the little mining town foreigners were rare birds; so while we dined the people, wonderfully silent for Chinese, edged in and lined the walls, to gaze at us and our queer table manners! Our boys were kept busy between serving us and inviting the crowd to depart out of its own temple.

The next day's journey took us over a beautiful pass. By this time I was an expert donkeywoman, but at the first steep place very nearly came off, saddle and all, over my donkey's tail, because the collar had been forgotten—the owner's scarf answered the purpose for the rest of the way. The paths at the summit had been described to us as good. They may have been good by Chinese standards, outcrops of rocks in the shape of miniature dolomite ranges about a foot high serving as stairways up and down steep slopes and varying the monotony of flat stretches. Such as they were I occasionally preferred my own feet to the donkey's back, indeed for the last one and a half hours I do not believe anyone could have ridden, and with my host's shoulder for a second staff, I scrambled down on foot.

Our night's lodging, when we reached it after dark, was a nightmare temple tottering to the coal mine beneath which caused its subsidence. So insecure did it look that we all preferred to sleep in the open under a gorgeous but very cold moon.

The next day brought us to the goal of our pilgrimage, a very fine old Buddhist monastery owning extensive lands farmed by the monks. The other temples in which we had lodged were just the homes of the village gods with a monk in occasional attendance. Here beautiful buildings housed altogether superior deities, served by learned men—sages, I had almost said. In all the temples I was much struck by the number of images, always, I think, of Gautama Buddha, or Kwanyin, that by any standards whether of the East or of the West must be considered beautiful.

The monastery guest rooms were magnificent in intention, but whether the wealth of the community was chiefly of the past, or whether it was merely habitual lack of order, here, as in every other Chinese temple, the mixture of disrepair with grandeur was incredible!

The only Buddhist missionary I ever met was here. He had watched me sketching, and after approving of my efforts in dumb show, he fetched a book illustrated with some appalling Western pictures of the life of the Lord Buddha. Excepting on one page the text was Chinese, but he elaborately pointed out an announcement in Roman characters saying that if the reader should be interested and wish for instruction in Buddhism he should write, etc., etc. It seems probable that so much enterprise originated in America !

Most courteous monks all. One who received us and seemed to be in charge of the guests we at first took for the Superior. We had come in the name of an Englishman well known at the monastery and a *persona grata* with the monks. In our party several could talk Chinese with inferiors, but it was a misfortune that there was no Chinese scholar. None had the necessary vocabulary to converse with equals without danger of using disrespectful locutions instead of the customary elaborately ceremonial and flowery phrases. By way of showing that we had manners we collected all the visiting cards available—mine rather grimy from long living in my purse, as an identification card—and sent them before us. We could not have been more kindly received, so judged that our effort had been appreciated. The Superior, generally in dignified seclusion, once came to see a sketch I was making, an honour brought home to me by the sight of a monk who approached to address him, and kowtowed to the very ground while so doing. Instinctively one would keep at a respectful distance, for, on the tapering scholarly hands were the longest nails I have ever seen other than in a Chinese picture ! Wayfarers have little opportunity of meeting natives of social standing. Not only is there the language bar, but their introductions are generally to fellow Europeans. It is a matter of great regret that, except for a very few educated in the West, I hardly met any Chinese of quality and learning. Indeed, only twice did I see a courteous old man shake himself by the hand. It is sad to have brought away the impression of a people of shopkeepers and coolies, the only people I came across.

The monastery was an enchanting place, and in wanderings up and down its many courts terraced against the hillside I constantly discovered new material for sketches, many more than could be attempted in one short stay. It was tantalising that my feet were not yet equal to walks, for this was a valley of trees, woods and streams, alluring to explore in so denuded a land.

This monastery, like one much nearer to Peking, is celebrated for a drum solo played as part of its ritual late every evening and in the hours before dawn; thrilling rhythms to hear from a little distance, and a marvellous performance to watch.

The musician sat opposite the great disc probably nearly three feet in diameter, for the drum practically filled the upper room of the little tower. He played on it with flat sticks, of which he used the sides or the edges, not the tips. Often the stick in his left hand served only to limit the space set in vibration by the other, thus giving a quite wonderful variety of tone and colour. To the ear it was much pleasanter from outside, but I wanted a sketch. The expression of the whole, certainly not its details, brought the Pitti 'Concerto di musica' vividly to mind, and still does whenever I recall the scene. On our way to the monastery we had for some time followed one of the great high roads of North China. Perhaps eight feet broad, it travelled alternately over loose earth and live rock in the shape of miniature dolomites, as described above. Into these little mountain ranges generations of cartwheels had worn two deep ruts. It was disappointing that we never met even one cart much less saw two carts meet. Shockingly hard on the mules it must have been in any case, but to see the solution of that Chinese puzzle would have been interesting.

My last trip in the Western Hills was in late October, to the great pilgrimage temple of Miao Feng Shan—the Mountain of the Marvellous Peak. To go there we followed the Pilgrims' Way. This, while not much more than a path in width, is one of the very few made roads in North China, paved in its whole length. In the first stage my vivid recollection is of persimmon orchards. The trees, far larger and more bushy than any to be seen in an English orchard, were laden with large golden fruit, brilliant as oranges among sparse crimson leaves—the sight of the orchards alone would have been well worth the journey. The stage ended at the house of our host, Lo Ching Shan Chai, so christened by the late Emperor. In English the name sounds elaborate, though it is certainly appropriate, the Nature Lover's Mountain Lodge. It was situated in Ming Tao Kow, Cherry Glen by interpretation, the leaves, autumn-tinted, still made the foreground brilliant as it fell rapidly from us.

Below a mountain stream rushed, tearing its way between trees and boulders, with here and there a smooth sheet of water where the Fairy of the Pool might disport herself. Nearby she and other gracious spirits received due homage of incense and flowers each at their own shrine. The view from the dwelling house itself was broad, enclosed by fine outlines of ordered hills, blue and purple at sunset against a primrose sky. Half a mile up a steep glen on the other side of the stream the temple of our host was dedicated 'To all great men who loved nature.' The tablets of Keats, Shelley, Walt Whitman and Shakespeare, among English-speaking nature-lovers, and many another great one from every nation, were there in company with two fine old Buddhas who, when the village temple was overtaken by destruction, had found a refuge here.

The villagers, following them, burnt incense and made offerings to images and great men alike . . . till such time as their own temple, if ever, should be rebuilt.

One pleasant day, then we again took the Pilgrims' Way up and up almost treeless hills, through villages guarded by groups of poplars planted to furnish the villagers' coffins. Death and the preparations for death take much more room in the life of China than with us. It is not left to an undertaker to prepare a coffin in emergency, but every man of substance has one ready prepared, made of good young tree trunks and of fitting weight to receive him and the quicklime in which he must lie. As in China to be bodily substantial is a mark of a man of substance the coffin must be broad and deep ! A European might have some difficulty in providing himself according to his taste, and it may be that hospitality in coffins does not appeal to the Chinese mind. To picture one's feelings, if presented in life with one's coffin is difficult. Thus it happened to a young man who fell ill while working for the A.P.C. alone in a remote part of China:

Such alarming reports of his health reached Shanghai that a coffin was sent with the man who went to relieve him. And by the time the sick man was well again, relief—with coffin—arrived!

To return from a deathly digression—

At the Temple of the Eight Holy Ones the hungry were fed. Hardly more than a cabin, the worshippers must have been poor. After sketching the Ming tomb of some long dead abbot, one of a group dotted over a lovely hillside among scattered cypress trees, there was still a stiff climb, and at the top of the hill a donkey awaited me. Astonishingly, in view of the treatment usually received by dumb animals in China, it seemed to be the custom to spare donkeys on the Pilgrims' Way. I had found it was usual to dismount at the steepest slope on the first day's journey. I was glad to see this donkey, and mounted, but a couple of hundred yards astride on a wooden saddle not too well covered, and without any kind of stirrup, quite rested me, and made me most thankful that my feet were sound. So I walked the whole way. The last lap was a climb of over 2,000 feet, through sparse trees and scrub, a glory of autumn colour, to our goal, the pilgrimage temple on the summit of the bare Mountain of the Marvellous Peak.

Through the autumn dusk, and from our height of 5,000 feet, the view opened austere and chill far below in the broad valley framed with mountains to the plain twenty-five miles away, where twinkling lights just began to show. Regrettably we had to leave next morning early, so I saw no more of the temple than the guest rooms on the very edge of the cliff. A reassuring pine spread its arms just below to break a fall. My recollection of those guest rooms is ungrateful. The commissariat was wonderful, so the inner man was at peace. Oyster soup that night I remember. But the atmosphere of the place was eerie. Praises of Miao Feng Shan, left by masters of the art of caligraphy in gratitude for benefits received there, hung on the walls, and to my eye, devoid of understanding, the characters looked somehow evil. A stone floor of the coldest—the end of October at 5,000 feet is not balmy—and the flap-flapping of broken paper in the window screens throughout the night, made the icy wind more dreary, and sleep was scant.

A gorgeous sunrise called us up to the last of a wonderful four days' pilgrimage.

Endless in my vision of that day's march is the descent to the plain. First 2,000 feet down to the valley, and up again to a higher level than Miao Feng Shan, and after this suddenly the Pilgrims' Way, which we still followed, turned into a staircase. The work, it must have been, of that heavenly official, ubiquitous in Buddhist lands, the Grand Provider of Opportunities to Acquire Merit.

Slippery, utterly irregular, impossible steps ! Certainly much merit accrued to my companions for their patience in bearing with my slowness. Probably the staircase only occupied 1,000 out of the 5,000 feet down to the plain, perhaps even much less, and the rest of the walk was lovely. We even found a few belated mauve anemones on the windswept hilltop. All the same, great was the relief of arrival at Chueh Ssŭ, the

MINING VILLAGE IN THE WESTERN HILLS.

To face page 28.

Temple of Great Perception, on the edge of the plain, although with no energy left to perceive anything beyond the fact that it would have been a perfect place for a long stay, while inexorable Fate drove us on !

There had been doubt as to whether donkeys would be procurable, as the peasants were timorous, and feared their beasts would be impressed by the soldiery. My host, too, was expecting his pair of ponies, and felt anxious on the same score. Providentially we found the donkeys (this time with saddles and stirrups), and the ponies had arrived also, owing to the forethought of the groom. He had once served in the German Legation and still possessed some kind of an identity paper stamped with the Legation seal. This he had had the good sense to bring, and the sight of the seal had served to awe an officer who tried to take them into letting man and horses go ! Happily he was unable to read the document ! In Peking we had been living for some time under martial law, though I was unaware of it until I read the statement in the English papers. It had, however, long been brought home to the unfortunate peasant. We had noticed that ricksha coolies were getting scarce on the streets. Tourists had all gone. When the fighting came so near us as to be between Tientsin and Peking, the American Legation had warned its nationals that the train service would probably be stopped. In consequence there had been a sudden exodus of the many military on leave from the Philippines to whom Peking is a shopping centre. To some it seemed to be little else ; they came for rugs, furs, beads and curios, and time left over, if any, was devoted to sight-seeing. So had the ricksha coolie been allowed to choose he would have found himself in a quandary—either starve in Peking or go untrained as a soldier ! Happily Wu Pei Fu gave him no alternative.

That night we gained an unexpected pleasure owing to martial law. Before returning to Peking we were to have dined at the Summer Palace, but we arrived there late, and Peking gates were closing early, so it was arranged that we should spend the night camping in great comfort in the newly opened restaurant in the theatre near the stone boat.

On the occasion of my first visit to the often described Summer Palace, I was nearly the victim of an up-to-date version of Mr. Punch's picture showing an old gentleman who ran with his fourwheeler long ago, when its floor dropped out. One of a party of six in a closed hired car, I was sitting on a movable small seat and was suddenly alarmed to find myself sinking while my partner sank faster. The bumpy rattling road had been too much for an already delicate floor, and it had given way. The noise made it terribly difficult to get the driver to notice our signals of distress, and there was an uncomfortable interval of hanging on to nothing with our finger nails before the car could be stopped and we redistributed.

It had been summer then and the lotus in flower on the lake—derelict lotus only on this exquisite autumn morning—and we returned to Peking just in time for the Christian general Feng Yu Hsiang's *coup d'état*, when next day he quietly took possession of the city, and none but the authorities knew anything about it until the deed was done !

CHAPTER III

SOUTHWARD—THE YANGTSE TO CHUNGKING

I HAD decided to stay in Peking till mid-November, because an exhibition of my sketches had been arranged for me by the Peking Institute of Fine Arts at their gallery in the old Austrian Legation, but I was most anxious to get south before the really cold weather set in ; moreover it was likely that the difficulties of travel would increase.

It was already long since it had been possible to get to Shanghai by rail, and when fighting began between Peking and Tientsin, trains ceased running on that line too, except that every few days an ' International ' would come in. These trains were organised collectively by the foreign Ministries, and run by each in turn from Tientsin, in accordance with the agreement after the Boxer rising that communication should always be kept open with the sea.

At Peking it seemed as though they appeared and disappeared as they listed, and nothing could be learnt of their movements from the Ministries nor, of course, from Cook's. When one came in, *if* you could hear of its arrival *and* had your permit *and* could find room in it *and* discover the time of its departure, you might travel to Tientsin for nothing. And if you were lucky enough to have a friend on board, or at the particular Ministry in charge, you might be able to take your luggage at your own risk !

The engines made a brave show, draped all over the front with the flags of the Powers ; a rail-laying carriage was attached, and an armed guard carried. Naturally no undertaking was given as to the time taken over the journey, normally one of three hours. My permit was procured from our Ministry—rather, it was a request that I might be allowed to travel—but, in face of all the 'ifs' it was a great relief when suddenly we heard that traffic had resumed. I had meant to allow a few days for eventualities between leaving Peking and the date of my sailing, but Tientsin was overflowing with travellers, and I was glad to wait comfortably at Peking till the day before my ship was due to leave, intending to spend that night on board.

To take the morning train was a wise precaution, and the kind American missionaries, with whom I had been living, took me down to the station. It was lucky that I had interpreters, for it turned out that no train had come in for a day, and so there was none to go out, the military beyond Tientsin having commandeered all the rolling stock ! All the officials seemed to know was that there would be none that day or the next, and they would not even take charge of my luggage. So I left it at the Hotel des Wagons-lits close by, and we returned home to await developments. The first news we had next day was that a train had been seen to go out, and, a little later, that there would be another in an hour. Down we rushed to the station again, this time to find their money being returned to people who had bought tickets, because the train had been commandeered by the military !

However, the next morning there really was a train. I was introduced to a charming American going back to her home in Tientsin, to which she hospitably invited me, and we managed to get seats. The train was naturally heaped with people, and probably looked like one that crossed us, with people on the front of the engine, running boards, etc. We were among the lucky ones in being only three on a seat for two. Europeans on the train were few. No Chinese had been allowed to ride on the International trains, and crowds of them were waiting to travel. We were fortunate in our opposite neighbour, a courteous Chinese gentleman of the old school—he was one of the two who shook hands with himself in return for some trifling service, and I felt inclined to thank him for being so truly Chinese. Sad that so pleasantly characteristic a custom should be lost in favour of Western manners misunderstood, as to which misunderstanding no wonder ! In Chinese eyes the European has no manners. He can hardly even bow ! In learning English for use among equals no flowery phrases are taught him. In consequence, the student feels that if he adopts the freedom of European dress in which brocades and silks are not called for, he can throw off the incubus of manners also ! At a missionary college in Hangchow (1924—what has become of it to-day ?) the teachers had been dismayed by the sudden transition from Chinese courtliness to apparently total disrespect when their students adopted European dress ; so the heads took the wise step of giving a lecture on the manners expected in people of their pupils' standing when clothed *à l'européene*—with excellent results.

We had taken our places in the train at 8 a.m., but at ten there was still no sign of departure, and then, to our annoyance, an International puffed self-importantly into the station, gay with the flags of the nations. My friend had no permit, and my luggage was booked, so we made no attempt to change, but sat on in faith that our train really would start some day, a faith soon afterwards rewarded, and we reached Fengtai, seven miles out of Peking. Here we stopped again, and the crowd stretched their legs in the bright cold sunshine for about four and a half hours. The rumour went round that we were waiting for the International to pass us, which, to add insult to injury, duly happened. After five hours' repose we again started and crawled on to Tientsin. The Tientsin station was so completely blocked with trains, nose to tail, that we were stopped a good mile out of the station, and found the International immediately in front of us ! I was glad then that my luggage was booked, so that, instead of spending the bitter, brilliant night mounting guard over it, we left it on the train and walked into Tientsin, with coolies to carry the small packages, and reached my friend's house before midnight !

My boat was well missed. Berths were scarce and travellers many, so that I was very lucky to get one in eight days, being, meanwhile, most hospitably entertained.

As though in spite at my longing to leave China the brilliant weather turned to a gale on the day of our sailing ; it was admitted by the Captain to be a 'whole' gale. The little ship was, as the Captain said, like a saucer on the water, being without cargo because of the war, and we sheltered twenty-four hours outside the Taku Bar. When we did start we were so knocked about that we ran for shelter back to within ten miles of our starting place. Eventually, after five days'

THE PYRAMIDS AT I'CHANG.

To face page 34.

voyage instead of three, we reached Shanghai, and in a day or two I found a boat on to Hong-Kong. There, in soft sunshine, away from the oppressive sense of imprisonment by a northern winter, and doubts as to whether the war would hinder my escape from it, I had time to wonder whether in any other city than Peking, and especially under any Chinese general but Feng Yu Hsiang, we should have known as little about an occupying army in possession of the town. To be sure we were not supposed to be out after 10 p.m., but if foreigners out after hours were stopped, it was only to ask for their name and address. True, too, out beyond Ssŭ Paillou there were three heads exposed to show the fate awaiting soldiers caught looting, but it was the only instance reported.

The Christian general had a wonderful reputation to maintain. Help and service had been *freely* rendered by his men in the disastrous floods near Tientsin the previous July. A reputation this almost unbelievable in comparison with the conduct of soldiers in general. At Nanking and Chungking the tales of cruelty and plunder were hideous. We heard a horrible account at Nanking of a theatrical manager who had insisted that some soldiers should pay for their seats at the play, and of the tortures they inflicted in revenge. Everywhere the barbarous tyranny of the soldiery over the civilian population was unbelievable. The sight of a uniform seemed to paralyse justice, and the poor civilian might beg in vain for redress when a soldier had wronged him.

At Chungking it was of everyday occurrence that a whole big boatload of market produce should be seized and no compensation given to the unfortunate cultivators, and of every man-load of coal or water, both of which came up from the river, heavy toll was taken by the guard at the city gates. The oppression of daily toil, as we saw it at all the ports on the river, seemed little less, unceasing drudgery to class the workers with their beasts rather than with men. The coolies, when taking off cargo or loading it, ran up and down the gang planks at a staggering trot without ever straightening their knees. It was impossible to go slowly for the weight they carried, and they were trained to utter strange sounds as they went to prevent stiffening and straining their chests. Small wonder that people who spare themselves so little should have but slight consideration for their beasts. Why should donkeys' legs not tremble under their loads when their masters load themselves till they must go or drop? Small wonder in face of such hardship, and with so little to lose, that the Bolshevism sown broadcast in their midst should have found fertile soil. That the worker should have his turn to rule and browbeat must seem the merest justice. Even had they knowledge of Communism's tyrannies these would still seem less than the slavery of their present lives. The toil is certainly no less nor are the soldiers kinder masters, but being Chinese they must have noise, and probably still lighten their labours with the everlasting chaunt we heard as the cargo was being piled in the hold. Every time it rose to a high note as the load was thrown into position. At some port where they worked practically all night there was a tenor with a huge voice; he was always one note higher than his mates and dwelt a second longer on the note, and always there was the click clickety-click, made castanetwise by the clerks with the tally sticks, as they were collected at the hold's entrance. All ugly enough, and both monotonous and disturbing, but unforgettable.

There was generally time as we touched at a port, when steaming up the Yangtse, to paddle round in the mud and see something of the town, the whole look of things wonderful and new to me.

Wu hu, where the beggar women come paddling round the ship in tubs with their babies to excite the pity of the charitable—the foreshortened view of them from above very comical. Picturesque Kiukiang, noted centre of a porcelain making district.

Hankow, from the sightseers' point of view dull and comfortable and European looking. Living there the comfort and clean pavements would have an altogether different value. Quite apart from political feeling, that the stability and opulent appearance of the British river front should awake covetousness was inevitable.

Between ports the landscape was the more monotonous for the unceasing rain—flat land under cultivation, occasional villages, buffaloes, peasants—all dangerously near the edge, it seemed, for, from time to time, the mud cliffs, undermined by the water, collapsed with a great splash.

Somewhere along the Yangtse I was first pained with the sight of small feet, a really ghastly deformity with all its implications of suffering. In Peking Western education for women is checking it. Also a clever Englishwoman, a *persona grata* among highly placed Chinese, persuaded some influential families to pledge themselves against it. Not only did they promise to leave their daughters' feet to nature, but also that their sons should not marry women with bound feet. So the fashion was turned against the cruel practice. One wonders how many generations it will take for the new fashion to filter down through the classes to the custom-ridden peasants whose womenfolk stump about the fields as on wooden legs—wooden legs, but alive and shockingly painful.

Most of the towns were full of beggars and of piteous, mangy, starving, pariah dogs. From one town, I'Chang, I think, both had been cleared by an enlightened Governor. The second change of boats for the journey up through the famous gorges is at I'Chang. Leaving the gorges just above I'Chang torment and turmoil cease, and the river widens into peace. Far across the water opposite the town are lazy-looking hills, Nature's first effort for some hundreds of miles to shake herself free of the endless plain through which the river had brought us. They are known as the pyramids and are of extreme simplicity. Peacefully we waited several days till boats of English or American lines kept at Chungking by a fall in the water's level should be set free to fetch us. No hotels at I'Chang, by the courtesy of their Captains travellers are passed on from one boat to the other, living in each for the length of its sojourn in port. Rather than spend my time in this way to the unceasing chaunt of the port coolies I decided to take the first boat to come down. This was the *Shu Hun*, the famous first passenger boat to travel up the gorges on her own steam. British built, and in her palmy days British owned, she had long been superseded by more showy and luxurious boats. Her record on the river, however, was excellent, and she had the great advantage of an observation chamber forward above the bridge.

HELD UP AT WANSHIEN.

To ace page 38.

She was now flying the French flag and sailing under a French captain, the property, so he told us, of a Franco-Chinese company. That the company was wholly Chinese, and the French flag and very entertaining captain theirs for hire, I discovered at Chungking. In consequence the insurance rates for goods carried were just double those obtaining on British or American lines ! Further we had the protection of armoured plating, behind which we were called at two places where shots were frequent. None came, however, on either voyage, although on boats before and behind us Chinese passengers were wounded, and we could see the brigands leaning on their guns.

Our single adventure was on the way down. No one travels by night on the upper reaches of the Yangtse, the river is too treacherous. Wanshien was one of our stopping places, both going up and coming down, and we tied up opposite the town about two miles out across the immense and rapid stream. On the up journey we stopped in early afternoon, and before we could go ashore were interested to see great commotion on land. Through the ship's compradore we were informed that there were public executions toward, and nothing would satisfy an American woman of the party but to try and see them. To my immense relief it turned out to be pure fabrication, but I narrowly missed running into some later at Chungking, and heard the shots. To see the corpses fell to a man of the party.

We wandered round the extremely picturesque but filthy town, where I was more disagreeably impressed than in any place I have visited by the unfriendliness of the atmosphere. This was an unpleasant recollection when, on the return journey, in the middle of the night, we were surrounded by 200 soldiers in lighters.

At 1.30 a.m. I was awakened by the cocking of a revolver and the Captain's voice:

'If you do not leave the ship at once I will shoot myself.'

Imperfect English, I realised, and no intention of suicide, and so too did those to whom he spoke, for several pairs of feet padded past my cabin with exclamations of: 'Hé hé hé hé hé.' The lights were switched off, grilles let down, and I jumped to my venetians to see what was happening. For a few minutes nothing more, but there were soldiers in lighters below. Then came cautious footsteps and voices: 'Don't shoot! Don't shoot!' and after that parleyings in the Captain's cabin which lasted till 4 a.m. Happily for my curiosity it was all in French through an interpreter. The soldiers said that they had orders to search the ship for opium. The Captain, 'that this was a French boat and his Admiral wouldn't allow him to tolerate a single armed man on board. If the officer would leave the ship and return with four men unarmed, the Captain himself would head the search, but not otherwise, because his Admiral, etc., etc.' The dialogue *da capo ad infinitum*, with but slight variation. And all the while *I* knew that *he* knew that *they* knew the "Admiral" was nothing but bluff!

It was certain the poor man couldn't be enjoying himself, because the line between soldiers and brigands is tenuous, and besides, his predecessor in command of the *Shu Hun*, while on another boat, it is true, had in January of the same year, been hauled out of his berth at midnight, put up against the smoke stacks, shot and tossed overboard to join the corpses which are a not uncommon sight in the Upper Yangtse. The *Shu Hun* was fortunately tied up just below our gunboat, the *Teal*.

At 4 a.m. the Captain lost patience and said that if all soldiers were not off the ship in five minutes he would megaphone the *Teal*, which he accordingly did. Her Captain at once offered to come over, and so the soldiers decided to believe the Captain meant what he said, and departed. Soon after I heard the search begin and went to bed. In the morning, lo ! lighters and soldiers still all round. Sufficiently remarkable on a Yangtse boat, no opium had been found, and the motive of the hold-up was still undiscovered. A messenger had been sent to the Commandant of Wanshien asking his leave to proceed, but the answer came presently that the Commandant had telegraphed to the General at Chungking, and until his answer came he could not take the responsibility of letting us go.

At about 11 a.m. we were surprised to see the soldiers loading their rifles. We could see no reason for this unless they had suddenly realised that the *Teal's* guns were turned on them. Wanshien has long enjoyed a bad name and no chances are taken there.

Unfortunately one of the rifles took matters into its own hands, and went off, badly wounding two of the poor half-trained lads who thought to manage it. Many of them looked no more than fifteen years old.

After that we had a guard of four British sailors from the *Teal*. I was the only British subject on board, but it seemed right that in so isolated a position all foreigners should stick together. At noon we were suddenly told we might go, and the Captain did not stay for a second bidding. It turned out that the company at Chungking had had the temerity to refuse a passage to the General and a hundred armed men, and this was retaliation for the slight. Except for the two poor wounded boys, and the Captain's hurt feelings; the whole episode had been farcical.

There was no time to get through the gorges, owing to the late start, which gave us the unexpected pleasure of a night in a very wild place. Normally we should only have broken the journey from Chungking to I'Chang at Wanshien; much too rapid a journey for enjoyment of the scenery. To come up the gorges takes only one day, too short for all there is to see, through water pitted with whirlpools. Even where no whirlpools are visible whole stretches of the river's surface are at a visibly lower level than others. The river was at mid-height. At that time the most dangerous of the rapids is the Yeh T'an (the word signifies Wild Waters), and to get through without hauling was a triumph for the boat. Most exciting to see the offended rapids rise high in a great wave above our bows, and wash over the main deck.

Corpses, human and other, seem to be the natural burden of the ghoulish stream, and we wondered how many were those of the patient fishermen frequently to be seen on the rock at the water's very edge. They appear to have stood there from all time, dipping their nets with a rhythmic movement unceasingly, only to be washed away by a freshet at last as a fish was about to be caught. Or they might be the victims of the reward offered for saving property: the corpses I saw were clothesless. There is a reward for saving life too, but that is not so large. And then ancient wisdom decrees

IN THE YANGTSE GORGES.

To face page 42.

that the life you have saved is yours to maintain, which, if the saved should be of an idle disposition, is a terrible tax on a poor man. After all, what is man to flout the gods who will to destroy?

But, in spite of tradition and rewards, there are life-saving stations, and little red life-boats which are said to do good work; though, in these days, steam has power over its parent water, and there is not nearly so much for them to do.

In anti-foreign movements one of the cries is always that steam has killed the junks, but the true murderer is squeeze. Every few miles through the Gorges, at any possible landing was a little white flag signifying 'Stop here and pay,' and woe to the sailing boat that disregards the notice! With so many calls for money it is cheaper and safer to convey both person and goods by a steamer, so we saw but few junks, and very little of the much described tracking, and never the enormous teams of coolies harnessed to their bamboo hawsers that we had been led to expect. Twelve to twenty was about the usual number. In many places it was hard to guess where man could find a foothold on the inhospitable cliffs. In one chasm, perpendicular walls on either side of it, a gallery for 'trackers' is cut high up in the cliffside.

On the banks the sudden change of level to slope, slope to cliff, cliff to flat rock or open valley gives the gorges their fascination. At one point peaks rise almost sheer 3,000 feet out of the river, and the variety of colour in the very rocks is amazing. Added to this it was May, and in that damp, warm climate the greens of the vegetation clinging to the rocks were at their most vivid and varied. On any gradient where cultivation was possible cereals were ready to reap. Every here and there, on some inaccessible-seeming rock a pagoda or temple was perched to gain merit for a pious builder and be a place of rest for good spirits. Every town on the banks builds one pagoda upstream and another down with this hospitable intent.

At one point in the gorges we had been amused to see a low rock covered with what looked in the distance like large yellow toadstools, and which turned out to be soldiers sitting under their umbrellas in the sun. An umbrella is part of every grey clad Chinese soldier's equipment, as also a fan, and why not? Only it seemed incongruous a little further up to see a squad doing the goose-step on a modern-looking parade ground.

Beautiful as it all was, and in spite of grumbles at modern speed, by the time we got back to the open the horror of captivity had almost descended on me. Consider that in a junk that journey would occupy weeks!—six to eight perhaps! To me less than adventurous, a vision of horror.

Outside the chasm there were probably bodies of man and beast, but there was space, and they were not aggressive. Although the sense of oppression is no longer there dangers are not over. Wrecks point a warning from perils of submerged rocks in a narrow channel.

It had been told me in Shanghai that the activities of the various war-lords might make it impossible to see anything of Chungking, our furthest point of call and one of the most important cities of China. Happily, though soldiers were everywhere, there was no fighting, and it was even possible to telegraph from I'Chang and to receive a reply at Wanshien. According to pessimists unless I telegraphed there would be no more than time at Chungking to present my letter, but, on the other hand, to telegraph was practically useless and a waste of good money. The military simply took treble rates for an urgent message, and put it aside till convenient ! However, luck was with me, and the pleasant result was a week at Chungking.

A huge, picturesque and altogether hateful town, squatting like a spider on its shelf above the river. From the water, then at about middle height, like most of the river towns, it appeared to be scrambling up the river bank on numberless toes ; the stilt-supported cabins built yearly outside the city walls by the river fishermen, and yearly swept away by the rising of the waters.

All Europeans leave the town for the summer, and come in daily to business from the hilltops across the river, carried up and down the precipitous 1,000 feet by four sure-footed bearers. The range is of sugar-loaf pattern, like nursery picture-book mountains, and follows the river. On its further side is a paddy-terraced valley, then another sugar-loaf range, and, after that, a deeper, broader valley and a higher, wilder range where the robbers dwell. My hosts were on a hilltop of the first range. They had gorgeous views of river and monster town, smoke-shrouded at their feet, with lovely distant hills to distract their thoughts from its dinge. A mere handful of Europeans lives in isolation there, amongst hordes whose tolerance turns not infrequently to definite anti-foreign feeling. To be one of them, and to keep a cheerful outlook on life, is heroic. Not only is there occasional definite danger to be faced—that is sometimes bracing—but any sense of security is constantly lacking. The week of most hospitable entertainment I spent on those heights is one of my treasured recollections of China, but as a home, with the thought of the gorges between me and the outer world, it would be a nightmare.

It often happens that some incident connected with a place stands for it in the mind as a symbol. Chungking is summed up for me by the recollection of an incense shop by which we passed several times. A vision of hopelessness—always the same four blind men driving a mill to crush sandalwood. They leant against great wooden spokes driving them round backwards, the despair on their faces clearly visible.

In contrast to this the pluck of my hostess, who never lived in the town if she could help it, but spent her days alone on the hilltop, except at such times as the various Consuls saw fit to call their nationals together for protection. On the hill her only guardians, besides her Chinese servants, were six or seven dogs of various breeds. Hearing them particularly noisy one morning, I looked out to see her taking a soldier by the sleeve with a gesture of right-about-turn, which she followed up by putting a stout staff in his hands. At the dogs' chorus she had come out to find him belabouring them, and had taken the stick from him. The Chinese are intensely curious, and curiosity had brought him to the house in spite of warning notices. So dogs had attacked, he had defended himself, and their mistress had defended them. Even Europeans are usually cautious in their dealings with Chinese soldiery.

Before leaving China for the enchantment of the tropics, one thing seen at Nangking must be described.

SUGAR LOAF HILLS ACROSS THE RIVER. CHUNGKING.

To face page 46.

Others have told of the sights of the town. That which most of all thrilled me was a modern Chinese parallel to the making of saints in the European middle ages; only this saint was self-adjudged, and called himself a god, probably better rendered an immortal.

Quite newly arrived in China we had been questioning the guide, a very intelligent man, a graduate of Nanking University, where he had learnt to speak fluent American, about the distribution of Buddhism, Confucianism and Taoism in China. In reply we were told that any Chinese who said he was of one religion to the exclusion of the other two lied. We had probably expected a less uncompromising statement! In any case, it was a hard idea for novices to assimilate, especially as the temples of each religion were entirely separate. Later he puzzled us by asking if we had ever heard of a man who became god in his lifetime. He explained that, conscious of having earned immortality by a holy and austere life, a monk or nun would, as they felt death approaching, ask for the test. The notabilities of the district were then summoned, and in their presence the dying man (or woman) was lifted into a huge jar where he sat in the attitude of meditation, the witnesses being present until his death. Still in the presence of the witnesses the jar was sealed and put into the temple, and if, in the course of three years no intolerable smell warned the temple goers that the would-be god had mistaken his vocation (this had happened a short while since with an aspiring nun!) at the end of the time the same witnesses were summoned to see the seals broken and the jar opened, and if no sign of corruption were there, 'not so much as a little finger nail missing,' it was recognised that the holy man was god indeed, immortal because incorrupt. Compare this quotation :

'Another kind of evidence once held in high favour was the incorruption of the supposed saint's body. Of the Blessed Charlemagne. . . . Otto III made search for his body and discovered that the embalmed remains were still incorrupt' (*Times Lit. Sup.* 30th Sept. '26).

If so proved immortal his mummied face was overlaid with gold together with his hands, and in fine raiment he sat in the temple for the worship of the people.

One whom the guide had known on earth as a virtuous and just mandarin, and also in the monastery whither he had retired about ten years before his death ; at whose death and sealing, and also at the breaking of whose seals, he had been a witness, was in Nanking, and might be seen by us. The guide was obviously and honestly sure that there had been no possibility of tampering with the body, which we were greatly interested to see. Under the figure seated in a glass case was a photograph of the mandarin ten years before he left the world, became a monk, and died in the odour of sanctity. But the likeness was still striking, and the golden face a fine one. At his shrine many miracles of healing and comfort were worked, and people brought him their requests from afar.

That in our thought humility was too much a part of holiness for the expectation of bodily immortality to present itself to the mind of a Western saint, although aspiration might carry him far beyond it, was as new an idea to the guide as the contrary had been to us. As he told his tale visions of surreptitious embalming crossed our minds, but he was so sure that there was no room for trickery of any kind that one searched for other possible explanations. After all, are there not at the Capucini of Palermo and in a monastery in Malta shrivelled remains dried up but not embalmed—a fact of common acceptance? Two doctors admitted that the following natural process was not an impossible one. If he sticks to the rule of his order the Buddhist monk touches no food from midday to dawn, and more and more as he advances in wisdom, the cravings of the body are denied, so that the saintly man is probably the dried and wizened man too. (There is a Chinese saying about a large body showing a large heart, but that must be for the laity!) In the monk's case little moisture is left at death to corrupt the body, and what proof is there that death really takes place until after the great sealing? The idea of a reward such as immortality might so hypnotise the man whose physical vitality is lowered by austerities, that he passes into a catalyptic trance, and so gradually into death, the jar being sufficiently porous to disperse the little remaining moisture from the tenuous body of the ascete. That the climate is far drier than ours must be remembered. I afterwards heard of similar self-canonisation in various parts of China. There is, for instance, a famous Emperor-Saint in his temple of the Western Hills near Peking, where his mummied body is still venerated. In that intensely dry air no jar even was necessary.

Quite an interesting cicerone, our Nanking guide. He gave horrible accounts of the oppression of the soldiery, and their cruelty towards the civilian population—probably due to the instinct of the ill-used in his turn to oppress whom he may. The guide's optimism suggested that things in China might take three hundred years to settle down ! At that time, 1924, there was no anti-foreign feeling. It would be interesting to know whether, at this juncture, he considers the prospects brighter for his country.

Anyhow, in China burlesque treads happily on the heels of tragedy, and to end my chapter I will tell about the railway station at I'Chang, which cannot be bettered as a tale of audacious disingenuity.

There was a scheme a few years ago to run a railway through the hills into Szechuan, where the gorges are now the only road. The undertaking was extremely costly and a subsidy had to be obtained. The very first use made of the money was to line the pockets of some local contractor by putting up a railway station worthy of so important a place, and in connection with which all his relatives and friends might find employment—from stationmaster downwards ! After that, as it was necessary to show a definite mileage before more money was forthcoming, they laid lines on the only flat ground available towards the hills, and then to make up the mileage without the cost of tunnelling more and more lines were laid, all parallel with these ! That at least was the tale as told, and I did not learn if the further subsidy materialised, but the railway station stands proud and lonely outside the town for all to see.

CHAPTER IV

ANGKOR IN CAMBODIA

AND at last towards Angkor the Beautiful and Indescribable.

Of the three places I most wanted to see Angkor is that to which I should best like to return. If possible I should go there the same way as before, the water way, because for the traveller who likes to 'see comfortably and write dangerously' (if need be !) there is nothing so pleasant as river travel. Over and above other advantages it gives the lonely traveller a chance of meeting with others and joining them in excursions which would be difficult alone, except possibly by the spending of much money, a thing I was greatly concerned to avoid ! It turned out pleasantly that almost the whole of the party with whom I was to see Angkor embarked on the same boat with me at Hong-Kong. Two French couples, Government employés at the end of their term of service, determined to see Angkor before returning to Europe, joined us at Saigon. The rest of the party, except for one fellow countrywoman, was American. It is truly astonishing to how few people in England Angkor is even a name. Is it generalising too much to say that in the Far East the British travel for profit rather than pleasure, and that Malaya is, roughly speaking, the tourist's limit ? Those countries which interest us materially are unavoidably those of whose beauties we know most. But never to have heard of Angkor ! To forestall a frequent question—Cambodia is a French protectorate north of Indo-China and south-east of Siam, and Angkor is a stretch of jungle north-east of the great lake Ton-le Sap, strewn with wonderful remains covering much ground and many centuries, roughly from the fifth to the thirteenth. Gorgeous temples chiefly, gateways too, and terraces, moats and fortifications, everything that was built of stone the jungle has both destroyed and preserved.

Here clearly are the remains of a great civilisation of high artistic accomplishment, yet, strange as it may seem, hardly anything is known of its creators. The people were called Khmer, and they still call themselves so, but to foreigners their country became Cambodia after their mythical founder Kambu.

Some will have it that Kambu was helped to civilisation and power by the Serpent Gods and married the daughter of Naga, others that he was the son of Indra's daughter and the Serpent King. Either version serves to explain the domination of Angkor by the Naga throughout the period of Khmer greatness.

Primitive Serpent-worship expressed itself later in the Hindu myth of the Great Churning, and in Buddhism the Naga was honoured as the Guardian of the Master. He is to be found in every temple, on the great terrace, and at every city gate, but most of all at the latest and most complete of the temples, Angkor Wat. There he remains undisputed master, his the one image that has remained in the temple, faithful servant first to Siva then to Buddha.

The race seems to have descended from a fusion of

ANGKOR WAT FROM PHNOM BAKENG.

To face page 52.

aboriginal tribes with invaders from Central Asia. In their type, as shown by the statues in the museum at Phnom Penh, the Cambodian capital, and in the temples, there seems to be a hint of Egypt, as there is also

AN OLD CAMBODIAN MONK.

a feeling of the Egyptian pylon (much attenuated) about the massive gateways. The first is probably a fanciful likeness, and the second quite superficial owing merely to the fact that the arch was never used. To support the weight of the superstructure on a lintel the walls are sloped on the outside so that seen in section they are like buttresses.

The most famous of the temples is Angkor-Wat, probably because it is the most complete, being also of the latest period, dating from the twelfth century, that is. The excellent little Bungalow Hotel stands just across the broad moat—nearly 700 feet wide—and opposite the main entrance so that the view of the temple may be enjoyed at all times, and it is easy to stroll in and out of it.

The walk is longish, across the causeway over the moat to the great portico and galleries, and thence straight on through the immense square to the three terraced stories of the great temple in the centre. If the explorer wishes to reach the central tower he must climb a very Jacob's ladder, great flights of stairs of unimaginable steepness, every step twice as high as it is deep and by no means regular. Was the idea in designing them purely architectural or was the ascent planned for the acquiring of Merit—Merit, fetish of the spiritually short-sighted the world over, of those people who would measure growth with an inch-tape. Anyhow, to walk instead of sitting my way down was a proud moment of self-conquest—but, then, what of the pride? But the tower is worth the toilsome climb, in any case. In pre-Buddhist days, so we were told, the temple was dedicated to Siva. The great central tower sheltered the *Lingam* and was open to the worship of the faithful on every side. It is now divided into four recesses, and in the one facing west is a gilt bronze Buddha of great beauty. The setting sun's last rays play on him like a golden searchlight leaving only the head always remote in mysterious shadow.

Within the great enclosure lives a small Buddhist community, their apology for a monastery a mushroom growth of wood and matting which seems to cringe to the great ruin now in the keeping of the state. The

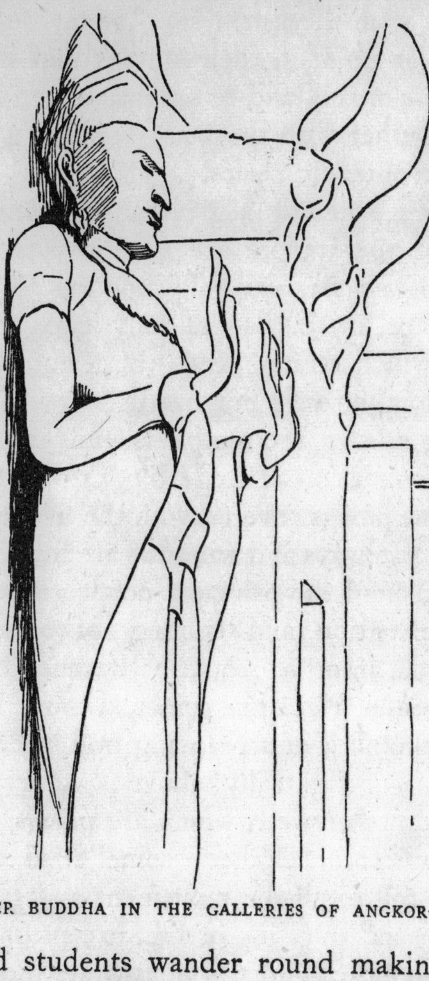

KHMER BUDDHA IN THE GALLERIES OF ANGKOR-WAT.

monks and students wander round making offerings to the Buddha of the tower and his satellites, and to another group on a lower level, which together with a model of the sacred footprint, a very moderate one, only 4 ft. 11 in. by 2 ft. 6 in., are for some reason more to be venerated than the many other fine ones in the bat-haunted galleries. The warm colour of the monks' robes is a welcome note in the grey buildings. The Cambodians' robes have more variety than those of other monks, even the Burmese. It may be to denote some particular point in their studies that many have an under-dress of red, and red sashes are frequent and delightful together with the many tones of yellow and orange of the outer draperies.

Tourists are evidently a great amusement to them, and many of the juniors are glad to practise their French. English was naturally not the *lingua franca* either there or in Java—the only two countries I touched in which strange and wonderful versions of my mother-tongue were not heard !

The great pile of the temple is built in grey sandstone on a foundation of huge blocks of laterite, and every available part is covered with the liveliest designs in low relief, gateways and windows are framed in them and every pillar of the principal portico is so covered. Gaiety of invention and subtlety of execution are perfect. Birds, animals, people, arabesques, everything is there. In one frieze the principal motif is a figure dancing on the neck of a prancing bull or other beast, and this runs delightfully above a series of sham pillared windows between which are panels of demure ladies magnificently clothed, some staid and some posturing, a foil to all the movement and gaiety. All is decoration and pure joy of life, except on the main building, where the history or at any rate the conquests of Cambodia cover the outer walls with glorious sculpture. Here the captured Siamese are led in

NAGA BALUSTRADES. ANGKOR WAT.

To face page 56.

triumph. They later avenged those humiliations, themselves the conquerors in the end, carrying off the emerald Buddha; it is to this day Bangkok's chief treasure, and Cambodia's king remained the vassal of Siam till in 1867 the French acquired the protectorate.

In these sculptures elephants, horses, chariots and men pass in ordered procession; further on is the wonder-working confusion of a pictured battle in which chariots and horses run and prance on the heads of other horses and chariots, and from these exploits the transition to mythological scenes is not abrupt! The whole series is executed with glorious energy and decorative power. Though now in decay a permanent spirit of youth pervades the whole temple, and it is difficult to imagine it more beautiful when it was young indeed. That there was much gold and colour faint touches remain to show. It is hard to believe that this early gorgeousness would not rather mar its present excellent dignity.

If Angkor-Wat had been, as we were told, a temple dedicated to Siva, the symbols characteristic of him either in his character of Creator or Destroyer are curiously absent. In the temple generally, overwhelmingly the most frequent sculptured motif is the Naga—the King of the Serpents—the multi-headed cobra. Manifold he edges and crowns every gable and is on every gallery of the many towers, and it is he who rears his sevenfold head as terminals of the balustrades in the causeway. He it is also who, his long body held by numberless human supporters, defends the gateways of Angkor Thom, the town of Angkor. But at the city gates it would seem he is no longer the Great Ancestor, or rather, that the emphasis is now on the Ancestor's great deeds, for demi-gods on one side and giants on the other take us back to the Churning of the Sea of Milk, vivid and detailed in the bas-reliefs at Angkor-Wat.

Beyond all other beauties of this temple are the grandeur of the whole conception and the wonderful proportions of the buildings. The moat is foursquare,

A CAMBODIAN PEASANT.

the outer enclosure being 6,060 yards round, and the causeway from portico to inner temple a quarter of a mile long.

The main group of buildings is in three tiers of galleries rising by terraces to that in the centre which culminates in a huge tower, as already described, and at the four corners of the pile are other smaller ones. None of these are towers as we know them, but rather domes drawn up by steps or galleries to a point; assuming the general outline of a rifle cartridge.

By the light of a half moon on the terrace of the great portico we saw a play by dancers, village girls trained by an ex-actress of one of the royal companies, the actors looking, both in dress and gesture, as though they had stepped from the reliefs on the temple walls. As usual the adventures of Rama and Sita fantastically unrolled themselves. The uncertain glare of torches held as footlights by a half-circle of crouching, grinning small Cambodians, was the most attractive part of the performance. Apart from the charm of the setting the acting did not impress me greatly.

A couple of miles away along a pleasant road is Angkor Thom. The walled city was the home of the Khmer sovereigns, though of their palaces little indeed remains beyond the gorgeously sculptured walls of the terraces. The city was built at the height of their power, in the astonishing limit of forty years between 860 and 900 A.D., and forsaken in the fifteenth century. Crowned ladies still sit in long rows on walls, and we have Garudas as caryatids and, better still, lovely Tewadas have descended from the Hindu heavens to lend themselves to the work. The most delightful of them all is at the prominent angle of a terrace, she, for the joy of holding a lotus-bud in her joined hands, supports the coping with her wingtips.

All these help to uphold the immensely long Terrace of Honour which forms the front of the Phimean Akas where was the king's palace. The terrace is 1,000 feet long and covered with a marvellous variety of sculpture in high relief. Here, side by side with conventionalised Garudas, semi-conventional Tewadas and portraits of

Queens and Court ladies, we have the magnificent record of an elephant hunt, exciting beyond all the rest because it remains topical to-day as it was then. Every animal is magnificent in character and realism so that certainly each owner would unhesitatingly pick out his own beast. A gorgeous procession abounding in life; some of the elephants carry not only masters on their backs together with their pets, but their trunks hold the game that has been killed, such as deer and other animals.

And, close by, flanking the central flights of steps which lead up to the terrace, there are the triple elephant heads to be found also in the recesses of the town's gateways. These heads are completely formal in style, each trunk dropped straight to form a column, and every tip curled round a bunch of drooping lotus-flower, while the heads are crowned as for some ceremony.

Chow Ta Kwan, with the rest of Kublai Khan's embassy, must have mounted these stairs to do homage to the Khmer King seated at the amazing golden window.

At first sight it seems strange that traces of human habitation should be so few. Only dwellings for the immortals, it is said, were made in the stone brought from afar. Perishable wood sufficed for mortal man; these wooden dwellings are delightful as may be seen to this day. The town is a parklike place, where the trees have been cleared from trespass on the many fine ruins, and a well-kept road runs through it, from which branch charming glades. In one of these sits a gigantic Buddha in meditation, while a little way behind him two disciples of much smaller stature stretch out their arms towards him. Some way in front two of the lion-dog variety called by the Siamese Norasinghe smile

GIGANTIC BUDDHA AT ANGKOR THOM.

ineffable satisfaction at their task of guardianship, and tall trees shade, without crowding, the Master.

It is a place to lure the wanderer, but I walked care-free only so long as I had the strength of mind to keep away from the dark Bayon. The Bayon dominates the whole town, and willingly or not most people succumb to its strange attraction. The smile on the hundred lips of its many towers—smile of derision, toleration, benevolence, who shall say? The expression of the one gigantic face (repeated four times at least on every tower and turret) depends on so many things—the changing light, the weathering of the stone, injuries from passing time, and not least the beholder's mood. It may be the face of Siva, or as some say, that of Brahma. Anyhow it has a fascination that is indescribable. The cumulative effect of the numberless heads, alternately beautiful and repellent, is tremendous. Four monstrous faces back to back under one lotus crown make the top of every tower and every turret; the great central tower built very much as children build sand castles with moulds from their pails, four or more as a base and one on the top, has many more than the crowning four. Evidently the original intention was that this tower should stand free; but its weight proved too great, and a platform (with more headed turrets) was added to strengthen it, thus, unfortunately, masking many exquisite sculptures on the lower stories of secondary towers surrounding it. On a postcard showing a general view of the temple from the north thirteen towers besides the great one in the centre are visible. There are fifty towers in all, so the hypnotic effect of the staring eyes may well be imagined. Actually the eyes look straight before them, but often the effect is as of downcast lids, and doubt grips as to whether or no one is being transfixed by the gaze above the complacent smile. Whether the heads be of Brahma or Siva they stand there in the forest timeless

BRAHMAN HEADS AT THE BAYON.

To face page 62.

symbols of ceaseless vigilance in the Creative Spirit. Four-faced heads are over all the gates of Angkor Thom, and deeper yet in the jungle are similar isolated gateways once guarding the entrance to great temples, now watching only the increase of nature as she strives to cover the very faces with the roots of her giant growth.

DANCING APSARAS, BAYON.

On the lower levels of the Bayon is life of a very different kind, light-heartedness pure and simple in the troupes of dancing Apsaras. On every side of every square pillar on the ground floor of the temple are three Apsaras dancing with the completeness of movement of a swimming frog. Apsaras dancing round the windows of shrines and round the shrines too. Their gaiety is infectious and takes no heed of the great faces. They might not even know they are there. With enchanting poses of fingers and toes, and a rhythm of movement that brings music to the ear, they dance upon their lotus flowers. Their dress is of jewels and crowns, and there is a suggestion of wings about the lower parts of their bodies—wings not growing from the shoulder blades, as we Westerners imagine them. With all their movement, wonderful to relate, they almost always manage to keep their crowns straight as they dance in bowers of branching arabesque! Not all the ladies dance, some are motionless, standing quiet with fascinating smile, doubtless waiting for their turn to dance. There are worshipping figures too, and many others and everything except the wonderful faces of the super-world is on quite a small scale.

Among the detached figures I remember one especially. He was at the end of a long gallery, a Buddha or a Vishnu sitting on the coils of the cobra and sheltered by its head. Seen from a distance he has the look of a living man in meditation, so that one goes quietly for fear of disturbing him. But in this Bayon as at Angkor-Wat the most important sculptures, excepting the great heads that *are* the temple, are on the walls of the lowest galleries. Scenes of marching armies with wonderful elephants, I recall. Nautical scenes, boats on river or sea, with fish in types and varieties to rejoice the heart of him who tells fishing stories. Scenes of work-a-day life among the people and of feasting among the great, also the preparing of their food by slaves who are divided from them by monkeys and birds in trees. To me the Bayon is the most fascinating thing in that enchanting Angkor. The hovering eeriness of the place took hold on me when one afternoon, lost in a drawing of the Siva heads, I looked up to see before me a tall Cambodian, his lower limbs wrapped in a red tattered cloth and on his head a high crown like those worn by the dancing divinities, only this was copied in wild flowers and leaves! He said nothing, but presently vanished as silently as he had appeared. . . .

Gorgeous as are the temples; it is their setting above all which makes Angkor unique. There is but one hill and that artificial, and of course temple crowned, but from its top, except for Angkor Wat and the long line of its moat close below, the view is across mile upon mile of tree-tops; and such trees! It was there that I first met the Giant Diptocarp, who stands head and shoulders above the other inhabitants of a tropical forest, none small, shaking himself free of them by dropping his lower branches and growing straight as a rocket till he can spread himself uncrowded in upper air. He is full of resin, and the natives make great holes in his flank to bleed him for their torches.

Ficus, as everywhere, were various and many. Many ruins half destroyed by boring roots in their young eagerness for life are now held together only by their grip as they grow through and on them. In one of the outlying temples—Greater Angkor covers an immense tract of jungle—were the biggest trees I have seen at all, the upper part of their roots consisting of buttresses such as are common to many tropical trees, but of enormous size, and the roots themselves running for yards along the surface of the ground, thick as a well-grown oak—the very image of the python of childish nightmares!

Not only were there trees, but flowers. It was nearly Christmas, and cold weather—comparatively. In the few other places, where luck has led me to the forest, it has always been said that only in the hot weather could I hope to see flowers. But here there was at least one creeper in full flowering. Less unlike ageratum than anything else I know, the blossom, insignificant but with a honey scent that filled the air, lay like a pale mauve mist on the tree-tops as they lay below us on the summit of Phnom Bakeng.

Blossoming out of time here and there were other things too, just to show what that land could do an it would !

As with flowers so with insects, I suppose, and I marvel what might be seen and heard there in the hot weather. On the day we came, standing by the moat not far from the hotel, we thought it irritating to hear an electric bell of particularly high pitch ring on and on, but soon discovered it was no bell but one of the myriad cicadas. Oh ! the din of their chorus and the relief of their sudden silence.

There is plenty of game at Angkor, but we saw no wild animals—except little bullocks which turned wild at the sight of us and whose antics entertained us vastly. The bullocks were harnessed in pairs to little carts not unlike unsophisticated *tongas* with a white umbrella growing out of their middle. These carts were advertised at the hotel as conveyances for tourists, and had been hired by some of the party, to the immense joy of the rest of us, for the lively scene it procured. The cattle would keep jumping round to look at the white horrors they were expected to convey, and their disgust was such that in spite of elaborate subterfuge on the part of would-be passengers who climbed in over the back of the cart, one yoke managed to free itself entirely and pranced off, so that the expedition had to be given up. Other means of locomotion were motor-cars (the roads were excellent) and minute ponies not much bigger than Shetlands, perfect mounts for an expert donkey woman, for, though they went a little faster than donkeys, being so near the ground one's sense of security on their backs was no less !

The two elephants must not be forgotten. Coming down from the top of Phnom Bakeng I had my first elephant ride, and much the most uncomfortable I ever remember, on one of those always uncomfortable beasts !

With them end my personal impressions, but two authorities must be quoted :

Chow Ta Kwan, the engaging Chinese diarist before mentioned, writing in 1296 A.D., and M. George Groslier, who, deciphering various stelae, has thrown fascinating light on Angkor in the heyday of its glory.

CHAPTER V

A THIRTEENTH CENTURY OBSERVER AND MODERN DEDUCTIONS

First, to give some idea of the fabulous number of people who inhabited temple precincts. There is a stele at Ta Prohm which gives a list of the temple's dependents. The whole number appears to be 79,265, of whom 12,640 lived in the temple. Of these 18 were principal officiating priests, 2,740 secondary priests, and 2,232 assistants, among whom were 615 women dancers. Within the temple grounds there must therefore have been whole streets of little wooden or bamboo houses on piles, such as may be seen at Siém Réap to-day.

Elsewhere we are told of hospitals within temple precincts which had doctors, assistants and nurses, both men and women. Amongst other duties they were expected to care for the infirm and old who came to worship.

M. Groslier has found corroboration of this information in the few débris unswallowed by the jungle, but of houses built of such perishable material naturally few traces remain. Moreover, Chow Ta Kwan in his notes says of private houses that 'All common rooms are thatched, only the family temple and private apartments may be roofed with tiles.' Here and below I translate from M. Pelliot's French version.[1]

[1] *Bulletin de l'École Française de l'Extrême Orient*, tome i. 1901. Hanoi: F. H. Schneider.

THIRTEENTH CENTURY OBSERVER

Practically nothing is known of Chow Ta Kwan personally, but his notes on Angkor are vivid. I am in full sympathy with his flabbergasted admiration for the lavish use of gold, even to such extent as it is to be seen to-day in Siam, Burma and elsewhere. At Angkor he speaks of two golden towers, a golden bridge, golden window frames to the Council chamber, and above all, the Golden Window within which the King sat to give audience :

'The Palace official dwellings and the houses of nobles all face the East. The Palace (Phimean Akas) is north of the Golden Tower and the Golden Bridge. . . . In the Council Chamber the window frames are of gold.

'In the Palace is a tower of gold at the top of which the King sleeps. The natives hold that the spirit of a nine-headed serpent inhabits the tower and he owns the kingdom. Every night he appears as a woman. . . . If a night should come when the serpent fails to appear it is that the time of the King's death has come.'

The King's dress was worthy of his golden frame. He wore a golden crown—a high pointed diadem like those worn by the dancing Apsara and their modern descendants, and the King of Cambodia to-day. This was evidently tiring, and on other occasions he 'encircled his chignon with garlands of scented flowers of a kind like jasmin. On his neck he wears nearly three pounds of large pearls . . . bracelets, golden rings set with cat's eyes. . . .'

The soles of the King's bare feet were stained red and so were the palms of his hands. (The noble ladies reddened their soles and palms too, but not any men except the King might use the stain.)

The golden sword, the 'Prah Khan,' in the King's hand was the legendary gift of Indra to Cambodia's ancient monarchs. It is now in the Palace at Phnom Penh. There it was shown to me as a piece of wonderful eighth century goldsmith's work. The hilt is of gold, and the blade, about one metre long, of iron, wrought near the hilt with figures of Indra, Siva and Vishnu in relief.

'The sovereign has five wives, the first of the household proper (*l'appartement privé proprement dit*) and four for the four cardinal points. As for concubines and others I have heard tell of 3,000 to 5,000. . . .

'For my part every time I had entry to the Palace I saw the prince come out with his first wife and sit at the golden window of the private apartment. The people of the palace held back under the window on both sides of the verandah and filed past to see. I was able to get a glimpse.'

Palace customs are among the intimate details about which, he naïvely remarks, more than once, 'It is hard for a Chinese to know these things.'

Although lost in admiration of the Khmer riches and grandeur he did not approve of all their customs. And he shook his head over all the bathing that went on :

'People often are ill, their too frequent baths and incessant washing of the head has much to do with it. Often they recover unaided. Many lepers take up their position on the roads, but though they live and eat with them people do not catch their illness. They say it is a disease they are accustomed to in the country. Once there was a king who caught it, he was not scorned for that. In my humble opinion it is excesses in love and abuse of baths that bring on this illness.'

'They have no coffins for their dead but only matting. They cover them with a sheet. . . . When they get far outside the town to some uninhabited place they leave them there. . . .'

The rest was for the dogs and vultures.

'If it is all over quickly they say their relations had acquired merit.'

Some people were already beginning to burn their dead. These were 'all descendants from Chinese,' he says rather proudly, though at the same time deploring the number of his fellow-countrymen at Angkor, as it tended to lessen their prestige. The Cambodian populace he thought very simple because of the 'respectful fear' they showed the Chinese, prostrating themselves to earth before them and calling them *Fo* (Buddha). Unfortunately the sight of a Chinaman was getting common and some Cambodians dared to defraud and deceive them !

We do not know whether Chow Ta Kwan was a big man, but he thought the horses very small and was astonished that they should have no saddles nor the elephants carry seats. He was much interested in plants, and enumerates those vegetables that he already knew at home : onions, mustard, leeks, aubergines, water-melons, pumpkins and marrows. There were also a few fruit trees common to both countries. Of vegetation generally he says :

'The kinds of trees are numerous, and flowers still more abundant, having beauty and perfume. Water flowers are of a thousand kinds, but I do not know their names.'

'The new Prince's body is so sheathed in iron that even if knives and arrows should strike his person they could not wound him. Thanks to this precaution he is able to go out. I spent more than a year in the country and saw him go out four or five times. When the prince goes out, cavalry heads the escort, then come standards, pennons and music.

'A troupe of from four to five hundred Palace maidens clad in brocades and with flowers in their hair, hold great tapers ; even in broad daylight the tapers are lighted.

'Other Palace maidens follow, carrying the royal plate of gold and silver and the complete set of ornaments, the whole of very various shapes and of uses unknown to me. Next Palace maidens carrying lance and shield who are the Prince's bodyguard form a troupe too.

'After that goat carts and horse carriages all decorated with gold. Ministers mounted go forward gazing afar ; their red parasols are innumerable. After them come the king's wives and coucubines in palanquins, in carriages or on elephants. They have certainly more than a hundred parasols trimmed with gold. Behind them is the Prince, standing on an elephant, in his hand is the precious golden sword. The elephant's tusks are cased in gold. There are more than twenty white parasols trimmed with gold, and with golden handles. Numerous elephants are round him and he is protected by cavalry.

'If the king should go to some place nearby he only takes a palanquin carried by four palace maidens.

'Most often when the king goes out he visits a little golden pagoda in front of which is a golden Buddha.

'Whoever sees the king must prostrate himself and touch the earth with his forehead ; this is called San Pa.

Otherwise he is seized by the Master of Ceremonies and not let off lightly.

'Every day the king gives two audiences for affairs of state. There is no set list. Officials or people wishing to see the prince sit on the ground to wait. After some time distant music is heard in the palace; and outside conch shells are blown to welcome the king. I have heard say that he only uses a golden palanquin; he does not come from far. A moment later two palace maidens may be seen to lift the curtain with their little fingers and the king, holding the sword, appears at the golden window. Ministers and people put their hands together and strike the earth with their foreheads. When the sound of conch shells has ceased they may lift their heads. At the king's good pleasure they also approach to sit down. At the place where they are seated there is a lion skin which is looked on as a royal appanage. When business is over the prince turns round; the two maidens let the curtain fall and everyone rises.

'Thus it may be seen that although it is a kingdom of "Man and Mo," they have a great idea of a prince's dignity (*ils ne laissent pas de savoir ce que c'est qu'un prince*).'

An *aperçu* of Groslier's theories about the Angkor to which he has given a great part of his life must be given for the light they throw on the wonderful group. His dictum that the Khmers were no architects is astounding to the lay traveller, but when the temples are compared with the churches and cathedrals of Europe at the same period it is easy to see that the Barbarians of the North had the science that was lacking in the luxurious civilisation of the tropics.

Architecturally speaking the plan only of the great temples is splendid. Groslier is the first to admit that the Khmers were great artists, but the construction remains infantine from start to finish and there is no development whatever.

The use of the keystone was unknown, so that there could be no arches, and vaults were built with overlapping stones of which the top one was a lid.

Another surprising observation is that, contrary to frequent statements, all that the Khmers took from India was their religion in the first days of their greatness and its mythology, in short, their intellectual equipment.

In architecture they only learned the use of stone for what had previously been made in wood, witness their use of stone as beams and boards.

In one important respect the idea of their temples was exactly opposed. In India tall Gopura surround a low sanctuary, whereas at Angkor the holy of holies is under the central and most magnificent tower.

The enormous extent to which Indian mythology influenced their art is seen in the great bas-reliefs. On the other hand, material things, weights, measures, and objects generally, seem to have come from China, as did also the first wave of Buddhism—Mayahana Buddhism—for in one temple Avalokiteçvara is specially honoured.

In Chow Ta Kwan's day he speaks of the temples bare of images but for one great figure, so that Hinayana Buddhism from the south reigned then as it has ever since.

According to Groslier there had been a revival of Brahmanism between the two, Vishnavite this time.

ANGKOR WAT FROM THE BUNGALOW. DAWN.

To face page 74.

And through all the changes the Great Ancestor apparently remained unforgotten.

Groslier tells us that the temples were twice pillaged. In the first invasion, presumably by unbelievers, altars were overturned in search of treasure, and at a much later date the appropriation of iron and lead was the cause of roofs being dismantled wherever the great T ties in use to bind the pillars were likely to be found.

In the days of Angkor's glory not only the town but the setting was strangely different. Round it, where forest now stands, was a great zone of cultivation. This was necessary for the people's food, but also, as Groslier points out, if only for use in scaffolding, trees must have been sacrificed for miles around. Then there were the wooden ceilings and floors of which only slight traces remain, destroyed long since by tropic insect life. His view is corroborated by the fact that for a largish radius none of the slow-growing trees which count their lives in centuries are to be found. Chow Ta Kwan says that Cambodian carpenters did not know the use of saws, and only used hatchets to cut wood.

East and west of the city were two immense tanks, probably fed by the Siém Réap stream. Now they hide under rice cultivation, and only archaeologists can trace them.

In the city itself we hear that the temples' tallest towers were crowned with flagstaffs flaunting waving banners—always beautiful (even on Selfridge's roof); but for my part I find it hard to believe that the lost grandeur can have approached the charm of the tree-embowered ruins as we know them.

The soul of the city has survived to tell of a nation of great artists, but though wonderful skill remained to them always, invention seems to have waned. Groslier comments on the extraordinary reiteration of motifs. They are very numerous, to be sure, but repeated and repeated in every temple with but slight variation. Nor does the skill increase through the centuries, for, at Angkor Wat, where decoration runs riot, carving sometimes suffers from a sense of slickness and recipe. The Apsaras' feet, for instance, beautifully foreshortened at the Bayon and other early temples, are here merely twisted aside. Yet, in the mind of its builders Angkor Wat was clear from its inception, therefore Groslier calls it the Triumph of Intelligence, whereas to the Bayon, where there are signs of groping and change of plan, he gives the palm for the Triumph of Soul.

It was almost a tragedy to discover, when the allotted five days at Angkor were over that, for Bangkok, it would have been easy to embark at Kep, travelling by bus from Phnom Penh, the Cambodian capital, instead of going all the way back to Saigon, to sail thence. Had I but known it when booking at Hong-Kong, this would have given me a week more at Angkor; but thrift brought resignation, because the passages back to Saigon and thence to Bangkok were already paid!

The same tiny lake steamer that had brought us up from Phnom Penh was to pick us up at Siém Réap, the port of Angkor.

From the modern Cambodian point of view Siém Réap is quite an important place and a headquarters of French officialdom. It is picturesque, too, which, from the traveller's point of view, is even better. An attractive wooden bridge spans the stream leading to the main shopping street. The stilt-borne wooden

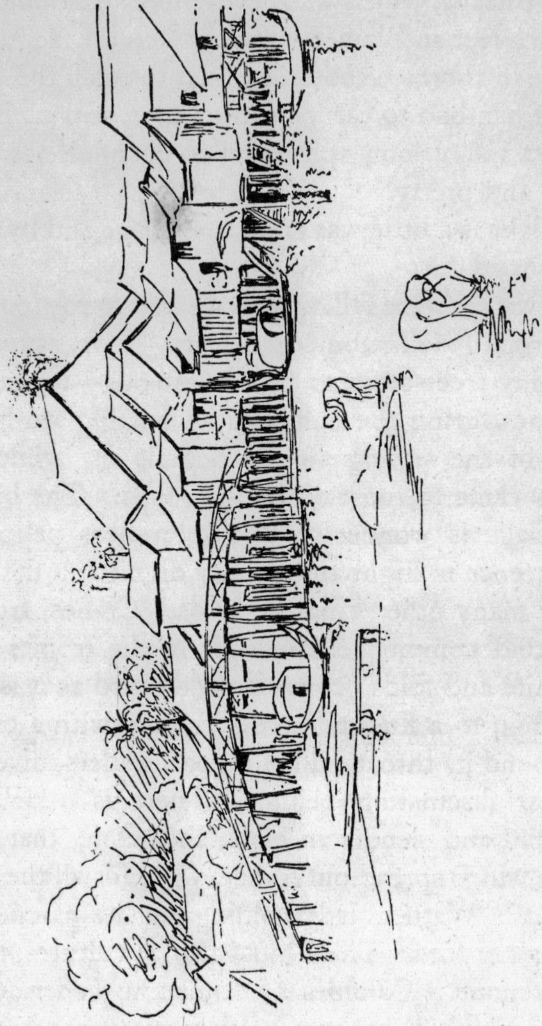

SIÉM RÉAP.

houses turn their varied backs to the water. All this may be seen at many a river town in Further India, but there were also water-wheels for irrigation, an Annamite device, I heard, which was new to me. The wheels are about six feet in diameter and two feet wide, and are set close in shore. Above each slat to catch the current is a half bamboo to carry up the water, and each pours its quota into a long split bamboo channel. A simple scheme and pretty.

The lake is a little way from the village and by a good driving road.

The waters were falling and we had to row out some way through half-submerged trees—it is astonishing how many trees seem to be amphibious—to meet the boat, and during the half hour of waiting we had the beauty of the setting sun to beguile us, while great pelicans came to roost on the tree-tops. The bird life of the lake is wonderful, and as well as pelicans all magnificence in flight and clumsy dignity on the water, we saw many other kinds of birds. Cranes, from the small kind common everywhere in the tropics which flies white and folds brown, a paddy bird as it is called very often, to a fine, tall grey creature with a crimson band round its throat. Flamingoes, waders, divers and countless fascinating beings. There is a delightful thing, tall and slender in black and white, that stands with its wings spread out to dry, with, for all the world, the air of a Watteau lady holding out her panniers and pointing her toes. There must also be vultures, though we saw none. Colonies of Annamite fishermen live on islets which, in the wet weather, disappear under the water, which rises to the very platforms of their little houses set on tall stilts. If death should come when the waters are high the body is exposed on the tree-tops.

The boat was really much too small for our large party. Coming up it had been no hardship for the

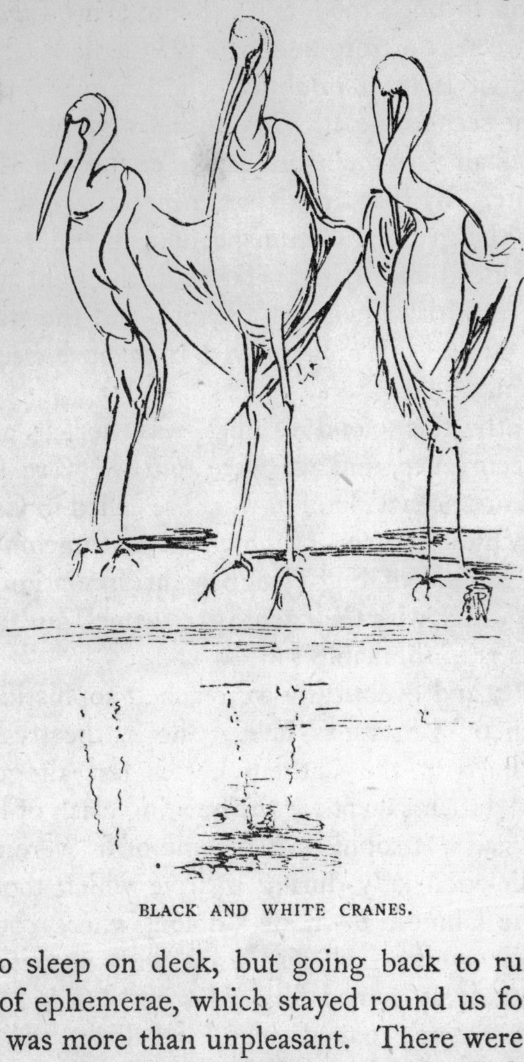

BLACK AND WHITE CRANES.

men to sleep on deck, but going back to run into a cloud of ephemerae, which stayed round us for several hours, was more than unpleasant. There were millions of them! Harmless quite, but how I thanked my stars that I had at once put up my little makeshift travelling mosquito net, and more that I was at the first of the two dinners necessary for our numbers. The lights above the table were put out so that the insects should not be attracted on to one's food, and I do not think I ate any, as, when we sat down to table the plague had only just begun, but it is most doubtful whether many people enjoyed the second meal! The sight of the walls alone furred thick all over their surface was enough to destroy any appetite. By that time it was necessary to walk on deck with the greatest circumspection, in order not to slip on the dead and dying. To be in the light was to be beaten as with snowflakes. Ugh—and the state of the decks in the morning proved it to have been no mere dream.

Apparently this cloud of flies was not at all an unusual occurrence, and we were told we were lucky that it had not been a cloud of what are called in Ceylon 'stink-poochies,' swarms of which are not uncommon. These are a kind of bug (English interpretation, not American) which with their acute green smell multiplied by millions is unthinkable!

Pleasantly and eventlessly we reached sophistication and Saigon on Christmas Eve. Shops, theatres and midnight mass at the Cathedral, this last altogether hateful and garish except for the opening clash of bells.

If the place was sophisticated some of us were not! One middle-aged lady during a drive which took us through the Chinese town of Cholon, where coolies, hot at their work, had dispensed with superfluous clothing, suddenly leaned forward with 'Oh! I have so wanted to see naked men,' recalling the old Limerick:

There was an old man of Samaria
Who would take his bath in the area,
Said Eliza to cook, 'Oh! do come and look,
Did you ever see anything hairier?'

but for the last line.

She was easily satisfied, for the Chinaman, as I ever saw him, clings to a good deal of clothing.

Saigon is pretty with boulevards and an air quite definitely French, and has a delightful Zoo. But I was not sorry to sail for Bangkok, and the voyage was a very pleasant surprise after the first rough night. The stretch of river had considerately given us time to dine before confronting the sea. By eight next morning we had reached Poulo Condor, with calm water under the lee of the point, and for the rest of the voyage we had perfect weather in ideal calm on a lovely island-strewn sea. Sadly these are not all isles of the blest. Poulo Condor is the French Convict Settlement, and we were told it was not possible to land without a special permit, half promised but never forthcoming; which was disappointing, as they kept us there all day. There, handling cargo, I was horrified by my first sight of a convict in leg irons, the heavy chain looped up to his waist. I got hardened to the sight in Siam where the convicts wear them with so determined a grace that one's sympathetic shame evaporates. After all, it procures them greater freedom in the open, and chains are certainly better than cells. An official of the island told us tales of the prisoners of Poulo Condor, who are of many nationalities and mostly serving long terms. The Malay alone does not survive imprisonment. We heard one tale of sinister humour about two Indian brothers, life prisoners for killing and eating *their fiancée*.

On our further voyage many sights rejoiced or pained us. An enchantment on a very still night was to sit in the ship's bow as we cut through numberless shoals of brightly phosphorescent fish showing like explosions of unearthly light in the water as they scattered before us. On the other hand, the very thought of a miserable cow being slung on board by the horns to this day makes my hair stand on end. The horns broke . . .

At the last of our stopping places, a tolerably long call, we enjoyed a walk. The place was called Duong Dong and the isle Phu Quoc. It was the hottest time of day, but the place looked too attractive to miss. Ye gods! how it smelt. The great industry of the place is the making of a rotten fish sauce . . . the more a taste *not* to be acquired that the noisome stuff is much appreciated by amateurs, for whose benefit we were shipping a quantity. But though the nose had to suffer to the eye all was charming. Water ways, little wooden houses, amusing barges, cocoanut palms and many other trees, and withal a pleasant air of prosperity. Not many people were out, probably it was too hot. As we passed a comparatively grand isolated archway where I paused thinking it to be an indication of temple grounds, a fine old native came towards us and courteously entreated us to enter his house. The invitation was interpreted to us by a young Frenchman with whom we had spoken on board. The old man was headman of the village, and rich, and his one joy was to entertain strangers, if any landed there, with sweet champagne! So sweet champagne we duly drank, sitting on Windsor chairs at a long table in a room in which East and West quarrelled as queerly as possible. Two altars with

Chinese tablets and ornaments fought for prominence with a large double bedstead draped with mosquito curtains—Western finery. Columns supporting the roof were cased in panels of mother-of-pearl inlay, but the joy and pride of the whole room was a large Western washing-stand, marble-topped, with a magnificent toilet set! It was really a very grand room. I hope he enjoyed seeing us as much as we were amused and pleased by him and his hospitality. But sweet champagne at two in the afternoon needed walking off, and the young Frenchman begged that we would visit his wife. Such an isolated life they led, with only one or perhaps two partly French families for company. The husband was in charge of the cable station. They took us to see the village temples, and up a pleasant wooded hill to show us the view inland over the forest. There was plenty of game, it seemed, but in the wet season leeches were the chief danger. As in many other parts of the tropics men may be bled to death by leeches in the forest.

At the temple in the hill-top we had to drink again, but this time from green cocoanuts offered by a priest whom I took for an old woman. Chinese Buddhism must have trespassed here, for his robe was grey and his long hair not shaved but twisted in a tight knot, and his fingers were adorned with claw-like Chinese nails!

Enhanced by perfect weather, with all meals on deck instead of in the stuffy saloon, the little boat had very pleasantly belied her rather bad reputation, and we were almost sorry to have reached the mouth of the Menam Chao Phya.

SIAM

CHAPTER VI

ARRIVAL

On nearing Bangkok one of the pleasures was to find myself in Conrad country, and although of his books only *The Shadow Line* has the Gulf of Siam as setting, many of the incidents he describes might have taken place round about the scattered islands through which we had just come, and many more along the banks of the Menam Chao Phya—Mother of the Waters Noble and Excellent—and on its numberless creeks. I know every corner of the landscape in *Almayer's Folly*, for instance, by heart.

Though small we were kept at the bar by the tide for some hours, ships of over 14 ft. draught cannot attempt the river. The tedious wait was a blessing in disguise, as it gave us daylight to see the river banks. The magnificent *Prachedi* at Paknam gleaming white reflects sunlight afar and smiles a first greeting. The river winds and winds, its wooded shores fringed with Nipa palms, tall fronds growing straight out of the water. Further back are real trees, banyan, ficus, feathery tamarind and casuarina and many another, punctuated with groups of various palm, lolling cocoanut, dignified palmyra, and graceful among all and straight as a dart, the Areca.

Every here and there are openings where some waterway joins the river, and at its mouth a village with little floating houses, while from the shore other small wooden buildings well raised on stilts above danger from the water's changing level seem to stride down towards them.

As in Cambodia and in many tropical river countries the wise custom of the people is to lift their houses from danger of flood. So it is too with the many monasteries on the banks where a landing-stage reaches over the water standing on long legs and ending on shore in a roofed *salá* for rest and shelter. Higher up the banks, clusters of stilt-carried cells for the monks lead up to the group of main buildings, also raised above the ground level, preaching hall and image house with the symbolic ship of the church usually built large in front of it, and prachedi large and small dotted all around. *Prachedi* is the Siamese name for the Buddhist *stupa*. They are solid blocks of masonry built round some sacred relic for the veneration of the faithful, and usually overlaid with *chunam*, a fine white stucco. To build a *prachedi* is one way of acquiring merit, and so shortening the ladder of lives yet to be lived by the giver before he can hope for surcease from the pain of living. Judging by the forests of these little monuments to be seen round every monastery, the amount of merit they bring must be out of all proportion to their cost.

Every Siamese man spends at least three months in a monastery as fully ordained monk, generally on attaining manhood, and to most monasteries a school is attached, so that monks and students form an enormous proportion of the population. One of the charms of the early morning river is to see the monks set forth with their begging bowls in tiny craft to collect their daily bread from the faithful.

Thus they follow the Lord's rule and give occasion to many to make merit by contributing a handful of cooked rice or curry stuff to his disciples. Every monk must partake of some of the food which has been begged, and it is the duty of the *nane* (pupil followers) to separate it into its various constituents and serve it up in separate dishes. After the monks the *nane* eat their fill, then the monastery hangers-on, then beggars, and finally the many and ravenous pariah dogs.

The river, at all times fascinating, is at its most charming in the early hours, when it reflects not only the gaily coloured clothes of the river folk but the yellow robes of the priests brilliant in the sun's level rays.

As we neared Bangkok rice mills became frequent. The Siamese, essentially an aristocratic people, like to have their work done for them, and the mills are generally the property of Chinese immigrants who are indeed the workers of Bangkok. As a result some have made big fortunes, and many have Siamese titles, and after a fashion to be seen also nearer home, lavish on the great what they have taken from the poor, the more willing to trample for having themselves been trampled on. The rice mills are modern in their equipment and turn out the polished commercial stuff that we eat in England, all starch and no nourishment, and also mill parboiled rice if the market requires it.

When three hours upstream Bangkok came into view. Not the walled Krung Tep (City of the Angels), that with its fairy towers of gold and porcelain was still out of sight up the winding stream, but merely the commercial part of the city, full of interest and liveliness if not of grandeur.

It is a dangerously varying and rapid river, but the population lives on or in it from infancy, and no one seems too young to swim ! Hundreds of these amphibious folk inhabit fascinating floating houses built on rafts or barges loosely moored by rings to heavy piles, that they may rise and fall with the complicated tides, much aggravated as they are by the constantly varying level of the swift-flowing stream. Fishing, washing clothes, and personal ablutions all go on side by side. It was a great pity that my companion of the Cholon drive was not there, for it would have delighted her to see individuals sitting on the cross-stays of a landing solemnly lathering themselves, the lather showing up splendidly on their dark skins, before plunging into the extremely muddy water. It was perhaps their sense of superiority that made it funny, soap is a Western luxury and not for the use of all and sundry !

The children were altogether amazing. On the klongs they may be seen two or three in a round bathtub just large enough to hold them, paddling about with not more than one inch free board, and here on the river were small things in minute canoes so low on the water that they seem to be sitting in it, speeding them against the tide, twisting in and out of the tremendous river traffic, tossed by the wash of tugs with long lines of paddy boats in tow, or by big steamers from far ports. We were told that the equilibrium of these canoes is so delicate that a European at his first attempt to manage one is upset time after time into the water, and seldom can sit in one for five minutes, even if he can work the canoe. On the way up we had met sailing boats of many patterns, mostly Chinese, some with their sails of the delightful mothwing shape common in South China, others tall and elegant like the Yangtse junk. And there were row-boats everywhere. Mostly they are built on the principle of a gondola to offer a minimum of resistance to the swirling stream. The oarsman stands like the gondolier in the stern and pushes against his rowlock, to which, unlike the gondolier's, his oar is loosely fastened by a bit of cord.

On landing it was a disappointment to find squalid pseudo-European streets, which moreover are spreading. Still there is plenty of room in the seventy square miles of Greater Bangkok, and to my pleasure I found that the mission which for the next eight months was to be my home was almost in the country. It opened on to one of the fine avenues planted by order of that fatherly monarch, King Chulalongkorn. I like the thought of his morning expeditions round the capital which he loved, planning a road here and an avenue there, and this at a time when waterways still carried all the traffic. His private family, large by European standards, doubtless fostered patriarchal virtues. Houses in this part of the town were almost all Western looking, but by no means all inhabited by Europeans; for though the left bank of the river is now fashionable among the Siamese, the beautifully fashioned wooden house of old Siam hardly exists on this side. In this Western quarter the more modern type of house seems to disregard the drawbacks of tropic sun and storm, while the older and more picturesque are lifted out of the danger of flood on columns and surrounded by deep verandahs to give much needed shelter from the sun and from storm-driven rain. The mission, I am glad to say, was definitely of the old type, and a stretch of paddy fields was separated from us only by a canal. Just across the canal were farmers living in little thatched wooden houses raised on piles out of the waters which follow heavy rain, and buffaloes trod out the paddy and soaked in the klong (canal) through the heat of the day.

Bangkok buffaloes are magnificent great beasts, none finer anywhere, with immense horns lying back, as they lumber along, chin in air, the whole length of their absurd long champagne-bottle necks. But though ungainly and stupid looking, the air of huge latent power about them recalls uncomfortably the force of inertia, and I had heard so much of the buffaloes' dislike of white people that their complete indifference to us was something of a relief.

The klong seemed a safeguard, too, and the whole farm colony pleased and entertained me till one sad day it began to melt away. The royal edict had gone forth; paddy fields were to become park, and the farmers must go. So on the first day announced by the soothsayers to be propitious for a move the little houses were taken to pieces and carried off—almost as easily as biblical beds! For the next few months hordes of Chinese coolies dug there in their stead. Happily for us their quarters were not near, but the exchange was for the worse.

Bangkok has always been different from other capital cities on account of the crisscross of klongs, still its salient feature, but now only on the right bank of the river does it deserve the name of Venice of the East. On that side the chief note of modernity is the terminus of the Southern Railway, soon to be superseded, and to

LITTLE FARM BY THE KLONG.

To face page 90.

this day there is no driving road, or so small a fragment that it is not used for driving. There are paths in abundance, but all the real traffic is klong-borne, and to see water life in its fullness no better place can be found than Klong Yai. On its banks some of the more elaborate wooden houses, beautifully panelled and fitted together, have a charming dignity and grace, and are happily lacking the tawdry fretwork eaves so dear to the Burmese.

On the bank too is a most interesting market, Talaat Plu, the market of the Betel leaf.

From the point of view of the sightseer the quantities of Manchester goods on sale, encouraging though they may be as to the prospects of British commerce, seem out of place; but in the flower and fruit sections it is a joy to linger. Here are flowers by the trayful, great mounds of blossom and of blossom only, never gathered by the spray as in the West, but picked flower by flower and heaped in gorgeous piles of colour and scent.

Sweet-smelling sacred lotus are almost the only flowers sold on their stems, and they are bound in tight sheaves. Flowers here are for offerings and are most commonly woven into garlands with which to decorate a friend, honour a superior or propitiate a god.

They are lovely, fat, close-woven garlands perfect to handle, but of a potency most trying to a sensitive nose! Their foundation is of a thick white bud of heaviest scent. Sometimes only the tassel at the end of a garland is of coloured flowers, or perhaps a coloured spiral line runs through its length, or an arrangement of coloured rings, or anything the maker's fancy may suggest, provided the scent be strong and full. To me it was a very doubtful pleasure to be garlanded, though the thought was kind and the act fitted with my surroundings. 'The Champok odours fail.' How I sometimes wished they would, when in class the schoolgirls wore one of the long, elegant blossoms dangling behind an ear, held there by a hair twisted into the slender petals. The difference in appreciation of scents as between Europeans and Siamese is in none so marked as in the smell of some flower which I have never succeeded in seeing, though at one season its rank smell of mouse attacked me in every road. A Siamese friend declared it to be delicious, and it is used as a base for other scents, much as musk is used in Europe. Still, an you like heavy scents or you like them not, the flower market is a joy to the eye that you may find in many parts of Bangkok if you know where to seek.

An opium den, under strict surveillance, as opium is a government monopoly, was one of the interesting things we saw at Talaat Plu. An uncomfortable-looking place even by the standard of a butcher's shop which it vividly recalled to me, only, instead of mere joints, *people* lay about the slabs, their heads on porcelain supports. They were Chinese, or Siamo-Chinese, almost all; and dreams were the last thing suggested by their attitudes and expressions. They would need to be particularly pleasant dreams to compensate the bleakness of their surroundings. The smoking, too, was such a restless performance. The pill to be made, two puffs to be enjoyed, and the whole proceeding over again. Even the pipe was not an old friend; it had to be hired and the stuff bought on the way in. We were at any rate a godsend to the curiosity of the smokers, who were quite as much interested in us as we in them, and we decided that the Englishman who showed the place in turn to us ladies would be credited with ar oriental number of wives !

The bliss of opium-smoking remains something of a mystery even to present-day science. What is there in the smoke to comfort ? I am told that, on analysis, there is little if any morphia in the smoke—the morphia is all collected in the large tubular cavity of the pipe stem as are the alkaloids of the opium.

Opium is a government monopoly, and can only be smoked under rigid rules, but the smoke which has condensed in the pipe together with the ashes of the burnt opium form a dark sticky mass, not under government control. So the opium den keeper sells it for diluting the pure government opium. He sells it for eating too, and as it contains a very large proportion of morphine, when eaten it causes very different effects from opium smoking, and is a very much more harmful method of drugging.

As in Europe strong spirits seem to have very different effects on the various nationalities, so opium appears to differ in its effects on various oriental nations. It is said that the native of Central India eats it with comparative impunity, the Chinese and Siamese seldom eat it, or do so with worse effects.

The Chinese appear to be able to smoke pure opium without very bad results, while the same amount will have a markedly deteriorating effect on a Siamese, morally and physically, and perhaps even worse on a Malay.

The whole of this side of the river has the charm of distinctive personality, and in appearance, at any rate, is almost unspoilt by contact with the West, for Europeans come here but little, although there are some fine temples to be seen.

CHAPTER VII

ON THE LEFT BANK

The Bangkok which comes first to most Western minds is that of the other bank. To a newcomer the impression of his arrival generally remains the clearest of memory's pictures. If he should be travelling to Bangkok by the Southern Express he will have been charmed with a glimpse of the river gay and busy, crossing it as he must from the railway terminus to the left bank, and then catching a glimpse of the beautiful group of spires of the old Palace across the Phra Meru. I was not so fortunate, for, after the river trip, to land in the New Road is disappointing and depressing. Characterless and squalid it straggles for miles, narrow and winding, bearing traffic undreamt of fifty years ago when it was made and christened *Chereun-Krung*, which means 'Opening to promote the happiness of the people,' that so novel a thing as a road in a land of waterways might proclaim its intention in its name. The buildings which enclose it can at no time have been impressive, but when new may have worn their stucco with a difference. Now dilapidated small shabby shops are looked down upon by great commercial buildings which, springing up with scornful irregularity and speed, push the little two-storied houses away. When they are gone the loss from the point of view of pic-

WAT PHRA KEO ENCLOSURE FROM THE OUTER PRECINCTS. OLD PALACE.

To face page 94.

turesqueness will not be great. To see into window after window of a low upper floor, all identical, each blocked with a shabbier and dirtier mosquito net than the last, is not inspiring. I wonder how much the net is for a badly needed protection and how much a sign of social status !

In its early days, doubtless, horse-drawn carriages with out-runners, and possibly rickshas too, were all the traffic the road had to carry. It was a surprise to discover that these hand carts for so long ubiquitous in the East were invented by an Englishman in Japan for his sick wife. Now, what the West gave, the West is destroying, and its motor-car is everywhere ousting gharry and ricksha. On the new road all three conveyances are present. Cars are numberless and driven with skill but small discretion, and as frequent and most useful trams take up half the narrow way, pedestrians and unfortunate ricksha coolies would go in terror of their lives if they were not so exasperatingly heedless ! Before my arrival I had been told that to go about Bangkok in anything less aggressive than a motor-car was impossible, nay, suicidal. However, gharries and rickshas better suited my purse, and so received the honour of my patronage, and the only accident that ever befel me was comical rather than dangerous.

I was in a gharry being driven down a little winding road unknown to me, which, at one point, followed a sharp turn in its accompanying klong, and then crossed it by a bridge raised a few inches above the road level. This was too much for the harness and both traces snapped with one accord, the pony continuing quietly over the bridge and we gathering speed backwards towards the steep bank of the klong ! The little driver was off his tall box in a trice and, hauling at the shafts, just managed to save me from a ducking.

I stepped out; the pony, waiting with calm indifference the other side of the bridge, was put in again, and we proceeded on our way, no sound having been uttered by anyone! The driver's only comment was a slow smile when he pocketed his fare at dismissal. True, he knew no English and I no Siamese.

To return to the New Road. Until recently it had one oasis, the British Legation. Brilliant with Flame-of-the-Forest in the hot weather, it stood on a beautiful site overlooking the river on its far side; a site which had been presented to the British by King Mongkut, a great, learned and good man, grandfather of the present monarch. It was probably intended as a compliment to her hosts that Queen Victoria should sit in a bay just outside the Legation Gardens, facing the street; but she wore our best inimitable English air of owning all she surveyed. This was not her fault, but the compliment rather missed its mark in consequence.

Though of stone she had, at one period, been bronzed, which was no doubt the cause of the following conversation overheard in the vicinity. Among the many foreigners in Government service at Bangkok is a well-known Asiatic doctor, one of a distinguished family all recipients of Siamese royal favours and decorations. A newly-arrived Asiatic with a group of friends who lived in Bangkok all talking English among themselves in the manner of so many loyal British subjects the world over, as they passed in front of the statue, asked whom the lady might be:

'Oh! don't you know? that is Dr. ——'s mother.'

The tale may be apochryphal.

Now the beautiful site has been sold for a large sum and the Legation removed to the new residential quarter, a practical step, but lacking in grace, as many think, towards the givers. King Mongkut's generosity also provided a chapel for the foreign community, which is in the care of the British and has an English chaplain, but all nationalities and every sect have the use of it if they desire.

In the New Road one begins to realise the extraordinarily cosmopolitan character of the city. Numberless Asiatic types throng the road. Indians from north and south, both Mahommedan and Hindu, but chiefly Hindus from the south. Burmans, Malays, Cingalese, and above all Chinese, who form one-third of the population and intermarry very much with their Siamese hosts, the children, *Luk Chin*, making excellent Siamese citizens.

From the winding, squalid, Chereun Krung straight roads run inland, and, cut at right angles by others, carve the residential parts of the town into plots nearly always rectangular. The roads generally form dykes running between two klongs which serve many uses. They drain the land, form natural boundaries, and are waterways connecting the tortuous course of the river. The deltaic country is utterly flat and the tides are felt far inland, so that when spring tides are out the canals are often left high and dry, or, rather, full of slimy mud on which it is far from pleasant to be stranded, a prey to voracious mosquitoes.

It is at such times that the fish walk, as they cannot swim, and stranded picnic parties, if philosophical, may find consolation in their antics. I was entranced, and without need for the support of philosophy, for I saw them at turn of the tide when only a little mud was uncovered, enchanting fishlings only two or three inches long and of a perfect sapphire blue. Their accomplishments are so many and their conversational attitude so serious that they must certainly be the intellectual *élite* of a most superior fish community. Not only do they swim, but they walk on two front fins, somewhat as a seal uses his flappers, occasionally interrupting a quiet stroll with a flying leaps sailiey. through the air with the help of a suddenly unfolded dorsal fin, sharp like a lateen sail, that disappears when the leap is made. To see two or three of them grouped in the queerest conversational attitudes suggested minute and brilliant mermaids, most unbelievable, jewel-like beings !

There is a big walking carp, but I only caught a glimpse of it in the distance. Fabulous reports of its prowess have reached the West, because the first European to write about it had met it climbing a leaning tree, and an amazing sight it must have been, but there is no doubt that in subtlety and refinement it is much below the sapphire fishlings ! The big carp is to be met walking (presumably not by his own will) in the fishmarkets, and there are plenty of other food fish in the klongs. Europeans prefer their fish from clearer waters and do not eat them.

An astute fish that I did not see is the shooting fish, which brings down the flies it eats by spitting at them ! The fame of the Siamese fighting minnow has gone abroad, indeed he has come himself to the London Zoo. He is a dullish-looking mite whose temper dowers him with rainbow colours, which become brighter and brighter as he gets more pugnacious, and I hear he will fight to the death. Those I saw in jars were only allowed a few bites before they were separated, but they kindly blushed to see each other through the glass. The Siamese keep them as in England fighting cocks used to be kept, for betting purposes.

The Siamese fisherman is to be seen everywhere, risking his place in the ladder of ascending lives that he may feed himself and others. Everyone eats fish, for in Buddhist eyes 'sin does not pass,' and responsibility rests solely on the doer (I wonder whether religion and the law see eye to eye, for instance, as to the receiving of stolen goods !) so I hope the fisherman's virtue of self-immolation may more than counterbalance the crime of taking (fish) life.

When the water is deep the fisherman may be watched by the hour standing on the bank or else far forward in his boat, throwing a circular net with a jolly gesture into the water. The throw requires skill and balance, for the weighted edge of the net which leaves the hand folded must reach the water in a widely spread circle. A tempting subject to draw, but impossible, I decided.

Another entertainment, though pathetic in its implications, was to see the peasants during the dry weather, when in some klongs and pools nothing but ooze remained, and that fast drying up, wading along in procession, each flinging a basket trap extinguisherwise before him into the mud. It was an unsolved mystery to me how the fish remained caught if they were covered, but considering the Buddhist horror of taking life this must be something more than a sport. Fish in the water, trees overarching and flowers floating, the klongs are fascinating.

There are great stretches of orchard in Greater

Bangkok which is famous for its fruit, and here the trees to be seen from the waterways are fruit-bearing. Wonderful mangoes, the much-prized durien, a stemless palm, its long fronds decorated with spirals of sharp thorns, which thrusts up from its root the prickliest fig-like fruit called *Salá*, *Lamut*, which is the West Indian Sapodilla, and many another too numerous to name, many of them, moreover, quite unknown to the average European. Europeans seldom eat *Salá*, not having the skill to avoid the million caterpillar-hair prickles of the outer shell, or to disentangle the delicious flesh from a clinging inner membrane. The preparation of fruit is part of the regular education of every Siamese lady, and it is served to the Siamese in exquisite fashion that the eater may have nothing to do but to convey it to his mouth. It is one of the ways in which woman may serve her lord ! Truly, it entails much handling.

Bangkok in the hot weather is famous not only for its fruit but for flowering trees too. The residential parts of the city are then on fire with what Europeans there like to call Flame-of-the-Forest, the Madagascar Poinciana. In Ceylon we know it as Flamboyant and in India as the Golden Mohur. Flowers come before leaves. In the older trees they form domes of almost unbroken colour of a nearly perfect umbrella shape, the outline sharp with the extraordinary precision of tropical trees. The bole and giant limbs, writhing uncannily, seem tortured to uphold such weight of beauty, in colour ranging from orange-vermilion almost to crimson, lightened only by the single yellow or whitish petal in each blossom. This at least is known to us all, flaunting its glories too vividly to pass unnamed by the least interested. The names of numerous other trees I asked, generally only to be met with a frankly acknowledged ignorance, whether by the European, interested chiefly in the shade they cast, or by the Siamese, proud to give the thrilling information that it was a Siamese tree—or flower—as the case might be! When names were forthcoming they were too often immediately forgotten, but to feel that one might know if one would is uplifting. Of one nameless flowering tree we knew too much. Its branches were on a level with our verandah sitting-room. It has large and remarkably handsome seeds, decorative and with a fine *allure* which made me wish to see the flower. One day an insidious and far from pleasant smell began to haunt us. The roof was searched and a few rats caught, but nothing specially objectionable was found. And still the smell grew, floating over in nauseating whiffs like nothing so much as poisoned breath.

On the worst day of all I was giving a tea-party to show some sketches. The smell was of a type which one instinctively refrains from mentioning, and I could only hope that other noses were less sensitive than mine. And then we discovered the guilty tree covered with thousands of utterly insignificant blossoms. In spite of fulminations against it, I hope, being no longer there myself, that the fine tree still stands. The scent must have been the noisome breath of its haunting 'Phi,' a terrible dragon, possibly, whose anger none would risk by cutting down its home!

Water flowers are many, and among them the water hyacinth is the ne'er-do-weel flourishing at the expense of virtue. Let it once get a footing and nothing else will have a chance of life, for it invades every corner.

It is completely indifferent even to adversity—spates carry great bunches of it out to sea, but living on floats and rootless, in the less frequented klongs it forms almost impassable barriers, and the peasant cultivator who clings to his waterways has much ado to push his flat-bottomed boat, produce-laden, through it to the market. The thrifty Chinaman is sometimes seen to collect it. I am told it is used in the manufacture of blotting paper, but in spite of its possible utility, and its charming mauvy-pink flower spikes, it is an unmitigated nuisance. It is said that on account of its pretty blossom its seed was taken to Florida with disastrous results. In contrast the sacred lotus, most exquisite of water-flowers, has become throughout the East the symbol of spiritual man. Virtuous as it is beautiful, blossom, seed and pod, root and leaf, are all of service to man. He uses the rose-coloured petals to roll cigarettes, and eats the seed, its pod, and the root, and the Chinaman dries and eats the leaf also. So by utmost self-sacrifice does it figure forth spiritual man, risen through slime and ooze to life in light and air. Its powers of growth are tremendous, leaf and blossom stand high above the water, and it is of all plants the most exquisite in gesture, colour and scent. Most happily in spite of the all-invading water hyacinth there are many small klongs where the rose-coloured sacred lotus still holds its own, and decorously riots, a joy to behold. The floating varieties of pale pink or blue with long narrow petals, and many other kinds of lotus, are to be found in Siam too. A very lovely white one must surely be that sung by Heine; by day it is close shut, but at night lies like a star on the water.

A place to visit in the cool of the evening after a hot

day was a pond near one of the royal palaces where thousands of these wonderful flowers lay serenely smiling.

The Victoria Regia is often to be seen, but Fate was not kind to me, for when I passed one there was never so much as a fisherman standing on a great leaf !

Happily the sacred lotus, the most common of all, is the most lovely of all too.

Along the canal banks the poorer native houses, little wooden buildings standing on piles, have each a plank to bridge the stream, with long stilt supports that storm-flood may not wash it away, or a bit of plank landing-stage from which fish may be caught and the person washed, and all of his possessions too.

And still within the limits of Greater Bangkok are stretches of paddy fields, orchards and villages—Siamese villages, Mon villages, Indian villages, its own centre for each race. The Indians are herdsmen, and to those who will take the risk, dairymen, but most Europeans prefer milk from the tin, while the Siamese make no use of milk at all, even for butter. Dhobies, washermen, particularly bad and rapacious, are low caste Hindus from the South, though more are Chinese. Peons, messengers in the various banks, and most of the night watchmen are Indian too. When the capital of Siam was Ayuthia there was an Indian quarter, but probably like the majority of Europeans in the East, Indians were not colonists, but had left home in the hope of returning with a fortune to lord it in their villages, or at worst of making a livelihood difficult to achieve at home. Meanwhile they care for nothing else and gain little but money from their sojourn in strange lands.

At the mission we had an Indian father and son who

were gatekeepers by day and watchmen by night. The old watchman, at any rate, took his duties seriously, tramping round the group of buildings with a big stick and a lantern, between naps in the lower verandah—naps merely suspected, for his snores, frequent betrayers of watchmen, were never disturbing. Of our other guardians, the pack of pariah dogs, fourteen strong, the same cannot be said. They would rush round in a body, several times in a night, a chorus of barking, howling fiends, and rouse every hound within earshot. By day they were quiet enough, just lying round inconveniently where one most wanted to step. The nuisance was admitted but suffered because, short of administering poison with their own hands, the missionaries had no way of getting rid of them. The Department of Public Health was making war on pariah dogs, but in spite of enormous numbers killed (70 to 100) every week, was unable to keep up with them, partly perhaps because, as at the Mission, when called upon to take action, the response was a notification of the day and hour of their visitation. In consequence, when its minions arrived, there was not a dog to be found in the compound ! The Siamese servants had seized the opportunity of making twofold merit—by saving the lives of the dogs on the one hand, and on the other preserving their employers from the crime of having them killed.

Alas for their schemes ! A few months later the officials were invited again, and this time were requested to descend on us without notice, and thus the deed was done, or almost done, for the servants succeeded in smuggling away two expectant mothers, who, later, laid the foundation of fresh packs ! The episode almost left us servantless, the whole staff being up in arms and aghast at the ill-luck to which we had laid ourselves open. One sad piece of misfortune it had certainly brought, for the good had gone with the bad, as the leader of the pack, almost, I heard, a pure bred Siamese hound and a fine creature to boot, had not been tied up and had shared the fatal morsel.

English people in Siam generally have Chinese servants and, as all the world knows, they can be very good indeed, in spite of drawbacks such as the secret societies to which they belong. However, they are very much more expensive than the less trainable Siamese, who have but little of the Chinese capacity for routine and detail. The Mission was poor—what Mission is not? So our servants were Siamese, and the national characteristics made domestic service there more picturesque if less regular than in most European houses. For instance, it was difficult to persuade the waiting maid that she should not clasp our plates to her bosom, a way of carrying them that we did not find appetising! We were busy people at the Mission, and it was not only through Western impatience of ceremonial that the servants had been shorn of their own manners without entirely acquiring ours. Respectful service, as practised by the Siamese, seems to Europeans exceedingly elaborate. To understand it, one must explain that in the Siamese idea, personal honourableness diminishes steadily from crown to sole, besides which the head of the short master must always be above that of his tall servant, of the old above that of the young, of the tall commoner below the short prince, of the prince far below that of the king. In fact there is always someone whose head has a right to be above one's own, so that safety from solecism is only to be found on the ground, and from the ground, crouching, does your servant address you. When he hands you food it is on his knees, and that being a slow mode of progression, the dish is apt to chill ! As before stated we were busy people, so that the cook was the only one of the servants whose manners had not been hurried away, and it never ceased mildly to surprise me to see her sitting on the floor while taking her orders ! One very pleasant token of respect in Siam is the lowered voice, which makes even holiday gatherings, gay though the Siamese naturally are, quiet compared to most crowds, notably to Chinese and Indian crowds.

CHAPTER VIII

THE OLD PALACE. OUTER PRECINCTS

THE sudden vision of the Old Palace, whether by good fortune from the river or across the magnificent *Phra Meru* (pronounced Premane) checks the breath and throws one back in thought to childish daydreams of a fairy prince and imaginary rides towards adventures in an enchanted palace.

It stands, an entrancing group of gold and coloured spires, protected by a fantastic girdling wall. Its crenellations are shaped like the leaf of the sacred *Bodhi* tree, and the gateways, to the newcomer, mysteriously reminiscent of ancient Egypt.

Disillusion lurks within the main gate, however. Here, unfortunately, are various Ministries erected a century or more ago under Western influence. They are still run to a great extent on Western lines with, in some cases, European advisers to help the Siamese ministers in their dealings with foreign powers. The intrusion of the European nineteenth century into Fairyland is distressing. An official car with a plaque of the bull's head attached to the front of the bonnet, that is the Open, Sesame. Without it the Palace is entered on foot. A bull-headed motor car is a poor substitute for a fairy steed, but disappointment is short-lived, for beyond the trimmed tamarinds which stand like trees out of our Noah's Arks bordering the drives, lo! another white wall, and beyond that again the gleaming spires of *Wat Phra Keo* on the left, and in front the gateway to the Inner Precincts of the Old Palace. Fairyland in being! To see not mere gilt but gold in the mass is an absolute revelation.

The great golden bell-shaped *stupa* that dominates the magnificent group is absolutely classic in form, surmounted by the thirteen rings of the Buddhist heavens, tapering upwards to support balls of diminishing size. The whole building is a symbol of Buddhism cased entirely in three-quarter inch square bricklets overlaid with gold leaf and glazed. The tropic sunshine strikes it with blinding force, and amazingly beautiful, it reflects every changing effect of sky and cloud.

Behind and above it is the wonderful Praprang of pale gleaming porcelain in green and rose, springing from the crossed roofs of the Pantheon, and its glory. In all that crowded enclosure seen from the outside these two monuments are the most wonderful.

It is a surprise to find that at *Wat Phra Keo* there is no monastery. It is what might be called the Chapel Royal, and except on occasions of ceremonial observance the yellow-robed monk is not more frequently seen there than gaily-clad laymen, who seem almost the more natural inhabitants of the fantastic buildings. Among them enchantment again closed round me. A shivering doubt as to its entire benevolence seized me as I passed the hideous guardians of the various gates, until the inimitable bland swagger of the *Kinorn* lined up round the terrace of the Pantheon brought reassurance. Delightfully funny and elegant these half bird, half human courtiers, early inhabitants of the depths of the primeval forest in the world's beginnings. There they

THE BLUE ROOF F WAT PHRA KEO, WITH KINORN AND YAK.

To face page 108.

consorted with the *Norasing*, lion-dogs who stand round the temple sanctuaries to fend Ill-luck's approach. Who hears the Norasing howl will never hear again, say the priests whose ancient Pali books disclose secrets of the past. The *Kinorn* are gentlemen and ladies of the court as to their upper selves, and most elegant fowls below. All of gilt bronze, each one is different in pose, gesture and features, and each quite exquisite, clothes and plumage set with glittering glass mosaic.

The lavish use of glass mosaic, not coloured glass but small pieces of brilliant colour glazed, is of immense charm, but, unfortunately, not durable, and the Siamese are immeasurably more skilful in handling it than anyone else. Everywhere the gorgeousness, brilliance and harmony of the colour schemes are unbelievable. Whole gables of temple buildings glow with these mosaics, generally used as a background for carved woodwork overlaid with gold, great scrolls of it supporting some central symbol such as Vishnu's *Garuda* or Brahma's *Hansa*, reminding us again of the ground from which Buddhism sprang and on which it grew here when King Asoka's missionaries brought it to the Siamese Kings of the north before the south existed as a civilized country at all. Here at the shrine of the Emerald Buddha, and in some other rich temples, the whole exterior walls are overlaid with mosaic, their background of pale gold, shimmering, dazzling and non-material. As clothing, too, mosaics are quite entrancing. The *Yàk* (giants), who do duty as caryatides with jocund mirth, are clad in mosaics, their dresses are of vivid and harmonious blues, greens and purples, which, together with the vitality of their poses, redeems the fantastic hideousness of their faces ! The expression of mirth is so refreshing in caryatides. How they would shock their European cousins of the Erectheum who stand through the ages bowed under their burdens in frozen dignity ! The *Yàk's* carry two large prachedi of gold leaf over copper, in which arduous task they are assisted by Hanuman, the monkey-general of the Ramayana, whose white face is to be seen in their midst. A constant surprise in this astonishing place is to find Hindu mythological figures and symbols in alliance with the purely Siamese. More of this later.

All around are buildings of extraordinary beauty and of a strange type individual to Siam and Cambodia. Amidst such wizardry, familiar forms of mangoes and other known trees silhouetted here and there against dazzling walls bring almost grateful recollections of everyday life, besides which, in glaring sunlight, their shade is doubly welcome, because dark glasses may not be worn within the Palace precincts . . . possibly in reminiscence of the days when disguise was frequent and deeds were dark.

Although their most obvious charm is that of colour, Siamese temples are fine in line and proportion. The steepness and importance of their roofs recall those of the extreme north of Europe. They rise stage above stage, double, treble, or even quadruple at the edge, each stage becoming steeper as it rises to the high line of the ridge, tipped with the Naga. At either end one gable grows out of another, each raking forward, again complicating and enriching ; and still further to enrich, each gable is edged with a flame pattern of prescribed design, one tall springing flame ending each series. It is either made in wood overlaid with gold leaf or encrusted with the all-pervading coloured glass mosaic.

Seen in section, walls of sacred buildings in Siam are like buttresses, with the curious effect that at a first glance, in spite of obvious differences, such as grace opposed to strength, and perishable material in contrast with everlasting rock, the body of a building, especially its roofless ruin, recalls the Egyptian pylon. The doorways and windows are also broader at the bottom than at the top, suggesting the side of a truncated pyramid. These features are clearly derived from Cambodian architecture. The Cambodians built their temples in stone, though handling it as if it were wood.

Wat Phra Keo itself, as the name implies, is the temple of the Emerald Buddha, the precious image which is all that now remains to Siam of her Cambodian conquests, the vassal state having been relinquished when the French took over the protectorate in 1867. Fittingly every resource of the national art has been lavished on this shrine.

The magnificent blue roof is its principal feature, but the walls and the pillars of the porticoes at either end, entirely covered as they are with designs of soft-coloured glass mosaic on a ground of pale greenish gold, make it appear a thing seen in dreams ; especially if you should chance to be there sketching alone at evening and the only sound that of softly tinkling silver as the breeze stirs the Boh leaf bells hanging from the temple eaves.

Every Tuesday I wandered and sketched at my pleasure in the magic enclosure, though my bodyguard was always within call. The said bodyguard consisted of a lieutenant from the Ministry of the Household and a clerk from the Foreign Office—kindly, patient young men, who, on my account, weekly saw their more fortunate comrades leave work at the usual hour while they watched over me till the light was too dim to paint. Whether their presence was for my protection or that of the Emerald Buddha I never knew.

English was our only means of communication. The clerk from the Foreign Office (not always the same) generally knew a few words of English or perhaps French, but Monsieur le lieutenant had only Siamese, of which I, unfortunately, had none.

At the end of my sojourn the only thankoffering that I could devise was to give them each a pencil sketch portrait made when thunderclouds interrupted my work. My efforts were most graciously received, although it was an obvious disappointment that they were not coloured . . . but life is short.

From earliest times magic and religion have been closely intertwined, so it is no contradiction to compare the atmosphere of this fairy place with that of the cloister as we know it in Europe, and a cloister does indeed surround the enclosure, carrying a sense of seclusion and secrecy. It is on the inner side of the gleaming white wall seen from the outer precincts, and is storied with the earlier lives of Buddha in a faded tapestry of painting.

On the anniversary of the reigning house, the past kings of the line in the persons of their golden statues in the Pantheon, which is open on that day only, receive the homage of all Bangkok, that of the reigning sovereign together with his devoted subjects. Bowers of Nottingham lace curtains draped up with sashes of bright colour are prepared for the reception of His Majesty, and seem to us, in such surroundings, the last word in incongruity. Whenever the king was expected we saw similar preparations. Europeans might consider the impression that their own use of oriental materials must make on the Oriental beholder in Europe. Oh! late wearers of the Bokhara skirts that are now my curtains, what would you think of their conversion to such a use?

It was a great disappointment to find that apparently all Bangkok freely entering, my way alone was barred—with gestures of regret and courteous smiles, it is true, but quite definitely barred. There seemed to be no official who spoke English, and, alas! I had no Siamese. However, an appeal thrown across the sentry towards a group of young men passing in found a student of English glad to practise the language. It appeared that, although open on that day to the public, without special permission foreigners were not included. . . . 'You do not appear to be Siamese,' was an amusing comment.

Still, there was hope. If I would go round to the main gate of the Palace, whence I could be directed to the office of the Major Domo (titles carefully committed to memory), he might give the desired Permit.

At the said office (the journey there had been long) it was sadly evident that it was holiday time even for Major Domos. No visitors were expected, and no one could understand any language I could speak, but a kind subordinate, putting the finishing touches to his uniform, evidently decided that the place for embarrassing foreigners was the Foreign Office, and led the way thither, beckoning me to follow.

The Foreign Office was closed for the holiday week and only one or two underlings, in various stages of undress, were to be found. Much explanation ensued, but, unfortunately, nothing that could be understood by me, and I was just turning away with despairing, but it is to be hoped polite, smiles, when, lo ! appeared my Friendly Student.

He translated : For sketching in the Palace precincts a special Permit was necessary. With some difficulty I explained that this was already in my possession, procured for me graciously by the Under Secretary for Foreign Affairs, but that clearly did not advance my immediate desire, which was to see the interior of the Pantheon. After further unintelligible consultations my Friendly Student led the way to the Palace Guard to consult the Captain. He, more than all the others, was apparently unready to receive visits, but fully equal to the occasion he sped us on (the day was hot) through interesting interior ways, where prisoners in leg irons were cleaning up behind the scenes, to the gate I had first attempted, only this time I was behind the sentry, and could sit and watch unnoticed while people of all classes passed in, dressed in their charming best, and carrying offerings of flowers. A welcome rest and a delightful scene.

Meanwhile Nai Friendly Student had gone forward to prospect, and at last returned with the news that permission was granted for me to go in, but not to sketch. So I drifted in with the crowd, through the cool cloisters, into the forest of Prapang and Prachedi and its permanent population of Brahminy cattle and elephant-headed *Ganesha* from India, *Norasing*, *Kinorn* and *Yàk* above described, Chinese sages and other quaint figures, and in quiet salà, disregardful of them as of all human effort, the Lord Buddha in deepest meditation.

The interior of the Pantheon was disappointing, not at all as purely Siamese or even Eastern as the exterior. There were interesting groups of Siamese soldiers in khaki uniforms prostrated in worship side by side with their fellow citizens in *panung* and *pasin* of gay colours, but in art the daily more inevitable trespass of West on East shocks always. Here lack of fusion is fatal.

It was a relief to follow with the crowd into *Wat Phra Keo*, where scene and setting were absolutely harmonious. Here was that combination of worship and pleasure-seeking completely absent only in Protestant countries. Their devoirs to the Lord of the Temple being paid, people rested, sitting in groups comfortably on the floor in those respectful attitudes' which demand the lifelong cultivation of double joints, and are excruciatingly difficult to the European.

The enormous temple teapot was in constant demand. It did not matter at all that cups were few, when necessary they were rinsed into each other, and a little tea spilled on the floor gave no offence.

The marvellous Emerald Buddha sits enthroned too high for worshipper or sightseer to admire the precious stone and workmanship, only the stillness of his pose arrests, as it always must.

Twice only have I been impressed with the intensity of utter stillness in a human being. At Benares a Brahmin pilgrim in meditation at the water's edge, and at Cairo a Mahommedan at prayer in the Zoo, who neither stirred nor gave any sign of having felt the paw of a big lion cub on his shoulder.

I was much interested in the figures of disciples standing in devotional attitudes at the feet of Buddha, and also in the endless offerings from all parts of the

Buddhist world of objects beautiful and curious that crowd the lower stages of the altar. Those that I remember particularly are tiny models of the sacred tree, the Master's shelter at the Great Illumination, the whole made in gold or silver, and covered with tiny leaves. The throne itself is of carved wood overlaid with gold and inset exquisitely with glass mosaic, or, as on one of the lower levels, with small plaques of mirror painted with curious figures.

Offerings which least commend themselves to European eyes are those brought from the West, such as vases of Sevres porcelain or Bohemian glass, and, as in all wealthy temples, a multitude of clocks of every description. There is apparently no sense of irony in presenting timepieces to One whose lifework was the quest for freedom from Time's endless cycles.

In a kind of ambulatory round and behind the altar is the Buddha's wardrobe. It was in his cold weather dress that I first saw him. The temple was empty then of worshippers, losing thereby half its charm, but there was leisure to examine its treasures.

Here are regalia for every season, and also in glass cases many of the smaller and more precious offerings. Endless minute figures of the Lord Himself, generally in attitude of meditation, each about two inches high and made in gold, silver or the perfect combination of metals—gold, silver, iron, lead, antimony, copper and tin.

After seeing the treasure, it is well worth while to examine the frescoes which cover the walls between the deepset windows, glassless but shuttered. These shutters, like the entrance doors, are gems of mother-of-pearl inlay on ebony, closely covered with amazing Ramayana episodes and beautiful design.

The general effect of the wall paintings is as of tapestry on a dark ground, and the scheme of decoration recalls that of certain mediaeval Italian pictures with crowds of tiny figures on a series of landscapes. Each landscape is the setting of some episode in Gautama's life, or his earlier incarnations as Boddhisatva.

The curious and amusing thing about the frescoes is the great sense of life conveyed by Devas and other mythological figures; also by most of the animals—elephants, tigers, dogs, etc., even though they should not portray quite the breeds to which we are accustomed. This is generally the case with horses, for instance, which seem to us diverting. Poor humanity, however, is left far behind, the figures being not merely faulty in drawing and proportion, but nearly always stilted, copied and without vision, while the artist's mental vision of the immortals has been clear and convincing. That the poses in a group of figures should be a matter of tradition, as are the component parts of a Siamese conventional design, might, one would think, dull the liveliness of the conception, although it should lend ease of execution. Instead, the effect is astonishingly lively, so long as the artist is not hampered by facts; at any rate by such obstinate facts as human beings, and can give free rein to his vision.

Naturally the standard of painting varies greatly in different temples, but it is very generally as above described. At Petchaburi in Southern Siam I met a Siamese painter, an interesting old man who had decorated many of the temples there with tiny but spirited renderings of the sacred stories, really delightful miniatures, and full of fascinating supernatural beings. He kindly consented to repeat a couple of little figures for me, one of them an enchanting lady frequently met in Siamese story, who, wringing a flood of turbulent water from her magnificent hair, thereby sweeps away all the Lord's enemies together with their armies, elephants and chariots. So charming was her face as he first painted it for me, that a cockroach took a fancy to it and ate it all away while the paint was wet. The distress of the poor artist was great. He managed, however, to repair the damage so much to my content that I can only wonder of what the cockroach robbed me!

The old man was anxious to see my sketches and, to my pleasure and admiration, liked them greatly. It bespoke a wonderful breadth of outlook in one whose chances of seeing anything other than his own type of work were so very limited. His own painting, he said, was to be seen in the hand, but mine to be admired from a distance. It was pleasant to rejoice him with pencil portrait sketches of himself and his wife.

CHAPTER IX

THE INNER PALACE AND SOME FESTIVALS

On a memorable occasion I visited the precincts of the Inner Palace. Here little may be seen even with a special permit. However, the courtyard alone is worth the visit, being just such a joy as fits in the Land of Faery, although the buildings are no longer pure Siam. In the courtyard imagine all kinds of trees transformed by the topiarist into a fantastic semblance of a giant juggler's game of ball. No mere shade is sought and the spell allows no individuality in the trees : they are all under the same enchantment, and the only one I could recognise was the tamarind, but they make the gayest decorative foreground for the Palaces, assisted as they are by low walls and beautiful coloured porcelain vases.

The only building ordinarily shown to visitors is *Maha Chakkri*, which does its utmost to draw the stranger back to the everyday world from the grip of the spell which already half holds him.

Maha Chakkri is frankly hybrid, the body being commonplace Mediterranean only redeemed by the beautiful Siamese roof, dark in colour with sparkles of mosaic on the central and two other storied spires which flank it. A *perron* leads into the galleries of pictures and curios collected in Europe, also portraits of princes and ministers in European style. It came over me with a shocked surprise that to the Siamese these things must have an exotic charm !

My special permit took me into the two really beautiful Siamese buildings which stand on either side of Maha Chakkri. To the right *Maha Dusit*, the old throne room, and to the left *Amarindra*, the hall of audience. Both are built of coloured porcelain, mosaic, and gold-covered carving on the outside ; within, the walls are frescoed with designs genuinely national, in which variants of the flame are the most frequent motif, while delightful figures attitudinise in antique attire on the window shutters. There are also gorgeous curtains of cloth of gold with coloured designs in appliqué.

The whole place filled me with a longing to sketch, but, alas ! no sketching permits are given for the inner courts of the Palace, and it was only just before I left Siam that a friend procured me that pleasure, and, as it turned out, for one evening only !

On that occasion, to the horror of my escort, I turned my easel in the direction of *Maha Dusit*, at that time of day a delight to the eye calling out to be sketched. But *Maha Dusit* was not named on the permit, of which the original was fetched to prove to me that *Amarindra* only was inscribed thereon ! So, as higher powers were all absent at the deathbed of a royal prince, and no appeal was possible, on *Amarindra* I set to work, only grateful that so jealously guarded a privilege had been granted to me.

Appropriate to their surroundings, brightly dressed people passed to and fro, notes of living colour. The regular uniform of Government servants of all ranks is a white full-skirted coat, said to be of Russian origin, with a *panung* of royal blue. The difference between

AMARINDRA HALL.

To face page 120

the dress of the lowliest employee and that of the head of a department is only in the material used, and in the wearing or not of shoes and stockings. The women servants, passing in groups, wore other bright tints; the elders were in *panung* like the men, and like the men had short hair. The younger, following the fashion preferred by his late majesty, wore the *pasin*, a length of cloth folded close round the lower part of the person from the waist to ankle.

Peculiar to Siam and Cambodia the *panung* is an adaptation of the Indian *dhotie* cloth, and consists of about four yards of material—rich silk for those who can afford it—put plainly round the back of the person up to the height of the waist, the upper edges near the body being caught together in front and tied. The surplus yards, which vary with the wearers' girth, are folded and twisted into a kind of rope, which is passed between the legs and tucked into the belt at the back. At a little distance the whole thing has the air of a very gay pair of 'plus fours' and is very smart when cleverly put on. Unfortunately, when worn with shoes and stockings it is as though the Eastern *panung* resented the European hose, and an indescribable hiatus results, for the *panung* frequently refuses to cover the back of the knee.

In the midst of the Palace the beholder instinctively tries to people the lovely buildings in imagination, and the courtly Siamese manners are well suited to so fairy seeming a place. But to understand their significance various laws of etiquette must be known; for instance, as before stated, the head of one to whom you owe honour must always be above your own. Not only to servants does this apply but to all classes. A prince will address the king from the ground, or even lying on the ground if His Majesty be seated, and, in that case, his approach will have to be made in lowly and snake-like fashion. So, too, does a commoner address a prince. The Siamese are convinced, as is every other people, that true courtesy is only to be found among themselves; but lest their customs should appear comical to the Europeans, whose seeming lack of manners they despise, true Siamese ceremonial is reserved for the purely Siamese assemblies, and is not profaned by use in mixed gatherings.

Once, by lucky mischance, we were present on such an occasion, we being the only Europeans at a Siamese rendering of Molière's play 'Les Amants Magnifiques.' It was given by the pupils of a Buddhist girls' school, and its principal, an intellectual Princess, had translated and adapted the play, turning it into a kind of operetta in which the words were set to Siamese airs, while the costumes were pseudo-classical. Moreover, with an eye to the edification of her pupils, the Princess had transmuted Venus and her crew into Charity supported by Faith and Hope. Let not Siamese magic spoil your rest, oh, shade of Molière!

Imposing-looking seats for the Court, thrones for royalty, the King having signified his intention of being present with the *Chow Chorm*, filled the front half of the hall. We, as only less respectable, were in the Great Gulf fixed between Court and people.

A mistake had brought us there that evening instead of the next with our fellow Europeans, but we were warmly welcomed, and I greatly prized the opportunity of seeing Siam at home. The King arrived two hours late, so, as we could not leave unperceived, we were there from 8 p.m. till 5 a.m., and to keep open eyes as the hours grew from late to early against a lullaby of never-ending Siamese tunes, heard without understanding, took heroic effort! Yet the scene was not one to be missed. Western touches transposed, and, in so different a setting, were almost as new and delightful as pure Oriental. The Princess played the serpent in her own Eden, and with her own hands served supper to His Majesty, ably seconded by favoured pupils, while others, less fortunate, respectfully stooping, bore trays to each Minister and Prince who had accompanied the King. We, too, had goodies brought to us, the only ones outside the Court so favoured.

Ungratefully, of the whole interesting evening the clearest picture in my mind is that of the King's departure, when he motioned the lady who had accompanied him to pass in front of him into the motor car, while she, not to be outdone in Western fashions, first dropped him a little curtsey. I fancy it was the same lady who, a few months later, was raised to royal rank by His Majesty in order that the son which she had promised him, being of royal rank on both sides, should be able to inherit the throne. Unfortunately nature once more played her well-worn joke and tricked the astrologers by sending an inconsiderable daughter. So, only a few days before his death, His Majesty's hope of a successor in the direct line was frustrated.

It is certain that Siamese manners are charming, and though thoughts of Fairyland were far in the blue distance of youth, I found myself back at its gates when some pretty child on bended knee presented me with a blossom, and it seemed fitting that younger people as a matter of course should take their place on the floor at my feet in conversation !

For me magic invested the Old Palace from my first view of it by the light of His late Majesty the King's birthday illuminations. In the face of so much beauty the saying of a Siamese student in England, that London had been fairyland to him when first he went there, returned to my mind as doubly astonishing. London with its noise, murk and mechanical brilliance ! It is a depressing thought that mere strangeness may itself cast the spell of enchantment; but no, for all its adoption of Western contrivances and modern methods Bangkok is still undeniably nearer Faery than dear comfortable Britain. Here at Bangkok electricity is almost universal, and illuminations grow yearly more vivid, so that the discreet and charming light of cocoanut oil lamps in decoration becomes sadly rare. Such is the melting quality of their light that buildings thus illuminated appear set into the velvet dark in a semi-transparent glow, while the cold glitter of electricity, self-sufficient and self-advertising, scatters the mystery of night.

Whether illuminated by electricity or with the soft glow of cocoanut oil, for H.M.'s birthday the streets in every direction were decorated as they might be in England on the occasion of a jubilee or coronation, as were also the palace gates of princes and nobles ; but best of all were the open spaces round the Old Palace, crowded with people in gay attire, the rich in cars and the poor in double rickshas or on foot. Everywhere bright-coloured *pasin* and *panung* were visible, and the priestly yellow ; for priests and students are prominent figures by reason of the robe that sets them apart. They

THE KING'S BIRTHDAY ILLUMINATIONS.

To face page 124.

strolled about in twos or threes, the tones of their draperies varying from orange to canary.

The fine old walls of the sacred enclosure carried above their leaf-shaped crenellations pennons alternating with three-tiered umbrellas in red, white, yellow or green ; and above and behind the multitude of *Prapangs* drew up their heads into the blue-green sky lit only by mysterious meditating stars.

In the streets were itinerant vendors, too, sellers of foodstuffs, sellers of sweetmeats, and, best of all, lithe men running in and out among the people, their hands full of those familiar joys, great brightly coloured air balloons, held high for safety above the heads of the crowd.

Few Western toys seem equally at home and appropriate in every part of the globe. The crowd, though so gay, was astonishingly quiet, even the Chinese, noisiest of the noisy in their own country, seemed under the spell of national quiet.

There were bands, and here I made my first acquaintance with Siamese music, very pleasing rhythmic melodies, in which the problem of perpetual motion seems to have been solved in contrapuntal themes of great charm and ingenuity. The interwoven threads of sound appeared to me to have much analogy with the beautiful designs on the lacquered bookcases, collected in the National Library by H.R.H. Prince Damrong, interlacing lines without beginning or end, enriched with a thousand fantasies.

In the orchestra the principal instrument, played by the leader and called *Klong Yai*, is a series of small connected gongs disposed in a circle which is broken in about a quarter of its circumference to allow the player room to sit, and demands of him acrobatic agility. There may be several in one orchestra, but those of other players are then of different pitch with sets of gongs larger or smaller.

Other important instruments are drums of various shapes and sizes, their insistent beat underlining the changing rhythms. The whole thing is extraordinarily fascinating to eye and ear until the fragile Western patience broken by iteration, the old *scie* springs to mind:

> Il était un petit navire (*bis*)
> Qui n'avait ja-ja-*ja*mais navigué (*bis*)
> Si cette histoire vous ennuie (*bis*)
> Nous allons la la *la* recommencer (*bis*)

On this occasion there were two bands, the second was military and brass, but happily it was not necessary to strain my patience by staying to listen to versions of well-worn tunes from home. The Siamese are an exceedingly musical people, and in spite of the fact that their own scale has about seven tones to our octave, and that in their own music only melody and counterpoint are considered, they enter exceedingly well into that of the West, as is proved by the excellence of the King's orchestra, though the conductor is a Siam-born Austrian who has never been to Europe, and all the instrumentalists are Siamese.

The illuminations last three nights, in order that His Majesty may be able to see and enjoy them both in the town and from the river, where the swift stream's eddying plays fantastically with the brilliance of the banks.

The Old Palace is but the most beautiful of many. Two more must be mentioned. The way to the *New*

Dusit Palace lies through the *Phra Meru* and a fine avenue of mahogany. The word *Dusit* means appropriately 'The Paradise where all desires are fulfilled.' The Throne Hall is a very handsome building by an Italian architect, and I believe a very clever adaptation of the monarch's desire for many domes, hampered by the royal amateur's indication of how the undertaking was to be carried out !

The roof is a wonderful vantage ground from which to see Bangkok—a town so flat that there is no place higher in the city, except the artificial *Pukao Tong* ('Golden Hill') with its crowning *Prachedi.* Inside the dome is splendour, but hardly a trace of genuine Siam beyond the great metal drums to announce the sovereign's coming, his throne supported by *Krut* and shaded with a many-tiered umbrella in white edged with gold, and the inevitable spittoons—a necessary concession to modern ideas of hygiene. I was told that the palmy days of betel chewing were past, but provision for its use is still very necessary, and black teeth are frequent among older people, though a gleaming white smile has long ceased to be a sign of depravity !

Among the Palaces that cannot go unnoticed is that of the Second King. The last to hold this title was one of the brothers of H.M. King Chulalongkorn, father of the present monarch. Theoretically, the function of the Second King was to hold the reins of government in the absence of the Sovereign ; but possession being acknowledgedly nine points of the law, there were occasional difficulties, and the political complications and rivalries were endless, especially in relation to foreign powers, when a Second King with a grievance would try to enlist the sympathies and help of a foreign minister, or even take refuge with him! So part of his Palace is now a museum and a fine setting for the precious things contained therein.

How long ago Hinduism came to Siam is, I am told, a matter of conjecture. There are Siamese Brahmins who have their own special temples; all that I discovered about them is that they are present at every big semi-religious festival connected with the crops or the changing seasons, as, for instance, the Swing Ceremony or the Ploughing Ceremony, which the King or his representative always attends, and here the Brahmins are diviners or interpreters of omens.

The setting of the Swing Ceremony, an exceedingly picturesque affair, is unique. A series of squalid narrow streets appear to lead straight to a blood-red scaffold which they serve to focus, then suddenly open out into a circular space in front of the particularly dignified and beautiful *Wat Sudath*. In the middle of the space is the tallest swing imaginable, the posts eighty feet high and painted scarlet. On the day of the ceremony it is crowned with honorific umbrellas, white and three-storied, fluttering in the breeze, and long lines hung with Chinese lanterns radiate from the top of the posts into the circus. On the far side, opposite the Wat, are the bowers of Nottingham lace as *de rigueur*, prepared to receive *Phra Isuen*, i.e. *Siva*, Creator and Destroyer, in the person of the King or his delegate. He has come down from his heaven to enjoy the sight of swinging.

Successively competing teams of six little men with queer red hats representing the *Naga* (Serpent King) climb into the seat ten or twelve feet above the ground, and are swung by a man who pulls a rope from below. As they swing their leader must with his teeth snatch

SWING CEREMONY.

To face page 128.

a bag of money from an umbrella-crowned bamboo fixed a few paces from the swing. Meanwhile the watching crowd seeks omens for the coming rice crop; it is good that the money-bag should be skilfully seized at the first try, bad if the swinging team should lose their *Naga* hats, and worse (especially for him, one would think!) if one should lose his seat. In Mr. W. A. Graham's book *Siam* are many interesting details of the ceremony.

At the Swing Ceremony was my first sight of a Siamese crowd, which I enjoyed under the most comfortable conditions, sitting in the shade of the great Wat among people of distinction and provided with chairs. We were offered refreshment, too; glasses of water, coloured vivid green or pink, which brighten Siamese ceremonial occasions; these are flavoured as well as coloured, but Europeans are cautious rather than curious and few do more than admire. I was incautious but not enthusiastic!

It seems that the original significance of the ceremony is lost, and all that the Brahmins now say in explanation is '*Phra Isuen* likes to see swinging,' which explains some swinging of a very different type, though swinging it was called, seen when I was at Tanjore in South India, in the great Temple of Siva. The swinger then was a temple dancer.

Brahmins are present at every royal ceremony, and in processions are easily recognisable by their white and gold cloaks and long hanging black hair. Mr. W. A. Graham says, that as long ago as 300 B.C. it is said of the monarchs of *Sukodaya*, who claimed *Kshatria* descent, that they surrounded themselves with the ancient Brahmin ceremonial of India, most of which is observed without very much change at the Court of Siam at the present day.'

Besides the semi-religious festivals and court functions Brahmins preside also on family occasions, as, for instance, when children at adolescence have to submit to three days' elaborate ceremonial at the cutting of the top knot. The mesh of hair is taken off by the noblest personage with whom the family can claim connection. If the unfortunate child be of high rank, it endures a time of intense discomfort in gorgeous raiment stiff with golden splendour. Special and beautiful vessels are set apart for the ceremony. I was shown a large shaving bowl of niello work, in which the Siamese excel, then in use as a flower bowl, and I fancy that is likely to be its future vocation, as so many young princes come early to England for education that among them the top knot cutting ceremony is falling gradually into disuse.

That Buddhism had its foundation in Hinduism is to be seen in Ceylon by the figure of Vishnu the Preserver standing in the image house of the temples. In Siam, however, Hinduism has a much bigger place. There is no art here which has not Hinduism as its base. *Krut*, the flying *Garuda*, vehicle of *Vishnu*, holds the same position as do with us the Lion and the Unicorn, and is the royal coat-of-arms. In the Royal Wats, as we saw at *Wat Phra Keo*, those Hindu personages, the cow, *Ganesha*, and also *Hanuman*, the monkey general of the *Ramayana* (always to be distinguished by his white face), are honoured in sculpture.

The classic school of acting and dancing too sets forth *Ramayana*, which are also found in wall paintings, inlays and other decorative designs. Especially is Hinduism seen in the architecture of the Royal Wats and the walls thereof; here Siva, the Creator and Destroyer, is represented by his symbol in the numerous *Prapang*, which rival in frequency the *Prachedi*, the Buddhist stupa form. So far as I know, however, worship is offered in one place only, at Wat Boh, where, under what I suppose was once the sacred tree, which gives the temple its popular name, stands the phallic symbol of creation, and here the people come to beg for sons, though it may be that their faith is sometimes tested by the gift of daughters instead.

This faithful *Boh* or *Bodhi* tree (in India called *Peepul*) is one of those under whose shade the Master received illumination. As in horror at such misunderstanding of His teaching, it has here allowed itself to be supplanted by a gorgeous vampire, *Ficus*, its cousin, which, sowing itself on the branch of some great one, clothes its trunk with roots, twines its branches round those of its victim, and lives with its life, while it strangles, breaks, absorbs and finally takes its place, itself in seeming, the magnificent tree!

The grounds of Wat Boh are an enchantment to the beholder, but to the painter a torment, as the richness of subject matter is only equalled by the difficulty of getting an uninterrupted view of what one wishes to draw. Here is a very forest of *prachedi* of all sizes. Four of them, built by various kings, are unsurpassable for beauty, height and elegance, and are built all of coloured porcelain tiles. In one the predominant colour is green, in one blue, in one yellow, and in one red. Springing from grounds thick with trees, and soaring far above the imposing roofs and glittering gables of the main buildings of the Wat, they are magnificent.

There is a most pleasant and rather melancholy quiet about Wat Boh on most days when once the guardian has silenced the chorus of pariah dogs ;—he collects the mangy pups and tries to sell you one—and if he has lost hope of you as a sightseer, you may wander unmolested. In the inner temple monks' mattins are impressive, both the rhythmic chant as they sit upright on the floor, bowing together with an occasional prostration towards the Lord Buddha high on his altar, and more impressive still the sudden silences . . . a delightful and spacious picture, spoilt only, to European eyes, by the false note of the very handsome rose red Western pile carpet.

The most interesting time to visit *Wat Boh* is at *Sonkran*, the festival of the solar year ; then the grounds are turned into a fair with all kinds of amusing things for sale ; also there are theatres and other pleasures. But that which marks the season is the making of miniature *Prachedi* in sand, one of the ways in which the monks take advantage of the New-Year rejoicings to collect money for the upkeep of the Wat. Merit-makers have probably presented heaps of sand for the purpose, and the monks sell it in small quantities to the faithful who, with the help of a little water, make it into miniature Prachedi, joy in making mud pies being universal! Whole families come down to the Wat grounds and vie with each other as to whose prachedi, or series of prachedi, shall be the most imposing. Maybe they will bury a coin instead of the relic, as in the grown-up *Prachedi*, that the monks may profit by that much more when the festival is over and the sand cleared away, but the real rivalry is as to whose Prachedi shall be the best decorated, and very gay they are. Tiny flags surmount or surround them, and rings of coloured wax candles and offerings of garlands are made, and sticks of incense burnt, or again they may be draped as the real ones often are, the material worn over the shoulder, so to speak, like a pointed shawl. Children and, parents all work together, and the scene is most delightfully animated and gay. Unfortunately I had to give up the attempt to make sketches, for, however quietly I peeped from retired corners, I was always discovered, and became to my embarrassment a centre of interest myself.

At this season the large building containing the gigantic sleeping Buddha, Phra Norn, is open to pilgrims who come to do obeisance and bring offerings. This building is one of the largest in the temple enclosure, and the huge image completely fills it. Phra Norn is, or has been, altogether covered with gold, which is now peeling off in places and hangs like loose skin above the level where the faithful, who bring gold, can reach to renew it. Many worshippers bring a small paper of gold leaf, and by applying it themselves gain merit for the act as well as for the gift. The next best thing to putting it on oneself is to hand it to one of the youths who have taken up their station on the raised dais to gain merit by helping others, but the figure is of monstrous size—72 feet long—and the gold is put time after time only on those parts that can be reached, which produces an appearance of muscle in unexpected places.

Many other occasions for acquiring merit are provided. Musicians, for a small coin, will soothe the Lord's slumbers with sweet sounds of tinkling gongs; stalls of flowers, joss sticks, and candles are there to be purchased for offerings; and, sitting round the temple in the half light at one's feet, are rows of nuns and beggars hoping for alms, and deeming that in the opportunity for acquiring merit thus afforded to the givers lies their own gift.

Probably because this view is held by rich and poor alike, in Buddhist countries and noticeably in Siam, strangers are remarkably little pestered for money, but it is a difficult idea for the average European to grasp, and he is apt to see ingratitude in the philosophical attitude of one who, having received help in his hour of need, just goes his way content to know that his helper is the greater beneficiary.

PHRA NORN.

To face page 134.

CHAPTER X

THE WAT

The Wat is the centre of village life, at any rate in the sense that every boy has his early teaching in its school, and every man spends at least three months of his early manhood as one of its monks, besides which village intrigue eddies round the election of the successor to the chief monk when his place is made vacant by death. So it was natural that when tying up at a riverside Wat, to stroll about its grounds, all the small boys of the village should seem to spring up like weeds from the earth.

The Wat is generally enclosed in an oblong space surrounded by a brick wall. The short sides of the enclosure face east and west and usually the principal entrance is in the east wall. Among the many buildings within the compound the Sacred Fane, the *Bhôt*, is easily distinguished, as a few feet from each corner and in the middle of each side, raised to about the height of a man, is a stone shaped like the leaf of the sacred Boh tree. These stones are called *Bai Sema* : they are covered with Pali script, and inside the square they mark all is sacred. The roof ridge of the Bhôt runs east and west and within the great Buddha sits enthroned, his altar facing the east. Though his altar is thus placed at the west end of the building, the reverse of the practice in Christian churches, the mystical importance of the east is none the less emphasised by his position. It was so 500 years before Christ, and for countless generations before Him men bowed before the mystery of the sun's daily rising.

A great stone boat standing among the group of buildings of many river Wats misled me into seeing a further likeness to the symbolism of the Christian Church—'that they . . . may be received into the Ark of Christ's Church . . . may pass the waves of this troublesome world. . . .'

But this boat is commemorative, not symbolical, and recalls a very remarkable boat in legendary history:

In olden days the sovereign of a large kingdom had two wives. The principal wife gave him a son, born with a caul. The second wife, who was childless, was madly jealous and persuaded the king that however lucky seeming this was a portent of disaster to monarch and kingdom. The king, impressed, called in a soothsayer who by his art foresaw great good fortune for the heir. Alas! for human nature, present benefits outweighed future good, and heavily bribed by the lesser wife, the soothsayer supported her and they obtained that mother and son should be banished to a far country (there are lucky cauls and also Hagars in all lands).

Years sped, and when the boy was seven the unappeased jealousy of the wicked wife discovered that he grew and flourished, so she commissioned murderers to rid the earth of him. A cunning plan was made that he should die a seeming accidental death, tusked by a wild elephant. But Meh Toroni, Mother of Earth, protects those of her sons destined to be great, and she opened the eyes of the wild elephant so that he knew the child as holy, and instead of tusking him prostrated himself before him.

So then, fear working with her jealousy, the wicked woman obtained a decree from the king that the luckless child should have a stone tied to his waist and be cast into the sea. And so it was done. Still Meh Toroni was watchful and she guided the sinking child to the very doors of the Naga King's palace—he is Phya Nák who lives in the depths of the sea. Enchanted with so beautiful a boy Phya Nák took him in and treated him as a son for six days. Now on the seventh day everyone around him must die, for Phya Nák must get rid of his poison. . . . As he loved the child, before the seventh day broke, Phya Nák had built a boat, put the child into it together with the prayer that anyone meeting the boy should care for him, and sent it up to the surface. Now near the place where it came up there lived a widowed giantess, and one of her slaves was first to spy the boat and the luscious morsel, and went towards it, happy in the prospect of a good meal, for those giants were ogres. But, seeing him come, the boat with its charge disappeared, and the slave went and told his mistress of the strange happening. The boat reappearing she went herself to see, and marvelling at the boy's beauty said she would adopt him. Then the boat came towards her and when the boy was taken out, its task being accomplished, the boat withdrew itself, and to celebrate this good deed people place it in front of the Wat to this day.

The rest of the story is long and full of adventure, and though nothing further is heard of the boat a little more shall be told for the interest of parallels in European fairy tale :

The giantess indulged the boy greatly and loved him dearly. Only two things she utterly forbade. There were two rooms into which he might not go, and a sheet of water that he might not touch. Now from time to time she left home to get a meal such as ogres love, and one day curiosity was too much for the boy, and he touched the water gingerly with the tip of his finger, which instantly turned to gold. This of course made it invulnerable and it was this that the giantess had feared, that, knowing himself protected, he would leave her. When the boy saw the gold tip he understood, and wound his handkerchief round the finger to hide it. When she came home his adopted mother asked what was the matter, and he said he had cut himself a little—but he waited with impatience for her next absence to explore the forbidden rooms. And when the giantess went away again he opened the first door and saw the portrait of a giant, and also a big stick and a suit of giant's clothes, but the second room was full of human bones. He determined to try on the clothes in the first room, and by putting them on he became a giant and understood what his mother was, and was filled with fear lest she should eat him. Fear urging him to escape, he first jumped into the magic pond and became gold, then put on the giant's suit and fled into a distant country.

Overcome with grief at not finding him at home the giantess followed, and begged him to return, promising him safety and forgiveness. But 'no,' he said, 'you will forget and eat me.' So she turned back, and, hopeless, died of grief at the bottom of the hill, and the boy was very sorry, and said he had not known she loved him so much.

The boy's other adventures, before he came into his kingdom, are endless and thrilling. I can only give the beginning of the tale, as told by the grandmother of the Siamese lady who told it to me.

The most important buildings after the *Bhôt* are the *Wihan* (Vihara), which is the image house, and contains figures of Gautama at various stages of his existence before and after the attainment of Buddhahood. There are images too of some of the disciples of Buddha, and of Brahmanistic deities, such as the Judge of Souls, the God of Rain, and the Goddess of Earth, Meh Toroni, through whose good offices the hero of the above boat story was saved.

Then come the *Rong Tam* or Preaching Hall and the school-house, and one or more *Sàlá*, raised and roofed but wall-less, which are rest houses for whoever will. In some Wats one thing predominates and in some another. And here is a true and tragic tale of woman's pride brought low, illustrating the place she occupies in Buddhist eyes:

Much merit accrues to the giver of any part of a Wat and most of all to the builder of a Bhôt. A woman of wealth who lives on the outskirts of Bangkok gave much and collected more money to build a Bhôt. All went well: it grew, and she gloried, till in her triumph at bringing the great work to a successful conclusion she presumed and herself helped to paint the ceiling—only to learn from the priest that her woman's touch had been desecration, and the building could no longer serve as a *Bhôt* and for the consecration of priests, but must rank henceforth merely as a *Wihan*!

The thought of the crestfallen dame, pursued by the anathemas of those whose contributions she had collected, fills one with the hope that pride so promptly punished left her, at any rate, great store of merit gained by the good and arduous work of collecting!

That the Master himself had very definite ideas of woman's place is shown by his rule for Buddhist nuns.

All Wats dwell in a forest of Prachedi, all, that is, that have had time to collect them, or that have not themselves fallen into decay, as so easily happens in a country where, unless he work for a parent's reputation, no merit accrues to him who repairs a temple, while so much may be gained by contributing to a new monastery. Although from the artistic point of view this is deplorable, psychologically it seems sound, for new enterprise has attractions and possibilities completely absent from humdrum patching. It would be interesting to know which best opens the pockets of the pious in this country, the new church badly needed in a populous district, or repairs to the old? Judging by an 'appeal' in a recent *Church Times* existing work begs in vain. '. . . Does no one care? . . . Last week we begged for fifty gifts of £10 each. We have received *not one*,' etc., etc. But then next to it—'£4000 wanted. Our *appeal* for the *Building Fund* . . . has produced no response up to the present,' etc., etc. So it is hard to say.

To return to the Wat. A monastery's chief monk is called *Than Som Pharn*. He is elected by the congregation, and the position is naturally coveted, for every man of the faithful who attend the Wat (generally in the persons of their womenkind) comes directly under the influence of its head at least twice in his life, as a schoolboy and as a young man in temporary orders. There are rival factions, therefore, that put forward candidates; but when the business of election is over there still may be room for much interesting wire-pulling, for the election has yet to be confirmed, and the dignity conferred by the Chief Priest of Siam, one of the royal Princes, and brother or uncle to the King.

The position of Second Monk, called *Than Maha*, depends on learning and degrees attained in the study of Pali, the ancient tongue in which the scriptures are written.

The head monks of the Royal Wats have a higher title, and it is from amongst their number that the chief abbots are selected, the *Chao Kana Yai*, under whom the order is divided into four sections, consisting of the north half of the kingdom, the south half, the brotherhood devoted to the purification of the faith and the simplification of its observances, and lastly, the head of the hermit monks, now few, who live entirely apart in the jungle. The King is the titular head of the Church, much as he is with us 'Defender of the Faith.' His rôle is entirely passive. As I understand it, his only active duties, if he should undertake them, would be distinctly unpleasant. If a monk commit murder only the King can execute him; but I have not heard of any such happening.

The grounds of riverside Wats can hardly fail to be beautiful. The clearing necessary for the buildings gives the tall tropic trees more space for their great lives in upper air, whence they pay their dues in shelter to small mankind below. The greater number of Wat buildings all over Siam, whether rich or poor, have beauty of proportion and dignity and a queer illusion of solidity given by their Noah's Ark shape, although they are frequently built of very perishable material.

Also they have certain most intriguing characteristics, things of which it took me months to discover the meaning.

That the great horns with which every building in a Wat decorates the ends of its roof ridge and of its many gables, represented the conventionalised Naga, king of serpents, was quickly realised, but I wondered why he should always be in so dangerously prominent a position in a country where Garuda, his arch-enemy, who preys on him for food, has the exalted rôle of Royal Arms.

Before he attained Buddhahood Somona Kotom (literally the ascetic Gautama) sat in meditation regardless of the outer world. And the power of his sanctity raised him up enemies, chief among them the Giant Devil, Phya Mahn, who, in no way underestimating the strength with which he had to deal, brought his armies with horses and chariots and elephants to destroy the Blessed One.

Beholding this Meh Toroni, Mother of the Earth, who realised that though Force could not destroy His Power yet through Force Earth might lose it, wrung out her wondrous hair, making thereby a mighty flood which carried all things before it and swept them to destruction. Meanwhile the Naga, seeing that the flood's edge might reach the Master, still rapt and regardless of danger, raised him on its coils, and to fend the deluge from above multiplied his hoods from one to seven, and with them all outspread sheltered the meditating saint while the stream overwhelmed the cohorts sent to destroy him, and elephants, riders, chariots and horses, were all drowned. A Red Sea story.

Even Phya Mahn was up to the neck in water and

like to drown, when just in time he repented him of his wicked presumption, and swore to serve instead of plotting to destroy that which was above him, and so received his pardon. And since that day, wherever there is Hinayana Buddhism there you find Gautama enthroned in meditation upon the Naga's coils and sheltered by his sevenfold head, but, so far as my observation goes, only in Cambodia and Siam has Phya Nák his privileged place on the temple roof ridge. Below him the gable edges are decked with flame which represents the fiery breath of the angry Nák, called Nák-phon-pid—a warning, I suppose, to Garuda to keep his place !

For while Phya Nák and his breath, menacing but decorative, are a feature of every Wat roof, the main ornament of the gable end at least is often a Hindu symbol. The most frequent is certainly Garuda, Krut they call him in Siam, in his quality of Vehicle of Vishnu rather than as the Royal Arms. The Vehicle of Brahma too, the Hansa (Siamese ' Hong '), is sometimes seen, or the head of the Norasing. Whichever may be the design it is carved in wood and gold-covered, and stands out gorgeously against a background of brilliant mosaic. Perhaps it is even more harmonious in effect when the gold having worn off a delightful greeny-grey is left upon the coloured background.

The temple walls are generally of brick rendered with *chunam*, excepting in the most sacred buildings and the richest—the Temple of the Emerald Buddha at Bangkok and the Shrine of the Sacred Footstep at Phrabat. They appear melting and insubstantial, covered with mosaic of pale green-gold patterned with soft colour. After these, the most beautiful walls I remember are at Wat Aruna where the *chunam* is studded with chintzlike bouquets in porcelain.

The general use of plain white is very satisfying, broken as it is with the elaborately ornamental window frames and handsome shutters (often of lacquer or inlay) set well back in the thick wall, and bands of dark shadow under the deep eaves, while roof and gables blaze with colour.

On the ground Norasing guard the buildings of every Wat, but many Wats have other animals too. At Wat Aruna, on the east bank of the Menam at Bangkok, are four beautifully modelled bronze elephants in whose favour the people have forgotten the early King Aruna, after whom the temple was named, calling it Wat Chang (Elephant Temple). There are elephants too in the niches of the four small *praprang* which strengthen the base of the magnificent *praprang*, one of the city's landmarks, standing in the temple grounds on the river's edge. Guides state that it was built by the fleeing Siamese Court as a thankoffering when they arrived there in safety after the sack of Ayuthia. The tale is probably pure fabrication to satisfy the amazement of tourists, and account for the very curious but exceedingly decorative use of fragments of china. Presumably the Court in flight carried their best china with them, which they offered to the gods in gratitude for their escape. Perhaps some of the most precious pieces may have been broken on the journey so that anything of less value had to follow suit. This would explain the curious way in which plates and bowls are used to decorate the *praprang*. It is entirely covered with porcelain cups, bowls and plates, many plates starred from the centre whence the fragments radiate like the petals of a flower, and embedded in *chunam*. It must be that some of the good pieces have been maliciously destroyed or stolen, and at the base, sad to say, the quality of pieces substituted suggests European imitation of the cheapest! All the same, whether the popular idea of its origin be true or not the decoration really does decorate a monument unique and impressive as a thankoffering should be!

Several of the Wats on the right bank are fine, Wat Chang by the height of its *praprang* and Wat Kan Layar by the magnificence of its huge roof are the most remarkable. The latter is the particular centre of the Chinese community and in their care. There you find them prostrated before a gigantic Buddha whose height it would be difficult to guess. Before him, as in their temples at home, they shake up bamboo boxes full of long sticks to discover what fate holds in store for their every enterprise. The Buddha is also one of the hopes of the childless woman, who brings him her offerings and prayers. Her thanks, when her petition is granted, take the form of gold leaf if a boy should have rejoiced her heart, while if it be but a girl she brings a scarf for the gigantic figure—something like fifty yards must be necessary to wrap him suitably!

It is one of my regrets that I was unable to sketch there, my lack of Siamese hindering, for to cross the river would have meant dealing with so many different sets of people.

Most of the temples in Bangkok are closed except at the hours of the monks' religious exercises, or at Wan-Pra—the changes of the moon—or on the great festivals. At such times the scene is tremendously animated, worship and social gathering being agreeably combined. At Wisaka Bucha I had the good fortune to be taken to several Wats by a Siamese lady. Each temple appeared to have its own way of honouring the Master's birthday, which is believed to be also the anniversary of His Illumination under the Boh Tree, as well as of His Death. The Pali ritual may have been the same, but there was no popular celebration in the same sense as at Wesak in Ceylon. There they have white-clad processions, and streets are illuminated as well as temples and their dependencies. One Wesak, which I spent at Kandy, had impressed me as full of what we should call the Christmas spirit and feeling, and the animation and delight in worship round the great Boh Tree opposite the Temple of the Tooth were popular in the fullest sense. Here at Bangkok the festival seemed less universal. It appeared to centre round Wats with individual tradition and congregations from markedly different social strata. The remarkable feature at the beautiful Wat behind the National Library was table after table of flower offerings—such flowers as do not exist in any land except Siam, and perhaps Cambodia too.

One of the social arts young ladies learn is the making of artificial flowers out of parts of the real blossoms. Cut flowers last but a very few hours in that hot climate, whereas the petals, being of a less delicate texture than those of northern flowers, last a much longer time in comparison. Hence the artificial-real. Their making gives great scope for invention, and it was most interesting to pass from table to table and see how each donor had been inspired. The weak point was always the setting of the blossom on its branch. Nature did nothing here to help but seemed to jib at the use made of her gifts—a lack of discrimination on her part, for not rivalry but the wish to preserve the beauty she provides explains the strange-seeming art. At this temple the congregation was of the *élite* of society. From there we went on to Wat Suket at the foot of the Golden Hill, where I was told to mind my handbag, but somehow felt more at home, and the People (with a big P this time) seemed extremely devout. The whole thing made a wonderful picture. At the west end of the church was the great golden Buddha on his high altar lighted with many lights. At his feet sat the officiating priest cross-legged, his ornate chair raising him well above the crowd all seated on the ground or pressed, like me, against the wall. Like his overawing Master he faced the body of the building, a midget above a congregation of midgets.

Then on to the Wat Suthas (pronouncedЮтha*t*) the beautiful temple facing the giant swing. Here it may have been that a different point in the ceremonies had been reached. The crowd made it hard to get into the court, an informal procession was in progress, and compact groups of the faithful, constantly increased by fresh arrivals, carried wavering tapers round the Bhôt —small massed lights, as always wonderful in effect. With the lights behind them the beautiful bronze horses, the most remarkable feature of Wat Suthas's inner court, stood out black and sleek. 'Pure Siamese work,' says H.R.H. Prince Damrong. Certainly they are in marked contrast to the merely grotesque Chinese figures also to be seen here, as in most of the Bangkok Wat grounds. On the same authority these figures used to be brought over from China as ballast by ships seeking grain.

The procession over we climbed the steep steps (they seem steeper here than even those of most Wats), unreasonably steep—narrow steps are one of the things their descendants seem to have retained from the Khmer architects. They must have some well-hidden virtue, or be for the architectural effectiveness of the abrupt rise. In the Bhôt, their prostrations over, the congregation conversed decorously and in low tones behind the pillars. It was an unexpected place in which to be introduced to a Siamese lady who had spent ten years in London !

On the terrace outside the scene was frankly social. Groups of monks or students with their families and friends drank tea, and helped themselves to the smokes or chews set out in elaborately embossed gold or silver tazzas. There were heaps of cigarettes rolled either in lotus petals or banana leaf. By the bright moonlight the place was full of pictures, but the thing I most wanted to sketch was a glimpse of the great gold Buddha on his altar within seen from outside through an open shutter. My impressions that night had been too many to attempt it, but it was cheering to hear that the place would still be open the following night if I could manage to come. So the next night, having collected two English friends, each with a little Siamese to his credit, I returned there. The scene was approximately the same, but, alas ! the shutter was closed. The Englishman, besought to put forth his best Siamese, instead feebly asked if anyone spoke English ! Admitted, excuses are many. Not only is Siamese a tone language in which it is easier even for the informed foreigner to make mistakes than not, but there is the added difficulty of polite address with different expressions for differing ranks. Someone *did* speak English; but according to him it was difficult or impossible to get the shutter opened, probably because it pleased him to converse with us affably, if somewhat lamely, the centre of an admiring group of friends. We were led to a table, and tea and cigarettes were pressed on us. The Siamese drink delicious clear Chinese tea. They are great connoisseurs in tea, but, like the Chinese, do not seem to mind whether or no it is really hot. It had been a disappointment to me in China to find Indian or Ceylon teas the universal drink for Europeans!

It was pleasant and amusing on the Temple Terrace, but our hosts wanted to see me sketch, and a monkling made a gesture towards moonlit gables, saying '*Kien rup*'—'draw a picture.' His rather charming aspect attracted me far more than the gables, and in response to my gesture of enquiry as to whether he would be drawn, he delightedly took his stand under a light, and stood like a rock for the few minutes necessary for a rapid sketch.

It is always paralysing and a penance to be watched at work by people crowding round, but to his pleasure and to the great excitement of the onlookers his portrait came off tolerably well. Then it was told me that he also was an artist and wished to make my portrait if I would lend my sketch-book. Accordingly the book went from me to the interpreter, and from the interpreter to him, as it is not permissible that a woman should hand anything direct to a monk, and oh! the half hour or more that followed. He had taken his rôle as model most seriously and I could do no less, but my cheeks ache at the recollection of the smile that grew more and more fixed with every minute that passed. Indeed, if the drawing handed to me at long last speaks any truth at all—and there were murmurs of approval from the crowd very chastening to my vanity—it looked as painful as it felt. My friends nobly said they saw no likeness at all. I could, alas ! and still can, but at this distance can laugh freely. . . .

For one youth who played the clown the interpreter's nickname was jokeman. We were willing to believe that his funny sayings lost in translation.

CHAPTER XI

DEATH AND CREMATION

It was with surprise that I learned that every Wat has its graveyard. It is tucked away in some remote corner for the paupers whose families cannot scrape together the ten ticals—about £1—which are the minimum fee for cremation. Until the Department for Public Health interfered, these burial grounds were apt to be a gruesome sight. The bodies were not buried with any idea of permanence, only till such time as merit-makers should provide the funds for their burning, and it is easy to visualise the result if half-starved pariah dogs or birds of prey discovered their whereabouts. I am glad to say I never saw one of these pitiful corners, nor did I ever see a poor cremation, which also may be very upsetting to the squeamish. For one thing, the heat gives a horrid semblance of life, so that the corpse writhes, and lifts an arm or leg out of the shallow coffin in seeming anguish, and for another, wood is expensive and not always sufficient to complete the job. The well-to-do can afford plenty of wood and a coffin sufficiently deep to hide the poor body's antics, while the really well-off provide shows for the people, and historical plays by marionettes worked from below after the manner of Punch and Judy. From the point of view of acting they are generally very superior to our last-surviving puppet play, but historically their value may be no greater, though legend may carry them back as far as Punch and Judy's supposed origin, if its distorted association with Pontius Pilate and Judas Iscariot is not imaginary. There are crackers, too, and sometimes fireworks, also presents for all friends and relations, generally a book commemorating the dead.

Just opposite Wat Suket is a big public crematorium, not inexpensive, I believe, but not fashionable either. It is situated outside the city wall and the gate which leads to it is known to the people as the Gate of Ghosts.

As in China conspicuously, and in many places nearer home, funeral ceremonies frequently involve families for years, far more show being made than they can afford. The show the Siamese must have, and their alternative to debt seems to us dreadful—the defunct must be kept until the money to give him a fitting cremation can be found.

In rich princely houses (the higher the rank the greater the expected display for the dead awaiting cremation) a special temporary building may be erected in the grounds and given afterwards to the Wat as a dwelling-house for a monk. Sometimes a special room in the house is set apart for such occasions, or, and in middle-class families this is probably the rule, the coffin is kept in the best room in the house! In such a house two ladies of the Mission were invited to the *fiftieth* day ceremony. Light refreshments served in such an atmosphere added to the horror for the Europeans, and they were not able to endure to the end.

So, occasionally, the dead may wait months and years for other members of the family to join them and share the expense of the ceremony due to their position. King Chulalongkorn, a careful monarch, put several of his relatives aside till the royal exchequer should be equal to the cost of a cremation suitable to their rank. They were almost forgotten, and he died first, so that the early task of his successor was a purification by fire.

The Siamese prince passes away in the presence of his assembled family. It must be an anxiety for people to whom manners are supremely important, lest pain or semi-consciousness should cause them to transgress. Inside the sickroom are the family, and outside a great assemblage of friends, relations and dependents, all there with tacit offers of help and ready to lament with the mourners at the bedside when weeping shall announce the spirit's passing. After the death all the relations in turn help to wash the body. It is then shrouded in a clean white cloth and in its mouth a coin is placed for toll at the Gates of Paradise. Meanwhile monks intone and a band plays to ward off evil spirits. Besides the expression of natural grief there is also spasmodic lamentation. For a king or queen a special chant is sung ornamented with groups of grace notes and with a minor feeling; the minor key, as we understand it, does not exist. The Siamese only use these conventional lamentations for the very highest, but a native lady told me that among the Mons 'They are used for the old' (of all ranks), 'for the young they really cry.' The world-wide tragedy of age that outlives those who would weep it.

Kings, royal princes and the highest among the nobles, those whose rank is Chao Phya, have no rest in death. They must sit up in copper urns for their cremation, knees to chest and hands palm to palm, as in worship. More lowly folk may lie at ease in coffins.

The Court undertaker's task is a gruesome one.

Probably in the second day after death, the first stiffening of the limbs being past, in the presence of the near relatives and dependants, he binds the body for the urn. And it must add abominably to the pain of bereavement to hear the hideous cracking of the joints, strained out of their natural position that the body may be forced into a close-fitting urn.

The copper inner shell is, I gather, individual, but there are various gorgeous outer shells for recurring use in the cremation processions of which one at least is gold, while all are of precious metals and fine workmanship. The most horrible of all the Palace undertaker's tasks is, on the eve of the cremation, to strip the royal corpse of its flesh, which is destroyed separately, the bones alone attending the cremation. This is done to facilitate and hasten the burning. I only hope that no unfortunate relation has to be present at the hideous performance.

The great season for cremations is before the breaking of the rains, in May or June. During my stay at Bangkok three royal cremations took place. They were most wonderful pageants, in spite of the fact that, greatly urged thereto by his financial adviser, His Majesty had ordered the strictest economy. Even the first cremation, that of the Heir Apparent, cost thousands of ticals less than is usually spent in such cases. The procession of the Heir Apparent was immensely long, and to eyes seeking beauty and loving peace, altogether overweighted by the military. All the regiments of which the dead prince, Asadang, had been titular head were largely represented in the dullest, commonsense European khaki uniforms, marching with arms reversed to military brass bands, from which strains of the 'Dead March in Saul' overlapped Chopin's Funeral March distressingly as at home. At long last, surrounding the urn, came eastern magnificence at its most splendid. The Heir Apparent was honoured with the finest urn of all, of pure gold and of wonderful craftsmanship, on a car man-drawn. It was the High Priest who made the pictorial centre to the procession. He sat cross-legged and god-like on a golden chariot, of which the seat was raised altar-wise upon tall wheels six feet or more above the ground. (That so oriental-looking a car should be the work of a British firm, as I afterwards discovered, seemed odd.) His hand held a half-open scroll which gave his presence an air of curious significance. Drawn by richly caparisoned ponies, yellow robe and golden chair, he was shaded by an immense golden umbrella shot with purple which was carried on his right, and balanced on his left by the emblematic screen in gold and red. Only the wonderful five or seven-tiered umbrellas overtopped him. All in cloth of gold they moved in pairs, each shot with different colours—to me those shot with red gave the greatest impression of richness and depth. The umbrellas were carried by men in mediaeval uniforms of astonishing colour combinations. I have a note of one whose coat was orange and red with a purple belt, and his short trousers cut Chinese fashion (the seat placed anywhere above the bend of the leg) being of orange and purple. He wore a bright red pork-pie hat from the centre of which thrust a sudden spire of about ten inches high. The mediaeval East, unfortunately, made way below the trousers for the utilitarian modern West—common cotton stockings and low boots, probably black and certainly very dusty. A certain number of these umbrella or screen bearers had bare feet, admittedly less hygienic but so much less ugly! There must have been at least a dozen of these wonderful umbrellas, each considerably taller than its carrier. Their effect is amazing, the rigid skeleton and slightly swaying flounces give a feeling as of living architecture. Of men in the procession the umbrella bearers seemed to be the lowest in the social scale. Younger sons of families of high rank carried curious emblems. Their hats were of the same spired pork-pie order in white or red, but they had white silk cloaks and handsome panung. Officers in blue and gold coats with gorgeous panung intrigued me on account of their close-fitting caps—ornamented above the line of the brow and curtained below it with points. Two of these points covered the ears, and from under them at the back a piece like a reversed Latin cross hung down. The whole seemed to be made of soft material, and one was at a loss to imagine its *raison d'être*. It would hardly have afforded protection from sword cuts. In its then surroundings, however, its picturesqueness was all-sufficient.

The Brahmins, easily to be recognised by their long, hanging black hair, were prominent. They walked together in long white lace coats edged with gold.

Arrangements and grouping were substantially the same at all three cremations. The grouping was excellently managed and probably significant.

When the military had taken their places outside the enclosure the musical part of the ceremony was taken up by a band of ancient Siamese horns and drums, a weird sound more indescribable than bagpipes, and as haunting. Then the King and princes joined the procession, and, H.M. at their head, marched three times round the pavilion built for the cremation before finally depositing the urn.

Royalty, and those whom the King delights to honour, are cremated in the beautiful Phra Meru, the immense grassed oblong in front of the Old Palace Group. Temporary buildings are here set up forming the sides of a large square. The pavilion reserved for the King and royal princes is in the centre of the principal building on the west side. The ladies of the Court, all in white, occupied the south side. European guests and officials wearing black were in the north wing of the King's pavilion.

With schemes for surreptitious sketching, I had brought a small, black-covered, dark-leaved notebook in which to scribble with an inch of yellow chalk, and hoped for the luck of a place on the outside of the pavilion. It was given me, and I rejoiced, though the mosquitoes—Bangkok's bane—seemed unusually vicious and quick in finding me out, till, looking down, I saw that I had put both feet in it with a vengeance—no vengeance quicker, for my ankles were covered with little red ants ! Happily we were promptly moved up, the acrobatic attitudes necessary to avoid the ants' indignant reprisals would have been more than difficult for the two or three hours we were at the cremation. That place was left unoccupied, I fancy.

There was much waiting and much ritual, which, to those like me devoid of understanding, seemed to be merely more waiting, and then at last the King, from his place, lit the pyre with an electric fuse. After this His Majesty, and after him the near relatives and other princes, went up in turn to pay their last respects, and lastly, the whole assembly. The King's lighting had been purely ceremonial, the actual burning does not take place till late at night, and then only in the presence of a few witnesses.

The Cremation Pavilion, though temporary, had all the appearance of durability, and was beautifully ornamented. A flight of steps led up to each of the three doors—that on the west side was used by His Majesty and the princes. They and all senior to the defunct wore black. The princesses and ladies of the Court seemed to have been his juniors for they were all in white. Carrying their lighted tapers, and looking in the twilight like a bevy of little white ghosts they drifted in groups towards the south door.

The north door was for the rest of the world, and at the top of the steps we received sandalwood and a lighted candle with which to take our share in the burning of the pyre. We put them in the space left for them under the urn, the candles being promptly extinguished by an attendant on the opposite side. After 'Wai-ing' each guest passed on and out on the east side. The whole thing was excellently stage-managed and decorous, and in complete contrast to my expectations, which were of a gorgeous fire, like that at the cremation of a high priest which I had seen in Ceylon, only far exceeding it. Here, instead, the burning is done in the secrecy of the night with intensive heat, and the sandalwood and corpse alone are consumed. That year two more deceased Royalties, a prince and a young princess, were to use the same Pavilion.

When the long string of guests had deposited candles and departed, it was possible to return and admire the interior in detail. The floral decoration was of peculiar interest and attraction. Nothing prettier could be invented than the three-tiered umbrellas flanking the urn. They were made entirely in the artificial-natural flowers described in the previous chapter. No need here to invent a new form of growth. Imagine bead weaving with flowers and parts of blossom for beads put together with great ingenuity and perfect decorative effect, the umbrella tops of flower lace-work and their sides flower fringes. Beautifully simple and distinguished in contrast to the massively embossed golden urn.

The ceremony was long, and it is not surprising that Europeans, whose official position compels their attendance, clad, *pour comble*, in cocked feathered hat and court-dress, should dread royal deaths. It was full of interest for a newcomer, and I found it hard to believe that the display was far less than customary, my imagination refused to picture it more lavish. The elaborately illustrated souvenir book which was distributed to us must alone have cost a large sum.

Outside the enclosure the crowd, that wonderful gay but quiet Siamese crowd, was kept at a distance, and seemed to have had little in return for its hours of waiting; but the endless tiny tuck stalls under the double row of tamarind trees must have done good business.

And after the cremation?

The ashes of at least one deceased royal prince are in a golden urn of elegant shape and workmanship, kept in a fine room of the family palace, a room dedicated to the dead of the family. In his lifetime the prince played a great rôle, and round the urn hang memorials of his various activities, with portraits. His many decorations, with the official cloak of lace and gold, are in a glass case. A great gold chair for the use of the priest at memorial celebrations is the only piece of furniture. It is a room full of memories threatened now by the West in the persons of the pleasure-loving younger generation. Regardless of the feelings of conservative elders they would like such memories to vanish with the past, or at least that their symbols should be banished to a distant part of the mansion.

CHAPTER XII

DANCERS, KINGS, AND COMMERCIAL HONOUR

Good fortune showed me three royal cremations, but, unfortunately, as the Court was in mourning, there was an absence of theatrical entertainments.

The best companies of actors belong to the Court, to the royal princes, that is, or to the highest and richest nobles. Plays were formerly given as entertainment for their friends and dependents, and held in the open air on moonlit nights. Until quite recently the stage was an oblong platform thrust out among the spectators. There was no scenery, and a raised daïs represented a cottage or throne, or anything else that the scene demanded. Behind the stage were the orchestra, dressing-room and greenroom, frequently not even screened off, the burden of the entertainment being thrown on the artists instead of on accessories, as in the great days of our own drama. Unhappily the East is borrowing the inessentials from us, and mechanism and its attendant realism threaten to invade even the *Lakon Luang*.

The late King was an enthusiast of the drama, and himself both dramatist and actor—this last to the great scandal of the old-fashioned. It is easy to sympathise with their horror. That the King, whose head was too high to be called by the same name as that of ordinary mortals, and to address whom a special vocabulary must be learnt and spoken from the very ground, should deliberately put himself on a level with a mere actor. . . .

In extenuation let it be explained that Western ideas of acting had at least for the past twenty years been gaining ground, brought home by the students whom the Government yearly sends to Europe. To act a play has long been part of the programme of their annual meeting in England, and through them a realistic school of acting arose in Siam, which His late Majesty did much to foster and direct. He built a theatre Western-fashion near the New Dusit Palace, and there his own plays were performed, with his own help. It was an expensive amusement and (low be it whispered !) princes have been known to grumble when invited to take tickets for themselves and their families, to see the Royal productions. Rightly, to my thinking, they preferred their own form of drama.

Invitation and command from crowned heads are synonymous everywhere.

I was present at an excellent performance of *A Pair of Spectacles* by the English Dramatic Society, to which His Majesty had leased the theatre. The King was present. The Royal box was above the parterre immediately opposite the stage, so that, as the Siamese National Anthem struck up, the audience rose as one man and pivoted on its axis. Commonsense, but comical.

Besides composing original plays His Majesty translated some plays of Shakespeare into Siamese, and acted in them too.

As You Like It was among the plays given. I should

much like to have seen a Siamese *Rosalind*, the charm that we associate with her is so utterly different from that which is expected of the classical Siamese actress.

In the *Lakon Luang*—the Royal Lakon—the repertory is Brahman mythology or legendary history, and the heroes all gods and princes, so it follows naturally that they act in a traditional manner, and conventional gestures be used to express the emotions. It must be remembered that in Siamese there is no voice inflection, as we understand it. In a tone language individual words are inflected, and according to the inflection is their meaning. With five possible meanings for many words, and for a few words even more than five, the inflection cannot be governed by emotion. Theatrical speech is further conventionalised by being pitched high and unnaturally. The Westernised theatre, in which speech is natural, is called *Lakon Poot*, the spoken play.

The convention in singing is peculiarly unpleasant to us, being loud and nasal, but although the spectator who has not the advantage of understanding what he hears may easily wish himself deaf, to the eye all is enchanting. The deliberate grace and exceeding suppleness, whether of the *corps de ballet* as a whole or of the *pas seul*, make an exquisite pattern, every line of which is carried to its logical conclusion, in a way impossible to the rigid Western. Not strength nor swiftness, but grace, is the ideal, and to the unprejudiced eye it is completely achieved. It is a grace limited as French poetry of yesterday was limited and governed by its prosody—a grace which has nothing in common with the quality as we know it.

The upper half of the body suggests the curving

petals of a flower. All expression is eliminated from face and feature. Whether or no with the deliberate intention of setting aside the personal in favour of the traditional, the make-up—layers of powder of an incredible thickness, black arched eyebrows, and scarlet lips—has almost the effect of enamel, and makes the face as blank as a mask. If one should press the flower analogy the head takes the place of the pistil, while the arms and hands are moving petals, and the way in which the weight of the body is thrown on the heel in many of the poses, suggests a rooting to the ground.

In movement the feet are as supple as the wonderful hands and arms. To throw the weight of the body on the heels, instead of on the ball of the foot, in dancing, is common to many Eastern lands, and in dancing of very various types.

The emotions are expressed by strictly defined gestures and postures, and the result is exquisite motion, especially of the hands and arms. Not merely can the hand turn right back to touch the arm, but individual fingers obey their owner in a way unbelievable to our stiff-jointed race. The elbow, too, moves in either direction, and grace forbids its sharp angle, so that, when leaning on one arm—the classic pose when seated on the ground—what we consider the inner curve becomes convex. Ancient sculpture shows how many a hundred year this ideal of a gracious pose has lived.

When their clothes are considered the dancers' litheness astounds the more. Made of gorgeous silks, heavy with jewels and embroidery, they set close to the root of the neck, tight to the wrist, and cover the leg to below the knee. The glory of representing God or

Goddess, Prince or Princess, must be more than paid for by having to wear a golden crown very like those of the Tevadas in the Angkor sculptures, and of which the spire is twice as high as the little face below it.

The clothes, like the gestures, are traditional and invariable, and their thickness suggests survival from the glacial period; and probably the human love of display, which makes it endurable to wear such clothing in such a climate, goes back nearly as far!

When all the characters are being played by girls, one of the signs by which the foreigner may recognise male parts is a pair of queer little wing-like epaulettes.

Court mourning was in abeyance during that great society function, the Winter Fair. It is a fortnight of delights, many of them forbidden at other times, such as gambling. Laws against gambling are set aside, to the profit of any cause that the King may wish to benefit. That year it was the scout movement, known as the 'Wild Tiger Scout Corps.' I had my first glimpse of the Siamese theatre, at a dinner-party in the Royal Restaurant, but it was tantalising that only a corner of the stage should be visible from where I sat. The restaurant took the form of a shallow lake, and we dined on barges, while a great banyan thrusting out over us, its limbs wreathed in coloured electric lights, illuminated the assembly. The lake was really a great tin bath, but the illusion was complete with fish and water-weeds!

The King was giving a dinner-party on one barge, and several of the Royal Princes had parties too. They and the nobles take stalls at the Fair, and arrange side-shows, vying with each other in the originality of their schemes. And so it happened that, later in the evening,

I went to Heaven, and saw a bevy of angelettes dancing. No other name describes them, because, though too young for angels, they had the completeness that is noticeably lacking in cherubs. Their ages might have been from six to eight years. They wore the wonderful dresses described above, and danced on the flat roof of one of the flimsy temporary buildings of the Fair, in a terribly small space. The way had been up the narrowest of perpendicular stairs, steep enough to satisfy the sternest moralist, and the possibility of fire forced itself on me rather hideously. We had come there by way of a maze, and had faced the danger of landing in Hell, if we had taken the wrong turning! Hell was represented by a bar, and certainly Heaven was much to be preferred by those who wished to see things Siamese.

The babies were delicious, and seemed most accomplished, but it was dreadfully young to begin their lifework.

Once I saw an even younger child dance. She was alone and quite naked, dancing to herself on the platform of a little wooden house. We saw her from our boat on the klong, waving her little arms, and turning back her fingers with entrancing aplomb and rhythm.

To judge from the Mission schoolgirls, who came from the extreme north and from the south, as well as from Bangkok, dancing and acting are inborn in the Siamese. From time to time they would give us a *Lakon*, in which we could see every variety of acting and dancing. There was broad farce and comedy and dancing in the classical manner, and other dances too, reminiscent of old English country dances. To me the most fascinating was the classical type, with the wonderful waving arms and fingers that made the dancers look like one of their beloved long, slender-petalled champak flowers, folding and unfolding at will.

When the Royal cremations were over, and Court mourning too, I was taken to see a play by the private company of a noble house. *The Dragon King* was its name, but though the story was as fantastic and exotic as one could wish, the stage, to some extent, was sophisticated and Western. There was scenery, and there were wings to the stage. In compensation, the actresses' dresses were adjusted in the wings which were open to view, and a small child played on and off the stage.

How hard a thing it is to be single in deed—let alone mind—was shown by the way the Dragon King's tail occasionally insisted on acting independently! This was not a classical drama, nor were the dresses those of mediaeval kings or gods, and most human was the way in which one small actress could not keep the pink knickers, which were the lower half of her dress, fastened to the upper half. Strips of brown skin would keep on appearing for all the hitching and mending that went on in the wings. A friendly incompleteness of detail mattered nothing so long as the exquisite art of movement and wonderful supple hands were there to fascinate. It took me seconds to realise that one gesture, as of a pianist with fingers turned down, about to strike a chord, was made with the reverse of the hand!

The *Lakon* may consist of men and boys only, or women only, or of both. When, in classical drama, the serious parts are being taken by girls, the comic relief is given by a few men, whose acting and dress are in complete contrast to those of the girls—especially the dress, which is practically non-existent. They are clowns representing country bumpkins, or slaves, etc. According to Graham they have very little to do with the plot, and are only there to tickle the audience with jokes more or less decorous.

There is also *Yi Kay* which acts farce and burlesque as well as serious drama. The chief difference between them is that in *Lakon* the actors are silent. The words are chanted by a precentor at the side, and the singing is done by soloists or a chorus of non-actors. In the *Yi Kay* the actors speak and sing their own parts, and may be men or women or both.

The Shadow Play, too, exists, much as in China and Java, and is here called *Nang Patalung*. My knowledge of its existence is from books. Graham speaks of it as Javanese in origin, and mentions the 'stiff leather figures.' The Chinese puppets are made of leather too—donkey skin reduced to a transparent vellum wonderfully coloured. The Siamese performance, according to description, seems to be much rougher and less skilful, but the exorcising of evil spirits by its help must be a wonderful sight. (*Siam*, vol. ii. p. 210.)

Marionettes, handled much as in a Punch and Judy Show, must not be forgotten. They are oftenest to be seen at cremations.

The great popularity of the Winter Fair is partly due to the variety of its amusements and the liberty of action in a society still ceremony-ridden. The Fair is organised by the Court, but patronised by all classes. Gambling is in the Siamese blood, and for the ten days of the Fair's duration gambling institutions, at other times against the law of the land, are not only permitted but organised. Slavery is also forbidden by law, but as in the days before King Chulalongkorn abolished both it and gambling, the not infrequent result of losses at the gaming tables of the Winter Fair, all else being lost, is the pawning of the person.

With the increased expenses of modern life and its levelling of fortunes, the great private theatrical companies, which played for their owner and his personal friends, are disappearing.

A distinguished nobleman of the old régime, noted for his private theatre, had always included all the younger and better-looking of the troupe in his family, though officially they were never recognised as wives. The result was a large family of over sixty children—not uncommon amongst the upper classes of Siam. He always attended Court functions accompanied by a number of his children, but never by their mothers, who were too insignificant to accord with their father's idea of his dignity. When asked by the King why he never brought his wives to Court, his reply, characteristically ready, was :

'Children, Your Majesty, I have in plenty. I have no wives.'

The limitations of matrimony in Siam are few. Any woman with whom a man lives is his wife. There are greater and lesser wives. The greater wives may be taken for the sake of family alliance, while the lesser may represent inclination rather than interest.

But the subject bristles with difficulties to the Western mind, for the 'hidden wife,' one with whom a man cohabits privately, not openly, is a recognised fact, only, happily for her children, there is no such thing as illegitimacy, and they have the same rights as the offspring of acknowledged wives, if the father should choose to recognise them. In this case they may, after the father's death, claim to inherit with the rest. The day of many wives, however, is passing, for they make costly households.

The opening of the country to foreign commerce, and the adoption of methods in trade founded on the acknowledged desirability for fair dealing, does not favour the accumulation of great fortunes to the individual. Buddhism makes no pronouncement on the subject of monogamy, so that the number of wives need only be limited by a man's budget, and men with moderate incomes are generally satisfied with one wife at a time. Divorce is not difficult, but in the case of the first and principal wife it is by mutual consent.

A Prince, Commander-in-Chief of the Army, made it a rule that officers should only present one wife to him. On the other hand, Royalty decreed that every wife of a person of princely blood should be registered at Court, which is natural, as, although His Majesty is the only person the number of whose wives is limited by law, his allowance of ninety-five official spouses is fairly liberal !

Naturally this allowance does not include the other ladies whom he might choose to favour, and such honour no courtier of an absolute monarch can afford to refuse for his daughter, although it should condemn her to life-long celibacy thereafter, and possibly to internment in the Palace too.

The Queens are of Royal blood on both sides, and are generally the monarch's half-sisters or daughters of some reigning monarch, and *Chao Fa* is the title of their children.

Those of the King's children whose mothers were

lesser wives have the title of *Phra Ong Chao*—the lowest title whose holder is addressed in English as Royal Highness. The father being either *Chao Fa* or *Phra Ong Chao*, the children's title is *Mom Chao*, addressed in English as Serene Highness. Their children again are *Mom Raja Wong*, and the next generation *Mom Luang*, while the fifth has no title at all. Marriage with one of higher degree does not confer the higher rank. The King's lesser wives are known as *Chao Chorm*, until they have been fortunate enough to bear him a child—they then become *Chao Chorm Mandaa*. By birth they are generally ladies of position.

Until the late King's reign, of the male sex only the King and his chamberlains had access to the inner Palace—it was a feminine paradise, staffed entirely with women from tirewomen to police, a rule greatly modified now.

There is no rule to prevent princes from taking wives from among women of any rank. As was the case with the little daughter of one of our servants, any child may be brought up in the Palace, or in the house of one of the princes, and among his children. If she is intelligent she learns manners that will fit her for a position as any man's wife.

The case of the princesses, down to the rank of Mom Chao, is very different. They may not marry beneath them, and as in these days of fewer wives there are not enough princes to go round, many of them are condemned to a life of celibacy. As a compensation to those who remain unmarried, women's interests are widening. More and more among them teach, and as possibilities of a larger education open out, they will doubtless find other careers as have their European sisters.

But, in any case, the movements of Siamese princes and princesses alike are dictated to them from the throne. For instance, no person with any title may leave Siam without the King's personal permission, which is by no means a foregone conclusion. That the King may be satisfied that the adventurous one is able to maintain the state due to a member of the Royal family, when abroad, is a reason given for the Royal surveillance.

That rank confers the right to take is a hard idea to uproot, as is proved by the following conversation held not many years ago between a European and a Siamese of high position :

The Siamese spoke of a mutual acquaintance in a subordinate position as a thief. In his defence the European pointed out that he was no more a thief than B., a high official, whose appropriation of government goods to his own use, was well known :

'B. is no thief,' said the Siamese, 'look at his position, he has the *power* to take, but A. is a thief.'

Such ideas are changing very rapidly, thanks largely to commerce, and because it is increasingly recognised that honesty is the best policy. Nothing but adventure is certain without an even standard of honour, and that trade for profit is impossible unless there is mutual confidence. Commerce leans on the state which, in its turn, tends to grow more stable, as less arbitrary methods than those of the past become custom.

There is a true tale of the *ancien régime* and a European government official of a generation ago concerning an incident the like of which could not happen now :

The official went monthly on a three or four days' ride to the chief town of the province, where the Governor had his headquarters, to fetch the money for his workmen's pay. On one occasion, after a pleasant evening with the Governor, he received and counted the wads of notes handed to him out of the safe, and the next morning started for home. When about to pay out the money he discovered, to his consternation, that he had been given wads of 100 tical notes instead of the 10 tical notes he usually received. There was nothing for it but another journey to put the matter right. The Governor was obviously surprised to see him again so soon, but until the evening was well advanced the European said no word as to what had brought him back. As he heard nothing to suggest that the money had been missed, he at last asked if anything had been lost—but no. So then he displayed the notes. Surprise was unbounded, but he received no thanks, the Governor merely remarking : 'How foolish of you to return the money. Nobody would have known !'

'But,' said the European, 'what about your accounts ?'

'Accounts—what are they ?'

'Well, double columns in which you put down what is spent opposite to what is received.'

It seemed an extraordinary idea to the Governor. What money he received went into the safe. Of that what he wanted he spent, and if any were left over it might go to Bangkok—a plan which certainly had all the merit of simplicity, though possibly it was not one of much help financially to the central government.

In spite of the Buddhist axiom that Sin cannot pass, since those days the recognition of a common responsibility has gained much ground in Siam, as it has need to increase all the world over, if we are to outgrow :

> . . . 'the simple plan,
> That they should take who have the power
> And they should keep who can.'

CHAPTER XIII

SUPERSTITIONS AND OTHER THINGS

WE are apt to label as superstition any belief for which no reason is obvious to us. Such beliefs in Siam are many and various, and among them the fear of ghosts stands first. They are called *Phi* (pronounced Pee) and not all of them are horrible; the *Phi Lawk*, for instance, are merely mischievous elves, and it is on their account that the solitary wayfarer by night sings to keep up his courage, and, if possible, make them believe him one of many. It is not pleasant to be pinched or tickled by an unseen hand. Although we give no name to the thing we fear, in childhood at least, most of us have known the feeling of someone just behind us in the dark, and some of us keep it throughout life. Perhaps, if we recognised their existence, 'little people,' still to be found in remote corners of Ireland, Brittany and elsewhere, might return among us too. The difficulty would be to discriminate, and to admit only those that are friendly. The *Phi Reuan*, for example, that good ancestral ghost who watches over the family, would always be welcome, nor would we grudge the *Chow Tee*, who owns our home, his own little house, a perfect miniature in teak, flame-tipped eaves and all, complete as for a human dwelling. *Phra Phoom Chow Tee* it is called, and a fitting place is chosen for it by the soothsayer whose wisdom no man can gainsay.

But if we welcome these, how exclude the terrible *Phi Tai Hong*, ghosts of women dead in childbed, and feared the Eastern world over? A curiously widespread terror, in its essence probably the fear of Fear. The ghost is that of a victim of untimely death, possibly carrying a second life with her own into the grave.

Yet the fear of her is most acute when the child has survived. In several countries the poor corpse is nailed to her coffin that she may not return for the babe. Among the Laos in Northern Siam the corpse is let down through the floor to bewilder the ghost that it may not find its way back, and many are the tricks to frustrate its longing for home and little one.

A woman dead in childbirth may be cremated, but her ashes cannot be preserved; they must be thrown into the water.

The child still-born is another source of terror. To outwit its dangerous ghost, *Phi Phrai*, in Bangkok the little body is given to the river without delay. It is put in a rice pot and floated on the stream lest life should be lurking. And it happens often enough that a cry is heard from the rice-pot, and the newborn child revived by the fresh air is discovered alive.

The suicide's ghost is a *Phi Tai Hong* too; a person self-slain must be buried under cover of darkness, and may not be cremated. The tree from which such a one has hanged himself is accursed and haunted, no one, even a robber, will brave its terrors at night.

At one time burglaries in Bangkok were very frequent, the burglars being not Siamese but Chinese or Lao. With the Laos a favourite trick is first to drug their victims with Datura smoke, and then to thieve at leisure, as happened to some missionary friends of mine.

In the early days of their work in Bangkok they were starting a school within the city, and themselves inhabited an upper story. Already they had heard much about thieves in Bangkok, and the Mission had been robbed several times, which increased the young wife's nervousness, so that in spite of the heat they slept in a closely shuttered room.

Awakened one night they switched on the light to see a grinning man squatting on his haunches. Seeing them awake he made his escape through the window, which he had broken open in order to climb in—happily leaving most of his booty behind. The incident left them strangely apathetic and inert, and it was midday before the staff, alarmed at their non-appearance, broke in and succeeded in arousing them.

Their precautions had made the burglar's task easy. He had only to drill a hole in the shutter and to pour the smoke through it into the closed room, but happily for his victims he had only used enough of the drug to stupefy them partially, though sufficient to make them ill for some days.

Naturally their fear of thieves was not lessened by the adventure, and they begged for a night-watchman. It happened that they were on the eve of moving into larger quarters, and discovered that although the house was also in the city no night-watchman would be necessary, as it was protected by a fine tamarind, and no robber would brave its *Phi*. Effectually they were left in peace.

Every tree has its inhabiting *Phi*. *Ton Takien* (Hopea) is amongst the most prized woods of Siam, and is especially used for boat-building. Its *Phi* is a lovely but redoubtable lady—her beauty strikes such awe into the heart of the amazed beholder that he dies. Woe be to him who rudely attacks her dwelling, though, when courteously entreated, gracious as beautiful, she is willing to yield it up for the good of mankind. So, when her tree is cut down, an elaborate ceremony of propitiation takes place, and again, while a boat is being built of it, strange marks in chalk are made upon the planks in deference to her love of good manners.

A sad tale, in illustration, is that of an unbelieving European who ordered his coolies to begin work without allowing time for the necessary ritual. They obeyed, but sudden death overtook them. Others were put on to the work and were struck down by fever. To show his scorn of the superstition the European himself lent a hand, and fever overtook him too. And while he hung between life and death pious people performed the rites, and the *Phi*, appeased, allowed the sick to recover, and her tree to be cut down.

The obvious deduction—the unparalleled importance of good manners—is a genuinely Siamese moral !

There are various trees that may be planted to bring good luck, but—which is genuinely Siamese too in its aristocratic exclusiveness—only by those above a certain rank.

Ton Sampoy, which is something like a tamarind, is a lucky tree, and *Ton Nard* keeps off ghosts, so, as dangers from *Phi* are endless, each Phi having its name and known peculiarities, generally unpleasant, it is good to have it in front of the house.

It is an essential canon of good taste that nothing is right or beautiful unless appropriate to its position. But it would be difficult for us so to identify any tree with religion as to feel it would be sacrilege to plant in our gardens. The *Ficus religiosa*, under whose shade the Master received Illumination, places many a good Siamese in an awkward predicament. It belongs to the Wat, but insists on sowing itself far and wide. Religion forbids that it be grown in a private garden, but it also forbids that it be pulled up, even when growing out of some cranny in a building which its strong roots must inevitably destroy if it be left to grow.

Perils are many, but fortunately much protection may be found in the wearing of charms—not those forerunners of mascots, tiny ornaments such as our mothers used to wear on their watch-chains, and not as in Italy, hands openly making horns against the evil eye, and other obvious devices. In Siam the charm is secret and known only to the wearer. It consists of a small slab of silver on which some magic sign is scratched rolled into a tiny tube and threaded on a cord, probably with many others, each affording protection from some definite ill. They look like long bead chains, and the schoolgirls used to wear them as necklaces. They are often put over one shoulder and under the other, or else round the waist.

Where magic begins and whether it is superstition depends on the point of view. Many a British man or woman, who unhesitatingly makes use of the supernormal by visiting a clairvoyant, would turn the eye of scorn on a Siamese wizard. The *Maw Dhu's* most profitable business is the concoction of love-philtres, but he is a doctor too, in whose prescriptions music for the charming away of evil spirits figures largely. He makes magic in a way old as time, and still to be met with in many another land:

Being charged by a client to rid him of an enemy or of some obstacle to his success, the magician takes wax and moulds a model, which he then wounds, sticks with pins, or otherwise injures, that the person represented may suffer similar hurt. And he knows the force of suggestion. In the case of a friend care was taken that the wife should know that magic was being used against her husband, in the hope that, through her, fear would strike him.

In another case a written curse was discovered among the papers of the victim-designate, after he had twice escaped the violent death wished on him. The paper being found and destroyed, the power of the curse was destroyed too.

Wizardry generally descends from father to son. The business is lucrative, for all mankind loves love, and philtres are in constant demand. The spice of secrecy and adventure, indispensable in the quest for a philtre, adds zest to undying hope and credulity.

One superstition is shared by Siamese and British alike, though its interpretation is exactly opposed. To the former peacock's feathers are lucky, while many of our own nationality fear them, though I have never heard that they fear the bird itself. In Siam to wake and see a peacock brings seven days of good luck, but I rather fancy the vision is rare, at any rate in my own experience of Siam.

If a sale be made early in the day some of us spit on the coin for luck—in the same hope the Siamese (and other Easterns too) will almost give goods away to the first early customer, more especially on the first day of month or year. Moreover, like our gipsies they believe in lucky faces, and will wheedle and wheedle that the possessor of a lucky face should buy, be it only a *satang's* worth.

The vulture is another and a loathsome dispenser of good and bad luck. If the bird perch on a house and turn his head to the west the owner's number is probably up. But if the unclean creature look to the east, and especially if it *vomit*, much good may ensue, if special prayers be offered up and candles be lighted.

It happened to a personal friend that three days before an unexpected, and in appearance untoward, event, a vulture sat on a tree in his garden. There was some uncertainty as to the direction of its gaze, but the servants took no risks, and the candles were duly lighted. The seeming blow, when it fell, opened out a new life to their master, but the doubtful prophecy being noised abroad, wise heads were shaken. . . .

Besides superstitions there are some charming legends about birds carrying pointed lessons. The Coppersmith, in a past human life, was a dishonest goldsmith who stole gold from a customer, and his penance now is to knock-knock-knock-knock-knock-knock-knock as fast as he can before every house. The Jungle Crow too, as he sits on the roof with his hollow hou-hou-hou, is mourning his past, and opportunities lost when the world was in the making. All the birds and beasts then gave what help they could, some bringing stones and some twigs, while he only held aloof.

When the *Chinchock* (tiny wall gekko) calls, to avert bad luck, respond at once. But should he call when you are making a bargain, postpone it—it could not turn out well. Gekkos are not disliked and feared in Siam as they are in Ceylon. In the latter place I well remember our dignified Appu's disgust when I pointed out one of the little creatures on the floor, lethargic from a changing skin. Head and little hands were already free, the old skin giving a quaint effect of ruffs round the hands and bonneted head. 'Those things should keep to the walls,' was his disdainful response in his excellent English. The effect is as of little hollow ghosts with goggle eyes.

In Siam, Cambodia and Burma a much larger kind of Gekko also inhabits the houses. Sometimes they are a foot or more in length. When living indoors they take up their abode behind furniture or in any dark corner. Ugly, awkward things, they make war on things still uglier which are plentiful in that hot moist climate; but the big ones are messy guests, and difficult to get rid of, as even the Chinese servants fear ill-luck if they kill them. They possess two beauties—their colour and their call. Their complexion varies a little, but is generally some kind of light buff, spotted with greeny-blue, and there is often red round their throats. Their name, *To-kay*, imitates their queer, oft-repeated call. The accent and a pause fall on the resonant *To*, then comes a big drop to a rather grating *Kay*. It is a lucky call to hear if the repetitions be uneven in number, and the more the better, so that one took to counting them. There were seldom more than four, however, and the creatures seemed to take a malicious pleasure in ending on a suspended *To* instead of finishing properly on the *Kay*.

I had a great wish to *see* a *To-kay* call; it was so constantly to be heard in that old house. But the luck befell a friend at the Mission, after my departure. She writes:

'We were in chapel when the creature suddenly

began to talk, and I saw it wedged on a ridge at the top of the verandah, its body swelled like a pair of bellows each time it to-kay'd. . . . I thought it would burst if it went on much longer.' Perhaps it stops when it feels that danger is near, but more probably when an appetising morsel passes within reach of the long lizard tongue.

If the *To-kay* were only a little less shy it might be a most useful pet for the dinner-table, on those nights when plagues of various insects make it hard to keep them out of the food. They are frequent when the rains are due ; one night it may be tiny beetles, another a kind of blue-bottle, ephemerae too, and cockroaches. The last-named, fortunately, are of a small variety about three-quarters of an inch long, but quite sufficiently objectionable. It is a matter for thankfulness that I only met the flying giant of sometimes nearly three inches singly. The big fellow with antennae nearly as long as himself is handsome, however much we may dislike his foolish face.

Revolting above all its kind is the red, flat, wingless cockroach, so hard to keep out of drawers and cupboards. I had some terrible encounters with him, but happily no losses. Choice clothes are the morsels in which he delights. He has the good sense to dislike napthaline, and in my warfare with him all sense of its fragrance was temporarily (and happily) lost to me. One piece of furniture in which he reappeared time after time must have been a breeding-place, and no napthaline could keep him away. It was finally freed of his presence by an internal scrubbing with the strongest hospital soft soap.

Those who study astrology may be interested in the

custom of wearing panung in regular rotation of colours. Its description shall close this chapter of odds and ends.

The custom is derived from Brahminism, and the colours are those of the planets. As in ancient Greek mythology they are seven, and include the Sun and Moon, all the heavenly bodies, that is, that are seen to change their places among the stars. But in Indian mythology two more have been added, Rahu the Invisible, who, in eclipses, swallows the sun and moon, and his assistant Kethu, the red serpent. The colours are those of the personifications of the planets, as their flesh is shown in paintings.

Siamese who can afford the luxury wear for :

Sunday - - -	Red
Monday - - -	Yellow
Tuesday - - -	Light Mauve
Wednesday - - -	Green
Thursday - - -	Dark Orange
Friday - - -	Blue
Saturday - - -	Dark Purple or Black

On *Wan Phra*—Holy Days—the days of the Moon's changes, Rose may be worn.

Such is the list as given by Siamese friends, and practised so far as my observation goes, although, according to Gerini, whose conclusions are reached through the study of Indian as well as Siamese documents, it is not quite correct.

Besides the daily wearing of prescribed colours, there is a ring reserved for wear at the Tonsure and Unction rites, and which may also be affixed to men's belts in war, that they may be invulnerable. It is called the Nophakau ring, because it is set with nine gems, and it has its origin in Siva's snake necklace, the skin or body of Vasaki set with nine gems or spots of coloured enamel.

> 'the toad, ugly and venomous,
> Wears yet a precious jewel in its head,'

shows that in Shakespeare's day the widespread belief that gems are found in the heads of reptiles was held in England. According to a quotation from the *Vishnu Purana*, the Hindu Snake Gods inhabiting the lower regions of the earth 'live in the light shed by rays issuing from the multitude of brilliant jewels in their crests.'

The nine gems of Vasaki are those symbolical of the nine planets, and therefore most auspicious to wear on the days over which they rule, and 'most efficient in averting the malignant influence likely to proceed at any time from any of them; and capable of ensuring success in all undertakings, prosperity and long life, which is further symbolised by the form of the ring taken from the body of the serpent, the time-honoured emblem of immortality and rebirth.'

So Gerini. His list of days, gems, colours and planets corresponding, is as follows:

Sunday	Ruby	Bright red or Sun colour
Monday	Moonstone	Silvery Moon colour
Tuesday	Hyacinth	Light Red, colour of Mars
Wednesday	Emerald	Greenish, colour of Mercury
Thursday	Cat's Eye	Variegated, colour of Jupiter
Friday	Diamond	Silver bluish, colour of Venus
Saturday	Sapphire	Dark blue, colour of Saturn

For Monday, Opal is given as an alternative, and for Tuesday, Coral, whilst the Diamond for Friday is 'of the kind like the colour of fresh cut lead or tin.'

The Gems corresponding to Rahu and Kethu would be respectively the Garnet and the yellow Topaz.

CHAPTER XIV

FROM GAMES TO JUSTICE VIA PUNISHMENT

Two sights spring to my mind's eye in connection with games in Siam.

The first is kite-flying on the *Phra meru* at Bangkok, and the second a game of *Ta Kraw*, played by laughing prisoners in chains at Chiengmai ! Both sights eminently characteristic of Siam.

Nothing could be more perfectly set than kite-flying on the immense *Phra meru*, looking down its length at the Old Palace, a wonderful background of golden spires glittering in the evening sun. Day after day in the windy season, all Bangkok assembles to see kites flown, and to back the favourites. In the shade of the wide avenue, which runs down the west side of the ground, are whole families in hundreds of cars. Under the double row of tamarinds, which surround the great grassed space, are endless little refreshment stalls of sweets, curries, seeds and what not. The sweets are on trays, the curries in the cooking on small braziers, and each has its group of patrons. On the ground itself is a huge multitude drawn from every class. Every kind of dress may be seen, and the gayest of colours, red predominating as always in the tropics, though here the yellow of monkish draperies, billowing in the strong breeze, is a keen rival.

KITE FLYING ON THE PHRA MERU.

To face page 186.

Family parties are headed by the stout old mother in panung, short chemisette and scarf, if she be well-to-do; in panung and breastcloth only if quite poor, and in either case her stiff hair short and standing upright on her head. Teeth, if any be left to her, are jet-black, and the mouth turned to a loose-edged cavern by the life-long use of betel chews. She is followed by her group of slender daughters, wearing the pasin instead of the panung, and more modern in head-dress too, with their hair rolled low on the nape of the neck, and teeth gleaming white. If becoming dress instead of fashion ruled, the mother should wear the pasin and the daughters the panung. Among the men, all in panung, the bright blue of government officials rules as everywhere in Bangkok. There are Chinese too in immensely wide trousers, which must belong to the extreme south, or to the Bangkok Chinese only. I never saw their like elsewhere. As with all Chinese trousers, the seat is placed anywhere above the bend of the leg, and they fall nearly to the ankle. Most of them are in bright colours, not in the everlasting blue of China itself, and Europeans often adopt them for undress in their homes.

The game that the crowd has come to see consists in fouling your adversary's flight, or in bringing him or her down, for it is a war of the sexes. The male kite is man size or more; it has five points and is white and tailless. The female, a skittish little thing not a quarter his size, is diamond-shaped and flirts a coloured tail. Both have crushed glass glued on their enormously long strings, in the hope of cutting each other down if the worst come to the worst and the little lady have not entangled the big man in her toils . . . sometimes the big man escapes scot-free. . . . As may be imagined it is a game of great skill. Manœuvre to catch and manœuvre to avoid, governed from the earthbound end of hundreds of feet of string, filled me with wonder, especially when dozens of couples fly all together and of course all in the same direction. The game is only possible in a high wind steady enough to lift the large kites above tree-level.

Skilled fliers naturally have great reputations, and their dexterity is watched with rapt attention. The whole crowd, head in air, might be awaiting the prophet of a fresh dispensation.

On one occasion the Red Cross organized a kind of kite carnival in which marvellous monsters filled the air. Instead of being flat, like the fighting kites, a good many were made on the principle of the Japanese box kites. Amongst many I remember a white elephant, a tiger, several peacocks, a whole family of cobras, a Red Cross nurse—doubtless there to salve the wounds of the animals after encounters—a terrific tubular python, a dragon of course, and many other wonders. The more complicated birds and beasts were really a series of connected kites, and must have been most difficult to manage. Except, perhaps, for the elephant all the creatures were life-size or much more !

In the same way that Sunday clothes more often mar than make, the usual kite games were more interesting to me than this great occasion. Yet, in spirit, it was quite as characteristic of Siamese inventiveness and sense of decoration.

Less spectacular, *Ta Kraw* has the fascination of lithe and rapid movement. The object is merely to keep a ball in play by hitting it with any part of the body excepting the hand. In an exhibition game by experts there are from four to six players, but no special positions at any time.

The ball is an octagonal skeleton of rattan, of which each face is a circle, and it is exceedingly light and about half as large as a football. The movements are very quick, one particularly clever and graceful stroke when the ball threatens to leave the circle is to kick it backwards over the player's head into the circle again. The game is popular in Burma and Cambodia too, and it seemed to me astounding that prisoners in leg-irons should be gaily playing it at Chiengmai.

The Siamese are great gamblers and love cock-fighting, fighting fish, and any sport at which they can back one side against the other.

While waiting in a side-street, mewed up in a car closed against a terrific thunderstorm, I saw the amusing preliminaries of a cock fight. As the rain cleared off, first two cocks appeared, old opponents evidently from the supercilious way in which they eyed one another. Followed two or three small boys who, in the most expert manner, began egging the cocks on to a round —but, alas ! for the urchins. Just as the beasts were getting really interested in each other, and had tried a preliminary pass or two, out stalked an indignant owner, and one warrior was carried off under an arm.

In less strenuous days and before motor-cars had ousted horses, French coachmen used to play 'bouchon' —much the same type of game as that played in Siam called *Law-Kang-tung*. A piece of board is raised at one end, and the players roll their coins down it in turn. The idea is to stop short of a line drawn across the track, and come as near to it as possible. The man whose coin lies nearest to the goal then flicks it towards those further away, and every coin touched is taken. There are seeds too.

In *I-kit-I-kian* a number of seeds are divided up amongst the players, and out of his share each contributes so many to the pool. The first player drops a seed on the ground, then, with one eye shut, drops another seed as near to it as possible, and so on in turn. The next thing is to hit the centre seed with your own by flicking it, and the owner of the first seed to touch it takes the pool.

Two games seen East as West are marbles and whipping tops, both played with a difference. In whipping tops, *Luk-tang*, the players try to smash each other's tops, while in marbles, instead of flicking with the thumb, as here, the middle finger is used as a hammer trigger and pulled back by the other hand.

The following list of games for small children may interest for their family likeness to those played in Europe, and forfeits are popular. In *Cham Chi* the little ones sit in a group and all hands are spread on the floor. The hands are counted out, and the penalty for the last left in is to go on all fours while the rest eat sweets off its back.

Some games are with nursery rhymes, and 'Oranges and Lemons' has a Siamese counterpart in '*Ri-Ris-Kao-San*.' The last-last-last-last-LAST head, when chopped off, has to repeat a difficult rhyme while hopping on one leg, and also answer a question correctly.

Ai-mong is Blind-man's buff and '*Ao-to*' Hide-and-seek. A nice version of Hide-and-seek is the Crow-hatching eggs, *KA-fak-kai*. A circle is drawn on the floor for a nest, and a number of small things placed in it, and over them a child crouches, blindfold. The others each seize something out of the nest and run to hide it. When all is hidden the crow seeks, and the child whose thing is the first to be found takes his place at being Crow. Bigger children have a kind of hop-scotch called *Se-bar*.

It must doubtless be because both derive from the needs of mankind's earliest forbears that the skeletons of most games are world-wide, as is also the framework of legends.

Among intellectual games Chess is prominent, though it is rather simpler than that played in Europe, which has certainly the same Indian or Persian origin.

A Siamese who takes Chess seriously, and plays both the native and European game, invariably prefers the latter.

The pieces are equal in number in both games, but have not the same value. The King is called Chief or General and moves as in European Chess. The Queen is merely called a Pip, and is not a powerful piece, for it can only move one square diagonally (as in the game originally played in Europe). As in other countries the Knight is a Horse, and moves in exactly the same way everywhere. The Bishop has a name entirely his own—*Khon*, which has no other meaning in modern Siamese. In all other Asiatic countries it is called Elephant, and it is possible that this word *Khon* may be a corruption of some old word meaning an Elephant or its rider. This piece moves in a peculiar manner, either one square straight forward or one square diagonally in any direction, but not one square straight back or sideways. It is, therefore, much less powerful than in European Chess.

The Rook or Castle in Siamese Chess becomes Boat. It moves as in the Western game, which makes it the most powerful piece on the board.

The Pawns are called Shells or Units and move as in European Chess. Promotion comes to them earlier however. Instead of waiting till the eighth rank they become Pips in the sixth rank. As the Pawns are placed on the third rank at the beginning of the game this is quick and easy promotion, but is of less value than in European Chess.

The arrangement of the pieces is the same in both versions of the game, with the exception of the Pawns and the Queens (Pips), which in Siam are on the King's right.

The Siamese board is only ruled, not checkered black and white. As there are no pieces which can travel long distances diagonally checkering is unnecessary. Both board and pieces have to be very substantially made, as the tactics of the game allow that a player who considers that the move is good, and more especially if it be check, may bring the piece down on to the board with a bang, by way of flustering his opponent.

Though further moves be patently hopeless, it is considered unsporting to stop the game, as that would deprive the winner of the chance to administer an artistically staged *coup de grâce*. It is by no means to be done in the quickest and most direct fashion, and for the sake of onlookers a prolonged agony is aimed at. Otherwise mate must be given in certain set positions which recall the art of composing problems in European

Chess, all of which adds to the pleasure of the winner, but is poor fun for the loser.

The Siamese take keenly to European games, and more than anything else they love the turf and its organised betting. Their own form of racing still to be seen in the country is really a match between two horses. A temporary course is marked out in a field, and the rider who snatches and holds the flag placed at the end of the course is the winner. The race, however, is lost if he fail to catch and hold the flag.

After the Turf, Association Football is the next most popular of borrowed games, and Tennis, Golf and Billiards are much played too.

The International Sports Club at Bangkok is a great institution. In its grounds are racecourse, golf course, football and hockey fields, tennis grounds, etc., while in the Club-house indoor games are played, and there is a ball-room which serves also as a concert hall, etc.

The King granted a charter to the Club, charging a nominal rent, Tc. 1 per annum, for its finely situated grounds. Siamese and all foreigners are eligible for membership, but the majority of the Committee and sub-Committee is European. The Club is a great boon to the numerous Europeans at Bangkok, comprising not only Diplomats and the large mercantile group, but Advisers to the Crown in almost every Department in which Western methods have been adopted. All use the Sports Club, which is a most cosmopolitan assembly, though it has a deplorable tendency to split into national groups.

Games and Punishments are in obvious sequence, and in penalties for little ones the family likeness to Western fashions persists.

Small naughtiness stands in the corner or else inside a circle drawn for the purpose. Or, to ensure stillness, it is tied to the nearest immovable thing by a thin thread that any impatient movement must break. Or, again, 'no pudding to-day' becomes 'only salt with your rice.'

To combine physical training for the suppleness so much prized with painful punishment, the hand is pressed back, as has already been mentioned. In a twisted pinch it is difficult to see anything but vengefulness, and a horrid punishment in favour with the lower classes is to burn a handful of cocoanut, or even chillies, and to push the culprit's head into the smoke.

Knuckling, as known among schoolboys here, has there the advantage of combining insult with punishment, the head of the punished being dishonoured by the touch. We here find it hard to understand how the Siamese respect the head. Gerini says that in Hindu law, on which that of Siam is based, laying hold of the hair of another is severely punished (*Manu*, viii. 283).

During the War I heard from a Siamese student, who had buried national prejudices under an English Public School education, how a newly-arrived Siamese officer felt about some of the things he had seen in Europe.

There being but one seat, he had seen the woman sitting while her husband stood. Well, a woman might be weaker, so let that pass. But that she should be served first at table was incomprehensible to one accustomed to be served first and alone, the womenfolk eating when he had finished. That which had chiefly outraged his feelings, however, was a *woman patting a man on the head* ! It is a relief to record that it was seen in Paris, not in London !

The Siamese carry nothing on their heads, flattened hand and shoulder is the highest they will lift their goods. It is generally women who run along the platforms with trays of sweetmeats and fruit, carried in this way, at railway stations. The Indians are easily picked out in a crowd by the loads on their heads, and in Bangkok it is generally the Chinese who are to be seen carrying heavy things, one at either end of a spring stick over one shoulder.

But punishment not work was the theme. That for seditious talk has passed into the language, and is not known now in any other way, if ever it was actually administered in the past. One who speaks indiscreetly is silenced by being told that he will have a young cocoanut put into his mouth, which would fit the crime faultlessly if hideously.

A good example and true of what a witty and absolute monarch could do by way of checking seditious speech is the story of what happened to the editor of a newspaper in King Chulalongkorn's days. The editor was not among the King's admirers, but knowing his tolerance consistently wrote against his doings. This being brought to the ears of the King, he said the editor's mouth would have to be stopped with a young cocoanut if the articles did not cease to appear. The King's saying was duly reported to the editor, who continued merrily with his abuse. Which, when the King heard—'Has he no fear of the young cocoanut?' said he. 'He must be mad. Let him go to the madhouse.' And to the asylum he went. It was from a much chastened journalist that a month later a very humble petition for release was presented. It was graciously granted, and the man gave no further trouble.

The Royal family is large, and it has happened from time to time that a Royal Highness has had to suffer the death penalty; but so that no drop of the princely blood be shed, he is executed in a sack, a wedge is put under his chin, and the neck broken by a blow. The last execution of the kind took place about a hundred years ago, and the criminal carried pride of birth to his death. A preliminary to execution is a certain number of strokes with a rod, which were duly administered. The executioner, neglecting to follow them up with the ceremonial *Wai* (bow with joined palms), was sharply brought to book by the Prince about to die! However unpleasant the punishment, ceremony was never neglected, and the *Phya* (noble lord) suffering imprisonment was accustomed to go out from time to time to see his friends, his fetters being carried behind him in a golden tazza!

These and other customs, some noxious and some picturesque, are of the past, now that the Penal Code is complete. It is the first part of the law as codified by a symposium of French lawyers. They have been at work since about 1905, and the laws of India, Japan, Belgium, Italy and Hungary, as well as France, have all been placed under contribution. The one code as yet in being is completely successful, and acknowledgedly suitable to modern conditions in Siam. It is hoped, therefore, that when the remaining codes (to include a Criminal Procedure Code, a Civil Procedure Code, a Commercial Code, and a Law of Judicial Organisation) are completed, Siamese law will be sufficiently clearly formulated for the abolition of all extraterritorial rights. Britain relinquished hers as long ago as 1909, her subjects being amenable to the International Courts or to the ordinary Siamese Courts, according to whether they were registered before or after the final treaties. France, Denmark and the United States have also relinquished their Courts, each country making what arrangement seemed best for the protection of its nationals.

When British subjects are to be tried in the ordinary Siamese Courts a European adviser sits on the Bench with the Judges, and, if the accused be a European, he acts not only as adviser but is a Judge whose opinion must prevail over that of the rest of the Bench.

'The International Court consists of the ordinary Court with the addition of the Consul of the foreign subject concerned, the Consul having the right to sit in Court, and act as an adviser if he thinks necessary, or to stay proceedings and transfer the case by evocation and try it himself calling the Consular Court out of abeyance therefore.'—(*Siam*, W. A. Graham, vol. i. p. 374.)

The old system ended in 1892 with the establishment of the Ministry of Justice, which came none too soon, for the elaborate system of checks and counterchecks, to prevent the miscarriage of justice, had been completely defeated by universal corruption. Even in the town of Bangkok reform hardly took hold before 1894, and it is from 1897 when His Royal Highness, the late Prince Rabi of Rajaburi became Minister of Justice, that reform really dates. During his ministry (1897-1910) he rendered immense services to Siamese Law by collecting and publishing in book form those numerous remains of the old Hindu Law of Manu, still in force to-day, as re-edited by various ancient Kings, notably by Ramathibodi, first King of Ayuthia.

'These compilations enabled the Government to carry out the first reorganisation of the Law Courts, placed the principal laws of the country within reach of the public, and provided textbooks without which no systematic teaching could be undertaken.'—(*Idem*, p. 376.)

But best of all for his country was the fine example of his forthright and energetic personality, and his death in 1920 was regarded by many as a national calamity.

As an instance of that with which he had to contend, see Graham's book as before quoted at p. 370 :

'In criminal matters it was customary to detain both the accused and the complainant, and sometimes even the witnesses, in custody, pending trial of the case, and as recently as the year 1900 A.D. the provincial prisons contained many persons who had got into them as complainants in criminal cases, and having failed to raise among their relatives and friends the funds necessary to bring their case to a hearing had remained in prison, in some instances for many years, working at prison labour side by side, perhaps, with the very individual against whom their complaint had been made.

'All prisoners were fed by their relatives, the Government not providing food. The prisons were small, dark hovels, always overcrowded, and without the smallest pretensions to sanitation. Discipline, however, being practically non-existent, the prisoners could often arrange to sleep outside the jail, whence, naturally, frequent escapes resulted.'

As advisers there are still numerous foreign Judges in the country, and they are among the wearers of the lace coats which intrigued me at the first Siamese ceremony I saw—the Swing Ceremony. There very grand ones with golden edges were worn by *Phra Isuen* and his courtiers. They covered but did not hide the silken panung underneath.

I next saw them at some public school sports, where they were worn by English schoolmasters over European clothes, and the effect was very different. The usual Nottingham lace bowers had been prepared for the King's reception, and so one's impression naturally was that His Majesty liked as much Nottingham lace as possible. On enquiry I discovered that it was not a matter of taste at all. In their origin the lace coats were Indian and worn only by kings. From the King they descended to the King's representative wherever his duties might take him. In the days of King Chulalongkorn they came to be worn as full dress uniform, and so they have remained and increased with the growth of officialdom. The lace coats roughly correspond to our silk gowns and hoods showing a degree in law, education, etc., and it is as the instrument of the Royal authority that they are worn by the Judge on the Bench, and the Schoolmaster—presumably only on great occasions.

CHAPTER XV

GOOD WORKS

COMMERCE with the West, commerce to the limits of the word in its widest sense of intercourse, has prompted Siam to some Western methods of self-expression. The Red Cross Society, for instance, which is powerful in Siam but not a Government undertaking, has found means of building one of the best-equipped hospitals in the East, the Chulalongkorn Hospital, built in memory of the present monarch's father. As a temporary measure, till a sufficient civilian staff be available, it is staffed by the military and subsidised by Government.

By diverting and canalising, so to speak, the universal desire to make merit, organising it to meet national needs rather than build more of the already multitudinous Wats, the Red Cross Society succeeded in finding money for the hospital and other public institutions.

It has been the means of important sanitary campaigns and has established an Infant Welfare Centre.

The Red Cross is also responsible for the only Leper Hospital in Central Siam. It is rather unfortunately placed between Bangkok and the sea, which makes Bangkok a high road for lepers journeying there. Leprosy is one of the country's great problems, as it has been estimated that there are probably 25,000 afflicted with the disease in Siam. I have heard of complete cures claimed by both English and French doctors. All the same the generally accepted conclusion, that leprosy is usually only catching by prolonged contact, is unspeakably comforting to the traveller.

One of the great difficulties in contending with the disease is its sufficiently early recognition. It is neither painful nor in itself fatal, so that in its early stages sufferers tend to conceal it, which is easily done when, as frequently, it first appears in parts of the body normally covered.

If he ever existed, the 'leper white as snow' has completely disappeared. Two main forms of the illness are recognised, nodular and nervous. Nervous leprosy causes complete lack of power in any part attacked; it is nodular leprosy in its advanced forms that is so horrible to see with its appalling tubercles. The two types when mixed, as generally happens, cause the ultimate loss of fingers and toes and even limbs.

It is interesting that modern methods of treatment are based on the drug most anciently known in connection with leprosy, Chaulmoogra oil. In Siam the tree from which it is procured is *Hydnocarpus Wightiana*, but it is taken from other trees in different Eastern countries. One of the great difficulties with regard to the certainty of cure is to manage to keep the patient under observation for a sufficient number of years to make sure there is no recurrence. When he thinks himself cured he frequently disappears.

The first Leper Hospital in Siam was established in the north at Chiengmai by an American missionary, Dr. McKean, who spent his life there, curing when he might, alleviating when there was nothing else to be done. To make the hospital, as far as possible, self-supporting, he taught the inmates trades, which became a means of livelihood to those who left it. A great source of income to the hospital is shellac; the lac-making insect has been found to work happily in that fine, quick-growing tree common throughout Eastern countries, the rain tree. At the hospital an avenue of them has been planted in the beautiful grounds, and is doing well.

The Chiengmai Hospital is only one of the many activities of the American Presbyterian Mission in Siam. At Chiengmai it has a native church and schools for boys and girls as also at Lampang, Chiengrai and Nan, and medical missions too. At Bangkok the 'Christian' college for boys and 'Wattana Wittaya' for girls are deservedly flourishing, while in the south it has at any rate a hospital, school and church at Petchaburi, and also at Trang. Of the non-Roman Christians the American Presbyterians are much the most numerous and the oldest established. The Roman Catholics have three bishoprics and many churches in various parts of Siam—also schools. In Bangkok there are St. Joseph's College for boys and the School of the Assumption for girls, and a cathedral. Roman Catholicism was first brought to Siam early in the seventeenth century by priests who came with the Portuguese settlers, but the first to come as missionaries were the French who, in the reign of the Grand Monarque, decided on Ayuthia, the then capital of Siam, as the starting point for their Great Enterprise—nothing less than the conversion to Christianity of the whole East!

Last of all with offers of Christianity came Britain,

who through the instrumentality of the S.P.G. and under the Bishop of Singapore established a church and two schools in Bangkok, which grow apace, and they would grow much faster did funds permit.

Wide and pleasant as are the grounds of St. Mary's Mission, which gave me a home as stop-gap teacher for the time I was in Bangkok, the quarters are quite inadequate to their schools' needs, and great efforts are being made to collect funds for a new building. The Mission already has a site well outside the town which draws daily nearer to the present school, and the missionaries look forward to completely modern buildings for which there will be no rent to pay.

The Mission Chapel is at St. Mary's, though services are also held at the boys' school in the town—about the latter more later. The congregation is chiefly Eurasian, who are by no means all *Anglo*-Siamese, so that no other convenient name exists to designate people of mixed European and Asiatic descent. It has never been clear to me why the name 'Eurasian' should now be barred in India. The fact is concisely stated in the name. That which we ought to face is that the quality of contemptibility is bred by contempt. What is to be expected of people held at arm's length by both their parent races?

In the schools the Eurasians are much outnumbered by the Siamese of all classes. One of the most unmistakable signs that Siam is a stronghold of the aristocratic spirit is the complete absence of any exclusiveness in school. Young princesses sit side by side with foundlings, and bring their little servants to receive identically the same education as themselves. In class the European teachers of course make no distinction, nor when a Siamese teacher interpreted my lessons as was necessary for the younger classes, did I notice that she made any. Outside lessons, however, the little servants are servants always, and the rest of their schoolfellows address the princesses as *Than Ying*. They may be deferred to in other ways hidden from me by my ignorance of the language. To the English idea a very curious custom is that of addressing every person be he child or servant by the prefix Mr. or Miss, Nai or Meh. I was told that it is because so very many names serve both sexes—but as most people know their own sex it more probably has to do with the national love of ceremony. Our maids, for instance, were Meh Mom, Meh Plaak (k not sounded), Meh Choi and Meh Chena. The two coolies were Chinese, but they too had prefixes, and were Ah Nee and Ah Joh. The teachers' prefix was Kroo, signifying teacher for either sex. As with us, at least some of the names have definite meaning. One of the teachers was Kroo Yim, a name meaning 'smile'—hard to live up to on hot afternoons with a somnolent class to be taught. Lek means 'little,' Muk 'pearl,' etc.

To give the servants their Meh was quite easy, as on first arriving I thought it part of the name. But among the girls I taught I learned their names before knowing the custom, so that from me they always had bare names. Towards the end of my stay I discovered a great many directions in which they must have thought my manners sadly wanting.

Discipline was generally easy, but naturally infants did not always respond to a word, and sometimes had to be punished. I peeped round the screen dividing my small classroom from a smaller, one day, to discover the cause of long-continued sobbing, and beheld a little boy made to stand on the table and curtsey ! Punishments which do not 'fit the crime' can be wonderfully stupid. I am told that this was probably of the teacher's own invention. She was Siamese.

Modern educationalists will commend the Siamese in that the slap is barred. A Eurasian teacher once slapped a small delinquent, and there was a terrible descent of indignant parents on the Mission. They acknowledged that punishment was deserved, and even requested that the culprit should be chastised, but to slap with the palm of the hand. . . . To our idea their choice of a suitable instrument was most strange—a bamboo or a piece of rope ! Either would be far more painful than the hand. It is necessary that foreigners walk warily in these matters, lest through ignorance they transgress. With cane, rattan, only criminals are chastised, and tamarind twigs are used to cast out evil spirits from the hysterical. It would seem that manners and superstitions are inextricably mixed.

I dread to think what effect a slippering of their offspring would have on the Siamese parent, while certain schoolmasters over here consider it better for punisher and punished than the use of the hand. Curiously, in the Siamese idea, the only reason I have been able to discover against slapping with the hand (the objection does not seem to be universal) is fundamentally the same as that of the slipperers over here, that the hand is not sufficiently elastic and that the concussion might be dangerous.

But to use that which clothes the foot, a member so low in the scale of personal honour, would horrify the

Siamese. The sole too! The sole when one is decorously seated must never even be visible.

Traps for the unwary are many and various in a land with traditions so different from our own. I must many a time have pointed out a wandering drawing-pin with the toe of my shoe, and sad to relate it was only at the very end of my stay that I discovered that to point with the foot is considered rudeness' depth. Most probably too I may have tapped the floor with my foot in efforts to wake up the class, which must have been paralysed with horror! The case of a man who divorced his wife for stamping her foot at him awakened me to my misdeeds. When seeking for models for the girls' drawing-class more than once I was glad to take a slipper from the row by the door—a ghastly solecism almost certainly, and now I wonder whether it was the blindness of ignorance that hid from me that scorn the class must have felt!

I lived at St. Mary's Mission, and most of my teaching was to the girls, but drawing classes had to be given at the boys' school too. The work at St. Peter's was very much harder, for quite a number of the biggest boys understood very little English, if any. Pupils in Bangkok have a delightful habit of *sampling* schools, in fact things had come to such a pass, no leave being taken of the last school before going on to the next, that they were required to bring a certificate from their late headmaster to the newly-favoured, stating their reason for leaving the previous school. A boy high up in his Siamese school might suddenly decide that a little English would be useful to him, and come to St. Peter's, where, for the continuity of his Siamese studies, he would be placed in the top form though not knowing a word of English. This was distinctly hard on the teachers of English subjects, and handicapped the other pupils too. Fortunately the Government standard for English was low.

In order to benefit by the Government grant it is necessary that the schools conform to Government standards, and in the infant classes, called 'pratome,' and throughout the junior and senior forms, 'matayome,' a set syllabus is followed. Naturally the greater part of the studies is in Siamese.

In such circumstances, knowing no Siamese, it was impossible for me to be quite independent, and it was frequently necessary for me to snatch Siamese teachers from their classes to interpret in mine, a sad loss of time to both. Drawing certainly improves powers of observation, so it is important to teach it to all children regardless of taste and talent, but the lack of a common tongue is a terrible handicap.

I allowed no indiarubbers in class, an unpopular ruling, but all thoroughly enjoyed the glorified freehand adopted to give them decision. The point was that the pattern, when complete, always made a picture, generally a double one, of some familiar thing or scene. I drew on the blackboard, and the pupils followed me on their papers, stroke by stroke, but the revealing strokes were left till the end, so that they never knew what they were copying, and a ripple of mirth went round when they saw whither they had been led, and laughter was general when I held up the results for the class's admiration. Of course very few got anywhere near the picture intended, but what mattered was that they were forced to *mean* each line as they drew it. Another great advantage was that after the first explanation to a newcomer there was no further need for an interpreter. In memory drawing too, which is a first-rate exercise for powers of observation, little interpretation was needed, and the class drew from memory both objects shown to them, and set subjects seen outside the school.

To give the lessons would have been quite enjoyable if my conscience had allowed me to let them consist of such exercises alone, but in all schools it is expected that pupils should learn to draw objects set before them, and as earlier noted, even artists in Siam are not good at recording their objective vision, so that in object drawing the majority were as bored as I was. In the big boys' class the probable free *mis*interpretation, through someone who knew nothing of drawing, was almost the last straw to the teacher !

The big girls all knew enough English for me to manage alone, but people who really enjoy drawing pots and pans and chairs and chests and books and boxes are rare in every clime. At least at Bangkok, there was no local Cambridge to force hexagons and pyramids in impossible perspective upon us. In Colombo I had suffered from these direly, and few indeed were the pupils I had managed to persuade that to draw them without the hindrance of an indiarubber was a really great game ! The Inspector there, at any rate, had been pleased with results.

At St. Peter's I was not the only one to suffer from the new big boy's lack of English. Imagine the catechism being taught in such circumstances—or any other English subject—but the catechism was particularly revealing !

It is good to hear that the school has been moved to

a far better site. At that time it was in the New Road, and not only the stuffiness of the town but the noise was detestable. Some kind of engineering shop set itself up just behind us, and we had to teach to the accompaniment of hammered metal. On the ricksha runs to St. Peter's there were amusing things to see—scenes of peasant life and street scenes, and it was generally then that I found the subjects for my freehand lessons.

The return journey to St. Mary's and fresh air was specially pleasant. The place, though built for a private house, afterwards became an experimental silk-worm farm under the Ministry of Agriculture, and the immediate predecessors of the Mission were the Siamese Police Cadets. Situated in a fine and treeful compound the main building consisted of two floors, both surrounded by verandahs. On the ground floor on a foundation raised well above the ground was the Chapel, etc., and behind it a small room used as a dining-room by the English staff who lived in that house. The upper floor was divided roughly into five. A large piece of front verandah projecting porchwise over the entrance served as general sitting-room. It was walled with Venetian shutters kept closed against sun and rain or opened to the breeze, as we willed. A verandah ran down each side of the enclosed building behind, and it was cut into four slices, of which three were very large rooms, and a small room at the end. Each of the large rooms had two big window doors giving on to the verandah at either end. The choice for the inmate was a considerable lack of privacy when the doors were left open, or stewing in artificial light if they were shut. The rooms were all provided with the swing screens common throughout the tropics to mask a door left open for the sake of air. But, stupidly, those of my room opened outwards, so that there was no possibility of closing them surreptitiously. To keep them shut meant blocking out too much light and air not to accept some risks, a midnight soaking among them. I made many a rush from my bed in the very middle of the room quite twenty-five feet from the edge, to close the verandah shutters against a horizontal wind-carried shower.

Mine was the furthest back of the large rooms, and in most respects the best placed for privacy, being behind the staircases. Privacy, as understood by us, is the comfort most missed by Europeans in a life in any small measure common with natives of the East. The room's drawback was that the small slice, the linen room, was beyond me, with a door between, and without keeping my room doors shut it was almost impossible to prevent the boarders from making a passage of it. This only happened once or twice a week, but quite absurdly, was an intense source of irritation. I had, for refuge, a beautiful bathroom with two windows, one or other of which could be kept open in nearly all circumstances. It was the best bathroom in the house, with a tin hip bath as well as the zinc sink, which served most people for their ablutions. The other rooms had worse drawbacks. Mine was the best room, given to a casual helper unprepared for the thousand discomforts which missionaries accept as being all in the day's work and as a matter of course.

There is now a separate sanatorium, but at that time the children lined up daily in the back verandah for the treatment of any small ailment, so that though it was not their house they were as much at home there as we, and in spite of the big rooms this gave a constant sense of crowding.

Missionary abnegation has no limits: it is considered a drawback in the present place (which it is proposed to remedy in the new school when funds allow of its being built) that the Principal's dwelling is not in the centre of the school group.

Except by special invitation for badminton, which was played nearly every evening, the children were not supposed to play about round our building, but although very easy to manage and docile in class, unless in the presence of teachers rules counted for very little with them. Another forbidden haunt out of which it was impossible to keep them, except by constant chasing, was our kitchen. Every Siamese is something of a cook, and their idea of cooking is much more elaborate than ours, akin rather to Chinese cooking and its delights. Siamese curries are tremendously hot as a rule, but very good, and some of the milder ones used to be sent in to us. Many of their fish condiments seem to us quite impossible, but they hold ripe cheeses in as great horror as we their ripe fish! Indeed 'cheese-eaters' is used, I believe, as a term of contempt for Europeans.

It was amusing to watch the school rice being boiled in the shed. It filled immense cauldrons over a charcoal fire. When it was nearly ready the cook would ladle out almost all the water and let it steam dry. Except for the two coolies we had only women servants. Her daily return from market in a double ricksha, and almost hidden under her purchases, made the cook an interesting person. Bangkok is one of the few places where double rickshas still exist pulled by one unfortunate

Chinese coolie. Marketing cooks make great use of them, and one also sees them piled up with whole families of poor Easterners, but the European avoids them more carefully than he avoids others. All Bangkok rickshas are uncomfortable.

We worked pretty hard at the Mission. I include myself, although, to give me time to sketch, by the Principal's kind arrangement only half of each week was given to school teaching. Distances in Bangkok are so great that an hour here and there would have been of very little use to me. The journey to the Old Palace in a gharry took nearly an hour each way, and most of my sketching was done in that neighbourhood. For studio work I had only the south verandah where the light was naturally difficult, the choice lay between too much light outside and much too little inside the room. But my chapter must close with the Good Works from which it has strayed.

Although no direct effort is made to convert the scholars besides caring for their minds and persons, the two schools give their pupils every opportunity of learning Christian doctrine and Anglican Church practice. At St. Mary's all boarders were expected to attend morning and evening chapel. To prayers before school the day girls came too, whether Christians or Buddhists, and all attended the Bible lessons. The sacrament was administered every Sunday and Feast day, and other services were provided both at St. Mary's and at St. Peter's.

CHAPTER XVI

EXCURSIONS

BANGKOK is full of fascination, but my wish is always to get further afield than the capital, and especially to go into the country. Less known places have the added attraction of more difficult access, particularly to the lone wanderer. Soon after my arrival in Siam the British Chaplain and his family went down to the sea for a few days' rest, long overdue, and asked me to join them at a pleasant little place called Nong Khae. It is on the east coast of Siam, two or three miles south of the popular Hua Hin, famous for its golf links and excellent little hotel, standing at the rocky point which separates two sandy bays. Hua Hin is a fishing village with shops, very fashionable and popular both with the Siamese aristocracy (several of the Royal Princes have houses there) and with Europeans too. Golf there is the best in Siam, views are charming, and there is bathing on the sandy shore.

Nong Khae is very like it, social attractions pleasantly lacking. It is chiefly a colony of missionary bungalows crowded in the hot season, but at that time empty, and it was in this group belonging to the American Presbyterian Mission that my hosts had taken a house built on a delightfully simple plan.

Instead of a ground floor tall piles, steps up to verandahs back and front, and a wide passage from one verandah to the other dividing the two rooms and their bathrooms which were the only enclosed part of the house. We ate in the passage, slept on the front verandah, and used the rooms to keep our possessions. In part of the back verandah was a small kitchen. My hosts had only brought women servants with them, and they slept on the verandah of the next bungalow perhaps fifty feet away.

On the second night of my visit I was awakened in the smallest hours by much low but persistent talking, of course all in Siamese, of which I understood no word. After what seemed a long time my hostess, who guessed me awake, and wondering, came along. She told me that the servant, sleeping on the outside of the group of three, had been wakened by a man holding a long knife, and who threatened to kill her if she woke the others. They were huddled for warmth—we had a real cold season that year, the thermometer even touched 50 degrees—and while arguing with him in whispers, she managed to wake the others undiscovered. The intruder's first wish was for information about us and our defences. These, in point of fact, were exactly nil; but the woman had the sense to dower the Chaplain with a gun and much skill in its use. And still he threatened till the one he held promised all he asked of her, but in her guile she discovered that she must first respond to a call of nature. He should go down with them to the beach, and for the beach just below they all started. But once down the bungalow stairs they risked a knife thrust in the dark and bolted for our house, and the villain, losing them, bolted too.

The poor girls tumbled on to our verandah half dead with fright but astonishingly quiet. Of course the Hua

Hin police were informed, but nothing beyond suspicion resulted. The gun fairy tale appeared to have been successful for we were never troubled. Needless to say thenceforward the women slept under our roof; they were out of the way before we wanted to get up.

Robberies are fairly frequent in those parts, and the population has not a pleasant reputation, using knives freely, though chiefly among themselves. It was the only incident to disturb our peace, and the days passed quickly between sketching, bathing and walking.

The coast thereabouts is a succession of very shallow sandy bays. The tips of their arms are heaps of rocks as at Hua Hin at the north end of our bay, or as at Khao-ta-Kiep at the south end, an isolated rocky peak apparently about to join the group of scattered islets dotted along the coast—unless the sand should conquer the sea and the islets become part of the mainland. In that quiet country time's passing could be felt and the gradual movement of earth's changes almost seen.

A belt of bamboo jungle bounds the sands. Just then it was wintering and quite bare. Never having seen such consistent wintering in the tropics, where each tree seems to take its rest at its individual sweet will, I thought the bamboo dying. Many of those that still had leaves were golden. Even freed from the weight of leaves their thorns made it advisable to keep to trodden tracks. The background of vegetation and shade was pleasant, but the feathery grace of bamboos, even giants among them (these were only between thirty and fifty feet), in no way compares to the soaring strength of real trees which were few and far between along the coast.

The nights were made more wonderful by the phosphorescent seas, great lines of luminosity breaking with the waves along the coast. While the Siamese, all perfect swimmers, bathed in it, the thought of that coast's two very real dangers, prevented my going into the water except by day. Deadly water-snakes abound there ; truly they are not anxious to bite, partly perhaps because nature has provided them with ridiculously small mouths, also they are sluggish in cold weather, but for all that a bowing acquaintance with two left by the water curled up on the sand at low tide fully contented me. Should I have had the courage to stand and wait, as did a woman bathing at Nong Khae when one of the reptiles curled round her leg ? Her courage was rewarded, for it presently uncurled and swam away. Others of the bathing party told me of the incident.

The second danger is worse because less swift in its effects. At times the water is full of a specially poisonous jelly fish, large as a football and speckled with red. Singly they are to be seen at all seasons. Here is no question of attack, but accidental contact causes terrible burns frequently resulting in blood-poisoning and death. I saw one or two dead upon the sands but never in the water. The only time I saw an immense ball of jelly in the water was after being touched by it. I did not wait to search for red spots, but swam my feeble fastest in the opposite direction. Had it been the poisonous kind my bathing dress would have been no protection.

Sharks do not seem to be dreaded along that coast, the water is probably too shallow. There was not even much fishing very near, an occasional boat with flares passed at night adorning our seascape, but Hua Hin was the place to see Siamese fishermen and their methods. A pleasant three-quarters of an hour's walk along the sands took one there, or else the train or a walk along the line; there was no road. There you could see most of the activities of which Mr. Graham gives such interesting details, fish-pickling and drying, Kapi-making—only the smell indescribable. There are fleets of fishing boats of distinctive cut. Whoso wishes to know of these should read Warrington Smythe's fascinating *Five Years in Siam*. It is not for the inexpert to attempt description of their subtle beauties.

In the hot season Nong Khae loses its charm and solitude. Then all the schools have their long holidays and everyone flies to the sea who cannot get to the hills, and there are no hill-stations in Siam. Many Europeans seek them as far as Bukit Fraser in Malaya—if they are so fortunate as to get a house there. Otherwise there is Mont Bokor, the hill-station behind Kep on the Cambodian coast, or Dalat in South Annam, or some go as far afield as Sumatra.

At the two S.P.G. Missions there were many children who only returned to their homes in the North at very long intervals. Some had no home but the Mission, so that the offer of a house between Hua Hin and Nong Khae for the long holidays was a godsend, and many of the children had never seen the sea. Most of the Siamese staff went down with the children while the Europeans travelled backwards and forwards, there being much to supervise and prepare for the coming term at Bangkok. Holidays are not times of rest for the heads of understaffed boarding-schools.

The British colony in Bangkok had for some time

past found it difficult to get the right man as chaplain, and had begged the priest-in-charge of the S.P.G. Mission to take over the chaplaincy until the right man should turn up. For the benefit of the Mission he consented, stipulating that its work should come first and turning over the chaplain's stipend to its use.

Responsibilities seldom come singly, and he and his wife, endlessly busy people, had been forced by circumstances to become acting principals of the boys' and girls' schools respectively, instead of supreme heads only. They were without helpers sufficiently qualified by knowledge of the Siamese and their difficult language to delegate this part of their activities. It will be guessed that personal holidays pure and simple hardly entered into their programme. During my stay one long-promised holiday they did take, and took me with them for two delightful days on the river.

It was at Khao Pansa, the beginning of Buddhist Lent just before the rainy season when all monks must return to the monastery. No more travelling for *Phra Todong* (Monks on Pilgrimage), as they may be met on the road each with the attendant small boy to carry his scanty luggage. All must return to rest as the Rule ordains. As the good Christian in his Lent so the good Buddhist in his season of abstinence forswears luxuries and, if necessary, vices—strong drink, for instance.

Before the Roman Lent comes Carnival, before the Buddhist Lent four days' holiday when all Government offices are closed and all the world makes merry.

To travel in a houseboat ! The perfect motion was revealed to me on that two days' trip—the sense of unimpeded movement dreamlike and quite silent, the tug's fussiness a long slack rope ahead and even its smoke carried off by obliging winds. The river banks sped past just fast enough to make sketching truly exciting, the sketches being largely from memory when they were not compound. River wats tree-embowered, river villages with floating suburbs, sailing boats, row boats, racing practice and many another interest.

The first stop was at the King's Palace of Bang Pa In. The curator was away holiday-making and it could not be visited. It was obviously much Europeanised, and in lotus-eating mood I merely felt it to be an illusion the less to leave in Siam and was quite content. We wandered about the grounds and picked up sweet-scented white blossoms fallen from tall trees unknown, before heading again for Ayuthia, Siam's ancient capital. At the full moon's rising we reached its outskirts and tied up at the pier of Wat Banen Choeng. Closed at that hour, its white gables gleamed in the moonlight, as we wandered round it half anxious lest the monks should come out and resent our midnight prowl—faint gleams of candlelight under doorways told of their presence. But we had the grounds to ourselves, and I sketched a gable with fantastic shadows thrown on its whiteness. And then to bed.

Six of us on that houseboat (more by day when the servants were there), so we were thick on the ground. The boat belonged to a Siamese nobleman, and was therefore arranged Siamese fashion inside with a gangway dividing two raised platforms, one narrow and the other wide; they were cushioned, and served as seats or couches as occasion required. Towards the stern was a bathroom of the water-dipping type. It was on a level with the platform, so that I who am tall could not stand upright there. Back to back with the bathroom a pantry-kitchen still under cover, and stern and bows were open. The sides of the room were all shuttered with venetians, and opened and shut at will.

There was only just room for us all extended, but it was well worth the crush to see Ayuthia in the right way. Ayuthia has always been a water town, built on and between the many channels into which the Menam at that point divides.

At early morning we steamed to the Old Palace and tied up opposite the ever-fascinating floating market. But here too the curator had taken advantage of Khao Pansa, and we saw nothing but the grounds. After all the most exciting things were out of doors, so we left the houseboat for a *rua chang* and were rowed up to the King's pavilion at the old elephant stockade. The pavilion is now a school, and it is said that the Keddah will no more be used for the catching of wild elephants.

Those were occasions of great splendour and courage certainly, but judging from descriptions not without unnecessary cruelty and baiting, often bringing swift vengeance in its wake, for few Keddahs ended without human sacrifice. Still it is well for the elephant that the King needs few now for use, and contents himself with those that are sacred to him, and called white. They and their whiteness have vanished from the country's flag, and their day of glory seems to be vanishing too. The Siamese white elephant has not even the white pig pinkness of the Burmese elephant that last year visited the Zoo, but is dark-grey, only less dark than other elephants. Although emblems of His Majesty's sacred descent, the King no longer keeps them stabled within the Palace precincts. Pathetic fall ! They seemed to have a sad and boring life, with little to do, and generally tethered. One I met out on the road had marvellous tusks reaching to the ground.

In Buddhist sacred story the White Elephant takes the place of the Dove in Christian sacred art, and announces the coming sacred and immaculate birth to Gautama's mother. The assumption of the title, 'Lord of the White Elephants,' by an Ayuthia king in the sixteenth century was the cause of a disastrous Burmese war in which the Burmese carried off the elephants, cause of all the trouble, and, as *they* claim, the King of Siam with them.

All wild elephants are most strictly preserved in Siam, only a proved rogue may be shot. To watch the destruction of crops by wild herds without attempting, under penalty of severe punishment, to drive them off is a tyranny to which only the most docile of peasant populations would submit. They probably regret the Keddah, but it is questionable whether the preliminary driving of the herd would not be of equal danger to the crops.

The Ayuthia Keddah is still worth seeing with its stockade of gigantic teak logs surrounding the enclosure into which the wild elephants were driven by a V-shaped approach. The palisade served not only to enclose the great beasts, but to make fast the rattan nooses with which it was the catcher's business to encircle the back leg of the selected animal.

From the stockade we went on to the ruins of Ayuthia as the Burmese left them after the sack of the city. These poor skeletons of brick stand gaunt and not very impressive in comparison with stone-built remains. It is a stoneless country and, like the beautiful temples in Bangkok, of which they are the prototype, they were once covered, at worst with fine plaster and at best with who knows what loveliness, gold, mosaic or porcelain.

No attempt at preservation of these historical buildings was made until the reign of the late King Rana VI., whose interest gave great impetus to the study of his kingdom's past. Up to that time only an occasional European student of archaeology, or venturesome tourist, had wandered round the ruins—what part of them, that is, the jungle had not absorbed. Many images, whole and broken, were carried off, none caring. It was suddenly realised to betoken a great lack of reverence that spoliation should be possible, and also that scraps—heads, legs, arms—of sacred images should be at the mercy of a chance step. It was not the Burmese, themselves Buddhists, who were responsible for breaking up the sacred images. Although these were known to contain treasure they would not take the risk of such impiety. But incursions of Haws, Mahommedan invaders from Yunnan, were without scruple, and if they ever came so far south as Ayuthia, the breakage may have been their doing. More probably, accidents apart, the pieces may be imperfect castings scrapped.

Whatever may have been their origin, when interest revived, instead of leaving the sacred débris among the ruins, they were collected, and all that was not specially worthy of a place in a museum was piled in heaps; and so they stand among the prachedi, that which is recognised as sacred is revered, is probably the argument.

One whole Buddha is to be seen there in his original place, though the setting is ruined. Perhaps his size —he is forty feet high—preserved him from destruction, and he has sat through the years since the blasting of his home, oblivious and disdainful of human vagaries. His undisguised scorn strikes as curiously lacking in the detachment preached by the Master. I had noted many times that although the shapes of hands and fingers, feet and toes were those prescribed by tradition for the Sacred Image, there was extraordinary diversity in the features of Siamese Buddhas. The reason, when discovered, proved to me once again that this is a world of miracles. There is a Siamese saying—and it would appear to be true if the diversity of the Buddhas speaks right—that the personality of the giver *may* be miraculously reflected in his gift. If the Merit-Maker is a very good man something of his benevolent features may be seen in the Buddha he is presenting. The sceptical whisper that the miracle is assisted by an extra fee to the founder; but if that is so how account for the fact that the Merit-Maker who thinks to expiate bad deeds by a gift sees his evil face also reflected in the bronze? Moreover, the image presented by a bad man is hard to cast. It has happened when the image has been given by a very evil liver that it had to be cast as many as three times.

The casting of a Buddha is a great ceremony to which all friends and relations are bidden. The image may be made of pure silver or gold, or of the perfect combination of seven metals. All invited bring gifts, of silver, of gold, and of jewels, to be encased within the image—or its pedestal—offerings repaid in store of Merit to those who bring the gifts.

Ayuthia was the capital of Siam until about 150 years ago. As such it had existed for over 400 years of prosperity. In the sixteenth or seventeenth century it was a flourishing port in trade relations with many European countries. Indeed, the cordiality of those relations nearly cost Siam its freedom when, through that prince of adventurers Faulkon, Louis XIV., by peaceful penetration through Church and trade (ships-of-war loomed large in the background, although they had ostensibly been sent as a threat to the Dutch who were making trouble from Malacca) almost closed his fist on the prosperous country.

The Church was represented by three Bishops and their satellites, whose grandiose main object had been to convert the whole East. The Romans have three bishoprics in Siam to this day.

Ayuthia was considered an excellent place from which to make a beginning, as its flourishing commerce had attracted a large population of Malay, Annamese, Cambodian, Burmese, Indian and Japanese settlers.

These glories are of the long past. The now ubiquitous Chinaman cultivates the land (rice-growing apart) and does other hard jobs. There may be a few Indian traders, and I know of one Englishman who has not only his business but his home there, but Ayuthia's interest at the present day depends upon its intensely Siamese character. The chief feature there now is not the court but a wonderful floating market. Each shop is the front of a little house on pontoons, with one or more sharply pointed gables with a flamelike curl to the lower ends of their fascia boards.

This flame is only symbolic of the national gaiety of temperament, not the fiery breath of an angry Naga. His place is on the Wat, and bad luck would pounce on the presumptuous citizen who should put it on his dwelling.

It seems that the floating house is not cheap. The

great teak logs to which it is moored need replacing at comparatively short intervals, and are expensive. For one thing the Government takes toll on each one. Still, they may be cheaper than buildings on shore, which must be strong to withstand inundation. The river is the very life of the people, and no slow one

THE FLOATING MARKET, AYUTHIA.

either; walking is sluggish when compared to the way they dart about in their minute canoes like little water-beetles.

The banks are comparatively high and well-wooded. In spite of the heat—Ayuthia is admittedly hot—it would have been pleasant to spend a few days there, but we had to be in Bangkok next day, and the too-quick return was all that was left to us, the swift stream speeding our departure.

That evening we did only two hours' steaming, and just before dark, because of great storm-gusts, tied up extra securely at the piles of a Wat pier.

The storm only threatened, and in the lovely early morning we strolled through the Wat grounds and in the near jungle. To reach it a perilous bridge had to be crossed, two planks *en dos d'âne* and without a handrail. The planks may once have been tethered, but nothing was left to anchor the ends to the ground. The centre of the bridge must have been quite three feet above the banks and eight feet above the water. Though full of qualms I had made up my mind to walk across, and arrived at the top with dignity unimpaired, but there it forsook me. The others crossed before me and I had enjoyed watching them, but had not meant that my own descent should so greatly add to their gaiety. . . . On the return journey discretion conquered valour and I crossed on all fours. The habit of bare feet would have made everything easy.

By midday, we were back in Bangkok with the recollection of two days' real pleasuring to cheer us in our work.

Two other excursions that travellers in Siam should not miss are to Phrabat and Lopburi. At both places the problem of where to stay was solved for us by Siamese hospitality.

Phrabat—the sacred foot—is one of the many shrines built over the footprint of the Lord Buddha when, by supernatural means, he visited Ceylon, Burma and Siam. As the means were supernatural it is only to be expected that the footprints should be supernormal; their size may have been a matter of the Maker's mood, and varies enormously. That at Phrabat was discovered early in the seventeenth century by a hunter who was clever enough to recognise it, although the imprint of the Chakr and other signs of sanctity always to be found on a Buddha's foot are missing. The footprint was discovered late in time, and the signs may, it is thought, have been obliterated by some accident. It is a comparatively small print, only about four and a half feet long, and though the pressure must have been considerable, the depression it caused in the rock is only about eighteen inches.

To atone for the long neglect a most exquisite little shrine has been built over it, all encased in glass mosaic with a pale golden ground, both the tiny square building and the pillars round it. These support the seven-staged roof diminishing to a tall and tenuous spire, roof and spire rich with gold and ornament.

The Temple stands on a little eminence at the foot of rocky hills, and a flight of steps recalling the Scala Santa at Rome lead up to it from the monastic buildings and booths and *salà* below. All round and above it are numberless votive buildings and prachedi, and here I had the good fortune, when sketching, to put my hand on the detached bronze head of a small Buddha. The reverent tidying into heaps had not yet begun here as at Ayuthia, but lest it should be considered ill-gotten, the head was promptly concealed among my sketching things where it stayed till we reached the Mission once more.

The shrine stands on a platform, and round it great gongs are slung that the pilgrim who has paid his devoirs to the holy place may call the angels to witness his Act of Merit. At the great pilgrimage season, unfortunately over when I was there, their clamour is constant. An Eastern pilgrimage is wonderful, the brilliantly dressed crowd devout and gay, and their delightful offerings of gold-leaf and incense, or (specially prized perhaps) some gimcrack European mirror or other article from the Bangkok shops. The account of this pilgrimage had fired my ambition to see the place, only for a solitary traveller the difficulties were many, not least the everlasting language question. It was through the kindness of a friend willing to repeat the excursion that my desire to see Phrabât was fulfilled.

The trip entailed a night away from Bangkok, but he was able, through a Siamese colleague, to get an introduction to the Chief Priest, who would find us a lodging and show us everything. It was pleasant to discover that we need not leave Bangkok in the early hours as the connection with the light railway from the main line to Phrabat was at a reasonable time—so the colleague assured us.

Alas for our information ! When we reached the junction of Ta-rua the one train of the day had gone !

My friend made much play with his letter to the Chief Monk. It was a matter of compelling necessity that it should be delivered that day, he said. And so it was if we were to see Phrabat ! There was no very obvious place for us to lodge at the junction, and the four or five hours' journey back to Bangkok with nothing seen was not to be thought of. The only solution offered was a special train at our expense, which sounded impossibly magnificent, but after a certain amount of bargaining we secured it for the modest sum of 20 ticals, about £2, with the cheering certainty that most of the money would go straight into the pockets of the stationmaster and his friends.

Amongst other pleasures we gave half the neighbourhood a joy ride, and took up a great deal of their furniture too. People so grand as to order special trains could expect to do no less. The guard wore a large revolver—against robbers, as he said. The line was through bamboo jungle, and in the grass half hidden there was a fascinating looking yellow flower which greatly intrigued me, but so pathetically unaccustomed was I to such grandeur that only long afterwards did it occur to me that I might have stopped *my* train to look at it !

The next blow was to find that the Chief Priest had gone to Bangkok. Happily his deputy had the power to receive the letter and us, whom he most hospitably entreated. The upper floor of the absent Head Monk's house was put at our disposal. It consisted of one room and a verandah, reached by a staircase from the ground. On the verandah there was a European table and four Windsor chairs, while the room was comprehensively furnished with a Spittoon !

We were immediately offered tea and the use of a big teapot and cups, and then our host showed us the shrine and its treasures, while the Chinese servant we had brought unpacked our provisions and set up the camp beds. He succeeded in borrowing an enamel basin and jug for us, which looked strangely out of place in those surroundings, but which were a godsend, as we had forgotten to bring anything of the sort, and they passed from room to verandah as one or other of us needed them.

The place was lighted by great incandescent lamps. We had one between us, and hung it in the room doorway that it should shed its rays on both. The place was spotlessly clean, and built of perfectly fitted wood—beautiful work. It was airy, too, as the room had a window in each of two walls and the door in the third. A locked door in the fourth wall led to an inner room not offered us. As we were upstairs the shutters could remain wide open, which was a great blessing. Downstairs the curiosity excited by strangers might have been tiresome. For one night's stay it was all quite sufficient. My companion discovered a bathroom of some kind but did not encourage me to use it, nor was I inclined to stand in the open and pour water over my person clad in a single thin cotton garment, discarding the wet one under shelter of the dry, as the natives so cleverly do.

The sightseeing did not take much time. The wooden casing which protects the sacred imprint was removed for our benefit, and the treasured silver matting which surrounds it duly shown and admired, and also the contents of a little museum.

The place itself was enchanting. To see hills after the utter flatness of Bangkok made me breathe deep, and it was the real country. Although the people were interested in us they left us freedom of movement, and when I wandered off next morning to sketch I sat peacefully and quite alone on the upper outskirts of the community, the only sign of life a snake spilling itself hastily away from my dangerous neighbourhood.

Happily the one train left at midday, so that I went full of regrets for so short a stay, and sophisticated European habits had no time to bring the sense of discomforts to the surface. Full enjoyment implies incompleteness.

On the Lopburi trip another man and woman were of the party too. This time we had been given a letter to the Governor of the Province, and hoped for a little floating house sometimes placed at the disposal of guests. Again the head was away, but his deputy offered us the little house, as we hoped. Everything necessary was there except bedding and provisions which we had brought. The plan was simple, a central sitting-room flanked by two bedrooms, and the whole surrounded by a narrow platform also under the shadow of the roof-eaves. A movable gangplank connected us with the shore.

Between us and the shore was the only safe bathing for any but very strong swimmers, for towards mid-stream the current was tremendous. The river at Lopburi appears narrow, being only the eastern channel of the two into which it divides. Tall bamboos and other luscious growth waved at us from the opposite bank and gave a pleasant expectation that something astonishing and exciting might, at any minute, break through. But the glimmer of a rushlight at night was all we saw.

We were tied up outside the fort, and the one unpleasant memory of the place is that of prisoners clanking their chains in the water when bathing, their armed warders awaiting them on the shore. There was a great deal of bathing, both of persons and animals, happily all that was within sight was downstream from us.

Besides the ruins, which are the main interest of the place to foreigners, there is a little modern town and market, and a fine prachedi on an island above the weir that so excited our branch of the stream.

From the train Cambodian remains are to be seen, but there is no hint of the sixteenth-century ruins of palace and fort, the King's summer residence, nor of the house of Faulkon. Though adventure was the breath of his nostrils, Constantine Faulkon was no common adventurer. His life was punctuated by shipwreck, and in the end his statesmanship was wrecked on adventure, but for all that 'statesman' is the word that best describes him.

After reading of his adventures, one physically a coward is left wondering how much of his varied life he felt to have been worth while as he died under torture. As a statesman Faulkon's praises are sounded by many contemporary authors, both French and Dutch. One of his great French admirers, the Jesuit Father Tachard, in his book, *A Voyage to Siam*, translated into English in 1688, says that Constantine's father was a Venetian nobleman, Governor of the Greek island of Cephalonia, and his mother a daughter of one of the 'Ancientest Families of the Country.' To repair the fallen fortunes of his family he went to sea, shipping with an English captain then on his way home to England. Other people say that he was the son of a Cephalonian innkeeper, and ran away to sea. However that may be, he had his own abilities to thank for his later marvellous successes.

While in England he took service with the East India Company and was sent to Siam, where he lived with a Mr. White, a merchant of position. In time he

FROM THE FLOATING HOUSE. OUR NEIGHBOURS.

To face page 232.

amassed a small fortune and decided to trade for himself. He bought a little ship but at first met only with ill-luck, being twice wrecked at the mouth of the Menam Chao Phya. His third wreck was the turning point in his fortunes. It happened miserably on the coast of Malabar, and all he saved from it were 2000 crowns.

Fallen asleep from sheer weariness on the shore he saw a Vision—a 'Person full of Majesty,' who, smiling, looked upon him, and said: 'Return, return from whence you came.'

Now Fate had decreed that the Siamese Ambassador, on his way back from the Court of Persia, should also be shipwrecked on that shore, and there, doubtless dripping and disconsolate, they met. Faulkon, with his habit of shipwreck, was of great assistance to the Ambassador, and when both had returned to Siam the latter, as a token of his gratitude and admiration, introduced Constantine to the Barcalon, King Narai's first Minister-of-State.

The Barcalon, an indolent and pleasure-loving man, was overjoyed to find so capable an assistant on whom to shuffle off unwelcome business, and so Faulkon came to the notice of His Majesty, who quickly recognised his merits. Indeed, the King would have made him First Minister in name as he was in fact, but Faulkon, aware of the jealous hatred his rapid success was arousing, refused to take the title of Barcalon until after the death of his first master.

Under the wise and energetic rule of the Greek, King and country prospered exceedingly. Many were Faulkon's inventions. There are traces still extant of waterworks devised by him to bring fresh water to the Palace. It came through earthenware pipes from a reservoir three square miles in extent in hills eight miles away.

His commercial undertakings were on the grand scale. Graham says that under his guidance 'The King himself became the principal merchant in his own country, and owned a fleet of merchant ships with which he did business greatly to the profit of himself—and incidentally to that of his First Minister.'

Political intrigue was his undoing. The French scheme under Louis XIV for the conversion of the whole East has already been mentioned. Through the missionaries Constantine Faulkon was put into touch with Colbert, great Minister of the Christian King. Faulkon was made a French Count, and became so much the creature of the French as to cede to them the ports of Mergui (then Siamese) and Bangkok, which were garrisoned by soldiers from the six ships mentioned earlier in the chapter.

By this time the Siamese were thoroughly alarmed, and even the King, who apparently still did not realise the material danger to which he and his country were exposed, refused to be Christianised against his will, in his message to Louis XIV, adding the following delightfully dignified reproof:

'After all it is strange to me that the King of France, my good Friend, should so much concern himself in an affair that relates to God, wherein it would seem God does not at all interest himself, but leaves it wholly to our Discretion.'

The patience of the Siamese nobles was exhausted, and as the result of a conspiracy led by Phra Petchracha when at Lopburi King Phra Narai was dethroned, and Faulkon lost his life horribly.

In the tenth century Lopburi was the capital of Siam, and it is important as the point of fusion of the various nationalities which go to the making of the Siamese as we know them now. The name Siamese too came from the neighbourhood when Lao-Khmer half-breeds took the name of Men of Syama. In the name 'Siam' it is still retained, but although in Europe we speak of Siamese they know themselves as Thai, and there seems to be some uncertainty as to whether this is the name of the northern branch of the Lao-Tai family, or whether the name came to them from that of an early capital, Sukhothai, together with the Brahman ceremonial still in use at Court. 'Sukho' means happiness and 'Thai' free—a wonderful suggestion to hold before the inhabitants of any city.

At Lopburi, as elsewhere, the Cambodian piles stand for strength and beauty. They are founded on huge laterite blocks, as at Angkor, and are often built with them too, but topped in some cases with sandstone and in some with brick covered with stucco.

For beauty of outline and situation the Wat Maha comes first in my memory, while in the Phra Prang San Yot, despite neglect and jungle, more interesting details have survived. Here three rifle-cartridge domes cover dark chambers in which some images have been left or replaced. The main part of the building is of blocks of laterite once covered with fine stucco, having itself too coarse a texture for the carver's decorating. Patches of the stucco are still to be seen here and there. That the apex of each gabled doorway is of sandstone finely carved I must take on trust, but the interior is largely lined with it, its presence a wonder in that stoneless country.

After the Khmer period stucco largely replaced stone, facing and protecting the brick core of all medieval and modern buildings. Among Khmer constructions, as at Angkor, only the habitations of the gods are in stone. It would be interesting to learn at what period kings had the audacity to forsake wood for brick. Anyhow, the gods have taken their revenge through the hand of Time, for the brick palaces have a look far more forlorn than the Cambodian temples more than twice their age.

If not beauty at least human interest is all with the brick and stucco remains of the King's Summer Palace, Faulkon's house and the city walls.

That the palace courts were once a scene of brilliance is obvious from the rows and rows of niches for cocoanut oil lamplets. The skeleton of the King's audience chamber is still interesting, his throne was in an interior window halfway up the wall, reached from a private stair and room at the back, and is on a much higher level than that open to the people. No risk here that any common head should be higher than His Majesty's, but prostrations were probably the order of the day for all that.

A visit of only two nights and so much to see left little time for sketching. Here is a portrait of our nearest neighbour at dawn, and another of a fascinating banyan which shelters one chamber, all that remains of a great temple, now the pile of stones from which the banyan springs and steps as banyans do, trunk by trunk, down steep sides to the ground.

Parts of various gods inhabit the chamber and still to-day receive the homage of the people. Their dwelling has been re-roofed with sheets of corrugated

BANYAN AT LOPBURI.

To face page 236.

iron—Sir Frederick Treves' 'Iron has entered into the soul of Burmah, corrugated iron,' is nearly as true of Siam. In this case the iron was almost to be forgiven for the fun it gave the monkeys whose home the banyan was. They swung from the branches, and came down again and again on the loose iron sheets obviously for the joy of the noise it made. Puck-like creatures, short-haired with sharply-pointed ears and 'a little button at top,' descendants perhaps of the Great Panjandrum? One of them seized a roll of cherished films, greatly to the dismay of the owner, and sped with it to the tree-top, an amusing last memory of two days that I, for one, should have wished twice as long.

CHAPTER XVII

NAKON LAMPANG

NOT very many years ago a matter of more than a month's journeying was necessary to go from Bangkok to Chiengmai, reached, since the opening of the last piece of the permanent way in 1921, in something over thirty hours. The journey used to be done by river, through the long plain up the endless swift stream, and when at last the Northern Hills came in sight, there was the prospect of dangerous rapids to be climbed.

In spite of all difficulties the American crusaders of the Presbyterian Mission, and the adventurers of British commerce seeking teak from the great forests, have long journeyed into the Lao country. Now the way is easy for the tourist, but to the writer the time spent in the journey was quite long enough.

The country was most interesting, and I was amused by my neighbour in the train, an Australian seeking in Siam a suitable investment for his savings. He was as keen as I to see everything, but one of the people who must at all costs have a listener; great at monologue, and under the impression that he gleaned information by his talk. The innocent enquiry if he had been to England shocked him into momentary silence, then, 'No! why should I?' And to my explanatory remark that to see Australia would interest me—'Oh! in that sense.' His British descent was apparently a sore point.

Too true it is that one man's meat is another man's poison. On this occasion my poison was Durien: passing from the famous Bangkok orchards to the unhappy north where no Durien grows. The possessor had it in his berth, two or three in front of mine, and it made the night hateful. The passage windows had to be kept tightly shut against its insidious smell, and as the outer windows must always be screened against mosquitoes, and more especially sparks, lest one wake in a fiery bed, as has happened to more than one traveller, the heat was hideous. The engines are run on wood, and tropical showers of sparks accompany the train. In such circumstances it was necessary to keep the most rickety fan imaginable going, which did not assist slumber.

To the greater number of Europeans, Durien is merely notorious, but it must be mentioned respectfully for the great esteem in which it is held in all the lands where it grows, hanging high from the branches of straight, tall trees. Natives have no objection to its smell, but Europeans, though devotees, admit that the stench is an almost impassable barrier, and also that it must be eaten with discrimination to avoid qualms and pains, though some think everything worth the feast. I had long promised myself that I would brave the perils of the Durien. True, only adventurers select their adventures, but let that pass. At Colombo the fruit had never pressed itself upon my notice—in Java it was in full season and the deed had to be attempted. Courage ebbed as, on our journey, each station we passed was more closely enwrapped in the indescribable smell than the last. At Djokja it was all-pervading: husks were in heaps at all street corners and piles of fruit filled the market, handsome and forbidding in its spiked shell: green, more or less egg-shaped and perhaps eight to ten inches long. The inner sheath is the most aggressively fragrant part. To give the order for one to be brought to my verandah was one of the heroic acts of a timorous existence. The landlady had been amused but encouraging, and for once virtue was rewarded. The fruit had been discreetly chosen at exactly the right moment of its career. It was, doubtless, one of those that grow at the end of a young branch and are considered the best of all. Hopeful greed gleamed in the eye of the boy who brought and opened the fruit for us. He helped us each to a tit-bit of the fleecy white flesh, studded with dark nuts, and waited and watched while we timidly tasted it, each looking at the other in anticipation of we knew not what, and he was obviously delighted that we refused more, and bore off the remains in triumph for his own delectation, leaving us considerably disappointed at the tameness of the sensation it had provided! We decided that both the delights of the nutty flavour and the terrors of the fruit at close quarters were grossly exaggerated; but then there is the after-taste, so let me warn other intending tasters that it is well to follow up Durien with black coffee and liqueurs. This was a first judgment, but I have since seen no reason to revise it.

My first stop was at Nakon Lampang to see the teak forest, easily accessible there for the solitary traveller, whereas from Chiengmai it is a camping expedition of several days.

A well-made road, at that time quite new, runs from Lampang to Chiengrai, with the natural and pleasant consequence that the completely modern and the utterly primitive met, and there were numbers of motor-buses, which made it prosaically easy for me to see the teak forests, and so realise my chief object in coming north.

I was also lucky in finding an acquaintance at Lampang. Unfortunately she and her husband were just off on leave, but able and willing to arrange that elephants should work in the forest for me to see and sketch if I could make my own way there. The 'buses made this easy, and though something of a gamble, one worth risking, being so much less expensive than to hire a private car. The advent of the motor-bus has had the demoralising effect of magic on the native, who looks on it as a means to get-rich-quick. Encouraged by the salesman he invests his savings in one of the marvellous carriages that go so quickly, carry so many paying passengers, and mean so little work to the driver. Never having hitherto seen any machine more complicated than a Singer's sewing-machine, which I saw in places incredibly remote—he learns to drive and to change a tyre, and do the roughest sort of repairs. Then he proceeds to drive his 'bus to death, sometimes, but wonderfully seldom, to its death by accident, afterwards sorrowfully awakening to the fact that he has killed the goose that laid the golden eggs and must return to labour or starve.

It will be gathered that 'buses were more numerous than reliable, but my hostess, an American missionary, in charge of the girls' school, knew a driver she could trust, and engaged the two front seats of his 'bus. In it we expected to proceed to the forest, and we also engaged seats for the return journey of the 'bus to Lampang from its destination at Muang Ngao.

'Buses in Siam are not too proud to step off their route to pick up a passenger, but next morning it was a strange 'bus that fetched us, the trusted one had sent it as something had gone wrong with his own.

The Manager of the Teak Company had left orders that a clerk who spoke a little English (to my comfort) should go with us to the rendezvous with the elephants, and introduce us. On the journey small transactions with village groups were entertaining, and we had uninterrupted views. At Bang-là, our stopping-place, it was a pleasant surprise to find fellow-countrymen, the manager of the Company's mid-forest station at Muang Ngao with his wife and one of the younger foresters, glad to meet messengers from the outer world. It was more than unexpected to find ourselves in the depths of the forest, yet not five minutes from the highroad.

Here, in a clearing, stood one of the Company's inspection bungalows. If I remember right, like many native huts, it was a basket-work erection made of laths of bamboo. In any case it stood on a foundation of tall piles. A steep stair led up to the platform where a fire might be lighted on a trayful of clay, and the whole front of the hut towards the platform was open. It consisted of one room, with a piece screened off at the back by way of a bathroom, the floor pierced to allow the water to drain off, and the back-door opening on a ladder to the ground. The Inspector's camping-kit furnishes the various huts in which he has to station, and the place was bare. It was put at our disposal as

IN MUANG NGAO FOREST. THE HOBBLED ELEPHANT.

To face page 242.

shelter from sun or showers, and the weather was prodigal with both.

It was immense fun drawing the elephants when they came from their real jobs much further in the forest, to haul and roll for my pleasure. The hauling was just a question of obedience to the rider's word, but to see the great beasts kneel to roll the logs, and use their own judgment in feeling about with their tusks to get the best leverage before making the final lift and push, gave the real sense of their power. The process was repeated over and over again.

More than anything else I had wished to see trees pushed down, and the sight fully came up to expectation, for to hear a tree of from four inches to eight inches in diameter crack like matchwood took away one's breath. An astonishing sight. The monster walked up to the chosen tree, looped its trunk, and with, so to speak, the bridge of its nose, pushed till the tree yielded. At the first tree I could hardly believe my eyes or my sketch, so the process was repeated. By this time our English friends had left us, with instructions to the gang foreman to do whatever I wished. When both the elephants and I had worked well, the poor beasts were hobbled by the chaining together of their fore feet, and turned out to get their dinners. They can go at a wonderful pace in this three-legged fashion, but it seemed the stranger that they should so quietly submit to the indignity when one heard that the elephant drivers in that part of the world, so far from having a traditional respect for their charges, and inherited mutual understanding with them passed on from father to son, were the merest casuals. They belong to a tribe which has no elephants of its own, but they are quite fearless of the huge beasts, and not even always kind, much less respectful.

When the elephants went off to lunch we climbed to our eyrie to eat too, and sketch the trees, till the clerk came to remind us that we must get back to the road

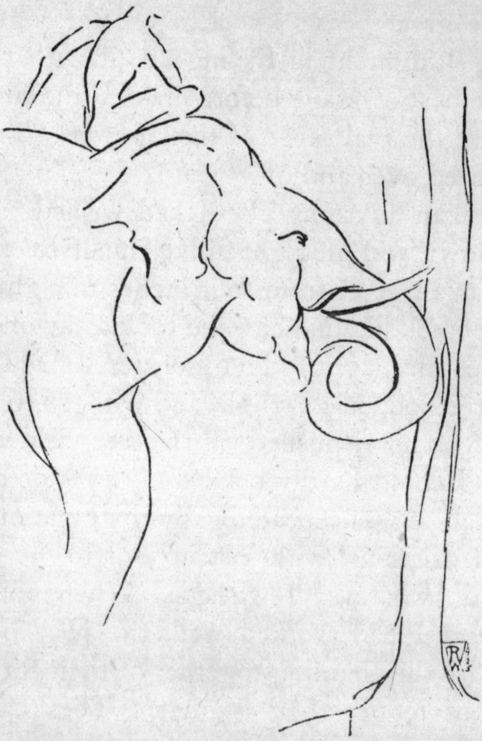

ELEPHANT PUSHING DOWN A TREE.

for our 'bus. The weather had turned showery, and we were glad to find shelter on the raised platform of a little shop by the roadside. The rain stopped. I wandered and sketched, trains of ox-carts full of grain passed, and we waited. The hours passed too, but no 'bus, and we began to wonder how to make the night in the forest hut tolerable. The little shop was full of American tinned foods, probably stale, and we might get ptomaine poisoning, but we need not starve. By way of wraps and furniture we had, between us, one thin silk mackintosh and a sketching stool. Our clerk spoke of mosquito nets to be borrowed from the coolie lines near by. Strange to say we did not find the idea much more attractive than the prospect of the mosquitoes themselves.

Late in the afternoon a car came, heading in the wrong direction, and at my companion's lively signalling it stopped. It belonged to the Chinese contractor for roads. No, he was not returning to Lampang. Yes, certainly he would tell any motor he might meet that we were waiting to be picked up, and so away. But in ten minutes he was back again, offering, if we knew of anyone who would give us shelter there, to take us on to Muang Ngao, as it was improbable that anything more rapid than a paddy cart at two miles an hour would pass so late.

We were the more indebted to his courtesy that he had to put down a packing-case to make room for us, and as we went deeper into the forest, and his judgment was justified, for we saw only paddy carts encamped for the night, our gratitude deepened.

On reaching the Company's Muang Ngao houses as darkness fell we found our deputy hosts of the morning rather relieved to see us. More conversant than we with the vagaries of 'buses they had been wondering how we had fared.

It was a most pleasant end to a wonderful expedition, and great fun and very flattering that the swiftly scribbled elephant sketches should all be recognised and named by their owner. To me they had looked so very much alike.

From my point of view it had been an immense gain to have the further drive from Banglà to Muang Ngao. By evening the forest was spangled with glorious hosts of Burmese rollers, flashing sparks of kingfisher blue, giving life to the still fascination of soaring trees. At clearings or some turn in the road there were glimpses of rocky points and noble cliffs where even the forest could not climb.

One problem was solved for me that day—how did the immense creepers reach from tree-top to tree-top? Instead of the monkey-like swing I had more than half imagined, in the clearing where we had met the elephants I decided that the only trouble that they took in the matter was in their eager early youth. On the ground they run on from sapling to sapling and so get carried up with the tree's growth.

Curious things were the living shells of ficus whose victims had been charred in forest fires while they stood on like empty and broken vases. All one could guess was that the dead tree burnt so quickly as to leave the vampire which had absorbed its life almost uninjured. A young ficus, at the beginning of its despicable and parasitic career, is to be seen in the forest sketch. Later roots and branches will completely enclose its victim, choking it, twisting, breaking and absorbing the giant completely, and producing in the beholder a most reprehensible sense of vicarious triumph mixed with a half contemptuous pity.

The only big teak in the sketch lies in logs on the ground; it is now rigorously preserved, and only that which has been girdled by a government inspector may be felled.

The Government of Siam was suddenly made aware a few years ago that through the greed of merchant companies, and the cupidity of the hereditary Lao chiefs, teak was threatened with extinction, and so the cutting was regulated by law, the owners being compensated in money, and the lessee's rights greatly curtailed. There is a government tax on every log, which is stamped all over its length with the name of the firm from whose concession it has travelled the hundreds of miles down to Bangkok. The journey from the time of felling to that of reaching the saw-mills is between three and four years. All the first part of the way each log travels independently. It is only when smooth waters are reached that they can be lashed together into the great rafts of between 100 and 200 logs, in which array they reach Pakret and await their turn for the saw-mills.

To girdle a tree is to cut its bark in a deep ring about two feet from the ground. It is left standing two or three years to die and get seasoned before being felled. Once cut down the elephants' work begins : they haul and roll it to the nearest watercourse, probably without water at that season. After the rains it floats down in company with hundreds of others to the main river, hurtling through rapids, guided in places where a jam is likely to occur by men and elephants whose judgment in such cases is said to be as good as their riders. Nevertheless sometimes an inextricable jam occurs, and dynamite has to be used to prevent disastrous floods.

I should like to have seen much more of the forest, but my hostess had to be back at her school. We had splendid views from the returning Chiengrai mail which took us back in the early morning, very lucky, unprotected as we were, in having escaped an uncomfortable adventure with its almost certain consequence of malaria. My companion had made many a journey to and from Chiengrai on horseback, so to her only the road itself was new with its consequent ease of travel. Hours now for distances that had lately taken days to cover.

The imminent expectation of the rains had thwarted my wish to go further to Chiengrai : there was scenery there, and on the way temples also, that I was most anxious to see. The 'buses made the journey temptingly easy, but on the other hand I had visions (if, for instance, a 'bus should get bogged) of myself stranded in mid-forest, neither understanding nor understood, and with no one there to interpret. Part of the road was acknowledgedly sketchy. Also my time was limited by the knowledge of extra work thrown on the missionaries during my absence from Bangkok.

Back to Lampang, therefore, and onward tamely by rail to Chiengmai, instead of going by road to Chiengrai —one more pleasant memory picture in my Siamese gallery.

Lampang has much charm. The river runs just outside the Mission compound, or rather at that season there was the wide sandy course dotted with great teak logs left behind by the last rains : logs waiting for freshets, and more logs to come, logs by the hundred. A few years ago the little town's existence was threatened by a terrific jam just upstream, dynamited to avert the flood. It would have been thrilling to see the river in spate, but at that season only a shallow, narrowish

ENTRANCE TO THE QUEEN'S PALACE MANDALAY.

To face page 248.

stream bubbled over the stones almost lost in the width of its course.

On the opposite bank the houses, backing down to the stream's edge, are generally perched on piles, and many have palisades of tree trunks to take the wear and tear of the flood-carried trees. The better houses are built of beautifully fitted teak, and roofed with teak shingles, but there is an occasional regrettable mend in corrugated iron.

For outhouses and sheds a kind of thatch is used that I saw only in North Siam, great leaves of bastard teak being used as tiles. The heart-shaped leaves hang stem downwards and the points are bent back round a lath and pinned into the leaves again. Each row overlaps the last. While new they seem to make a good covering and the roof is an easy one to renew—it gives an attractive silver note among the teak buildings, reddish to nut-brown according to age and weathering.

In recollection my first vision of the little town is always of these very picturesque backs piled one against the other, and broken by endless little galleries and sheds. In the river itself all the usual activities are in process, fishing, washing clothes or beasts or bodies, and on our side of the stream the various Mission compounds with beautiful trees, especially some wonderful tamarinds.

Between the inhabitants of North and Central Siam the one great difference is in their staple food. The Northerners eat a glutinous rice cooked and served in baskets bottle-shaped with a narrowish neck and one scoops it out by the handful—a queer sensation to the novice. As the name implies the grains all stick together instead of having that fine separateness so much prized further south, and naturally the people of each district maintain that theirs is the only good and digestible food ! Many of the mountain tribes, when on expeditions, carry with them their basket of ready-cooked rice, and live on it, a handful at a time, supplementing it with other food if occasion offers. If there should be nothing else there is sure to be the northern equivalent for the betel chew, which is far less universal in the north than in the south. That which takes its place among the people is the leaf of a wild tea soaked in brine, and with this stimulant travellers walk for hours.

Of course both these northern specialities had to be tasted. Of the chew it can only be truly said that I found it less distasteful than the betel. My hostess generally took her meals apart from the school, but in order that I should taste the excellent rice in its correct setting we were invited by the Siamese staff and schoolgirls to a meal in their dining-hall. It was an outer room with walls and roof of cocoanut matting, and at that evening meal a most lovely outlook on a lacework of tropical growths blue-green in evening light against the jade yellow of the after-sunset sky.

CHAPTER XVIII

CHIENGMAI

On the railway line to Chiengmai there are several viaducts bridging whole valleys, fine specimens of pre-war German engineering. The rails run over open sleepers and the bridges are without any kind of parapet. The builder must have had a monkey's sense of balance, and only travellers with good heads can enjoy the wonderfully unimpeded view.

The Chiengmai Railway resthouse has a reputation for cleanliness and comfort; but I was fortunate in not having to put it to the test.

The picturesqueness expected of a royal town, the home of the Lao hereditary princes, still exists. Within the ramparts are fine temples, but the railway has had its inevitable levelling effect, and that approach to the town is nondescript and Westernised.

A last representative of her line, one of King Chulalongkorn's Queens, has returned to the home of her youth, but past are the wild, gay doings of which the older foresters can tell.

When the British first discovered the wealth of the Siamese teak forests, hitherto only tapped by the people of the country, the foresters' leader, in fun as in more serious business, was a latter-day adventurer of the heroic type whose memory and doings are still green among all but the youngest of the Europeans in

Siam. In his long and most varied career, to borrow an expressive French phrase, *il en a vu de toutes les couleurs*. For the monotonous and exceedingly isolated

PHYA NAK, WAT LUANG.

life led by foresters of a generation ago, much compensation was needed. The missionaries were isolated too, but except to the few who have mistaken their vocation, the life has the wonderful advantage of being an end in itself, its interest never flagging. Misfits occur, however. I came across several such turned trader in China.

The river at Chiengmai is of the same type as at Lampang and also the houses on its brink, but the town as a whole is infinitely more interesting, with some really fine temples. In my short stay there was not time to do much sketching, though considerate hospitality made everything as easy as possible. It added greatly to the interest of the temples in Chiengmai to have as guides my first hosts, American missionaries of long standing in the Lao country, able to converse with the priests, and on friendly terms with them.

A giant Diptocarp, detached and magnificent in the Wat Luang grounds, was a subject not to be missed. Locally it was known as the Bee Tree, for the great honeycombs on its limbs, so big as to be visible even in the sketch. Wonderful trees in the exuberance and remoteness of their lives, their high branches a refuge for birds and monkeys where no shot can reach them. At the same temple the doorway and its approach were guarded by Phya Nak and his twin, wonderfully entwined. Crested and terrible he is, and in spite of his extravagant jewels, very impressive.

Chiengmai is on approximately the same line as Prome in Burma, and many of the temples in this part of Siam have Burmese characteristics of over-ornamentation, especially as to the prachedi which flourish metal umbrella-crowns and streamers on their spires. Nevertheless one of the most beautifully Siamese and pure in line is in this neighbourhood at Lampoon. One of the ancient cities of Siam, like Ayuthia and Chiengmai, Lampoon seems to have moved ground with the years, leaving fields of remains behind it—chiefly armies of prachedi now partly taken back by the jungle. We went to Lampoon to see the great pilgrimage temple. It probably stands over some far older structure, for at its river edge the wall is brought up to the present ground level with the great blocks of laterite, beloved of the Khmer builders.

After visiting the temple we went on to seek amongst the forsaken remains for a monument of unusual shape and material, not of the ancient Khmer type though built of stone and ornamented with portrait statues. We discovered it too late to do more than admire it and some sweet-scented flowering shrubs and other vegetation round it, but on the way back a vision of the great golden prachedi at the temple made it imperative that that at any rate should be put down on paper. It stood out against a storm-cloud, forerunner of the expected rains, and was lit with a last gleam of the setting sun. The sun's light had already left the young rain trees in front, and their closed leaves seemed drawn aside that the sacred pile should be better seen—an effect quite unforgettable, and happily the return next day to do the necessary drawing was made easy for me. The gold on the Lampoon prachedi has at any rate the appearance of being over copper, and the whole tone is of wonderful depth and warmth.

The upland valley in which Chiengmai is situated is so broad as to be almost a plain, and it suffers much from heat contrasted in winter with cold quite sharp for the tropics. In the hot season many of the Europeans take refuge on the principal hill of the neighbourhood, Doi Sutep, 5,500 feet high. There is no hotel, so it is

THE BEE TREE. CHIENGMAI.

To face page 254.

only sought by those people who have built themselves houses there, and scarcity of water is a difficulty when choosing a site. Still it is the nearest approach to a hill station in Siam.

My hosts had a house overhanging a stream halfway up the mountain side. Trees embowered the stream, using it as a staircase, finding foothold on ledge above ledge of its rocky sides.

MOTHER AND CHILD.

An elephant had brought me in a luggage carrier from the foot of the hill, grumbling all the way that she alone had been taken away from the herd to work, humanlike making the most of her grievance when the other elephants joined us halfway up, and escorted us. After that they paddled in the stream while I sat and sketched them, and their riders pulled their headgear to a coquettish angle—they had got hold of old European hats—expecting to see a picture of themselves, but my pleasure in their beasts' great size seldom left the poor lads room to exist, or if any part of them chanced to get on to the paper, it was not the sacred head.

In the days of carriage exercise it was the constant refrain of their happy owners that the horses must not be 'kept standing.' Quite naturally nobody likes it, elephants less than anyone, it seems, so my sketches that day were few.

On then up to the level where the scent of the pines carried one home to England, wide valley view and winding river far below. The return by another way was changed by the tropic shower from a scramble to a slide, but dry clothes and excellent lunch both awaited us at the house, also welcome rest till the cool of the afternoon. The walk down to plain level and the motor drive through the ruin-dotted plain back to Chiengmai rounded off the excursion.

At the foot of Doi Su Tep was the only teak I saw at Chiengmai, numberless saplings with gigantic leaves —one measured over four spans, about a yard. Though Chiengmai is a celebrated teak centre the forests are two or three days' ride away, roads quickly degenerating into tracks, and I was greatly impressed to find how isolated foresters still are. My then hosts were daily expecting one of their men taken ill in the forest, at that time being brought into Chiengmai on a man-carried stretcher, days on the journey. But things were much worse a while ago. In his youth my host, on one of his forest tours, was attacked and bitten by a dog in the jungle. His suspicion that the animal was mad was confirmed at the next village. The animal belonged to one of the villagers, but as Buddhists may not take life the dog, being mad, was merely chased into the jungle. Pasteur had made his great application of the proverbial cure with the hair of the dog that bit, but inoculation against rabies was in its very early days. The nearest institute was at Saigon in Indo-China, and the difficulties of travel so great that six months elapsed before the patient could get there. And when at last

GETTING DINNER.

he reached Saigon—what a welcome ! The hospital was composed of a series of sheds, and in the verandah where the injections were administered the chances of his escape from a horrible death were written up large, for his comfort, under each patient's name.

The chances diminished rapidly, according to the time that had elapsed between bite and treatment. After six months the chances were naturally all against my friend—still, if he should survive the next two years he might consider himself safe !

Returning from this digression to present-day Chiengmai. It has real native crafts and shops where they can be seen in the making and bought. So that the tourist can bring home more than mere memories of landscape and temple : he can find souvenirs to carry off.

Chiengmai is a great centre for lacquer, very like the Burmese lacquer in type, and like the Pagan lacquer it was formerly all on a ground of red. Recently they too have branched out into red patterned with gold-leaf or gold-leaf on black, which, if not a return to an ancient fashion, must be an adaptation to small objects of the fine work often seen on the temple shutters and doors, and on the wonderful Wat bookcases, of which a remarkable collection is in the National Library at Bangkok. The frame of box, begging bowl, betel set, tray or what not, is made of fine laths of bamboo plaited, and the lacquer applied in successive coats. Great skill is required to make the perfect shape on so uneven a surface and to retain the elasticity which is much valued. The designs are mostly traditional, but it is fascinating to watch the workman's unerring precision in spacing them—beautiful freehand work.

Small bronze weights, now superseded, in the shape of fantastic birds, dog-lions or, best of all, elephants, are delightful treasures still to be bought. Although the artists must constantly see elephants they have no copied air, but seem as much part of the artists' inner vision and as full of life as the gods and goddesses on the temple walls in astonishing contrast to their representations of mere human beings. The beasts of my own particular herd range in height from one and a quarter inches to six-eighths of an inch.

Much silk is woven at Chiengmai, a good deal of it like Korat, but less heavy and rich. Moreover it is made in short lengths of a little over one and three-quarter yards for pasin, the panung is not worn among the Lao. The range of colours is exquisite but fugitive like most Eastern vegetable dyes. Besides native cottons an immense amount of mercerised cotton is imported from Burma and is woven. It was to a Chinese merchant's shop that I was taken, but the weaving is probably Lao as much as Chinese.

Other souvenirs that may be bought are earthenware bottles for water, and beautiful baskets. Those that specially pleased me were made for marketing or carrying goods, strong and light and made of finely plaited bamboo. They are quite different in character, material and shape from the many Bangkok baskets.

The European community at Chiengmai is small. It consists chiefly of men connected with the forests, missionaries, consuls, and men of law, and when I was there the club state of development had not long been reached. Some people still regretted the days when the various inhabitants received the rest in their homes in rotation, and the club-house was not.

The situation of the Club is particularly attractive, and it has a golf course, tennis courts and a polo ground. There is pleasantly little of the spirit of exclusion, inhabitants of Chiengmai of every nationality are eligible for membership. A few among the missionaries who felt that there were too many other calls on their money, abstained from joining in paying for games which they had not time to play.

Just at that period the gathering at the Club was considerably exercised over the advent of an English bride whose husband was a Chinese doctor. They had met at an English hospital where the Chinese had a staff appointment and she was a nurse. The bridegroom's family at Chiengmai was well known to everyone but not among the Asiatics obviously eligible as honorary members of the Club.

The lady had only met her husband in surroundings familiar to both, and it had probably not occurred to her that traditions are a matter of moment, nor how much she herself was their creature. Nothing was known of the bride's individual background, but nothing was more certain than that, racially, those of the families of bride and groom were at opposite poles, and also that the Chinese husband might be expected to sink back into that of his people with disconcerting rapidity.

The question at the Club was whether to do anything to welcome her, and the general kindliness decided that she must be given the freedom of the European group.

Although the young couple were to have a house of their own instead of living with the man's mother, as was customary, the ideas of her family-in-law with regard to privacy, for instance, would not be those to which an Englishwoman was accustomed, and the tests of her adaptability were sure to be many and unexpected. It is to be hoped that all went smoothly. All I heard, after a first meeting between her and some old Chiengmaians, was her disappointment at finding neither electric light nor cinema at Chiengmai ! My regretful departure for Bangkok hid the sequel.

GC .N PRACHEDI, LAMPOON.

To face page 260.

CHAPTER XIX

IN SOUTHERN SIAM

Petchaburi and Trang

King Mongkut, grandfather of the present monarch and of the late King his brother, is one of the most arresting figures in recent Siamese history.

On the death of his father in 1825 he was the rightful heir, but the throne had been seized by a half-brother, son of a lesser wife. Instead of conspiring against the intruder Chao Fa Mongkut retired to a monastery, taking his younger brother with him, and became a monk, and it was not till the death of the usurper twenty-six years later that at the age of forty-seven he ascended the throne.

A man of large mind, profound study of the Noble Eightfold Path in which he became deeply learned did not suffice him. He himself founded a rule which is still followed in many monasteries.

He learned English in order to be able to study manners of government and customs of the West, as well as its science. Mechanics and especially astronomy were a life interest; moreover, modern Siam owes her position among the nations to his open-minded benevolence. It was he who opened the kingdom, where since the seventeenth century foreigners had received little more than toleration, to free intercourse with foreign nations.

The traveller from the south may see a favourite palace of this great King where the train comes abreast of the station of Petchaburi. It stands at the summit of one of the little isolated limestone hills, outposts of the range further inland, on the left of the line just across some paddy fields. The palace is uninhabited now and anyone can stroll round it and see the fine view from the Observatory top. When I climbed there a monk with his attendant small boy was in possession, but there was room for us all. My guide on that occasion was a Siamese pupil-teacher from the Presbyterian American Mission School, and with her as interpreter we talked a little. The priest was from Pegu in South Burma, and travelling probably the greater part of the way on foot. He had a very few words of English, which he was glad to air, but they were nearly as hard to follow as the unknown tongue he spoke to my guide. He was delighted to sit for a rapid sketch, and my landscape sketch also greatly interested him, dry colours as they called the pastels always intrigued onlookers. From that height the view was across the deltaic plain to the sea's blue line in the east and southward; inland the plain was dotted with other lonely hills closed in by a delightfully fantastic limestone range just then purpled by thunder-clouds. Immediately at our feet paths bordered with old frangipani trees—the Temple Tree of Ceylon—in full bloom, made clear the outlines of the wooded hill, and springing from its lower head sharp spires of tall prachedi cut the sky. Perfect peace on the Observatory top; but as our shadow grew over the rest of the hill and it was time to descend, not even the intoxicating scent of the frangipani delayed our headlong flight down through the wood, where we were pursued by clouds of mosquitoes as by furies. I thought Bangkok had taught me all there was to know about mosquitoes, but at Petchaburi they are far worse, and I have never encountered them in larger hordes than on that wooded hill—no place to linger as darkness fell.

The ruins of a tower halfway up the hill, doubtless once a part of the palace *chemin de ronde* and now a bower of flowering frangipani, were ideal as a vantage ground from which to see the detail of the plain below. Endless paddy fields cut it into shapes roughly square, edged with palmyra palms, their straight stems springing from the dividing dykes. Sugar palms they are called in Siam, which does not seem to know the Kitoul palm common in Ceylon, whose juice and jaggari is so much sweeter. The Palmyra's dignity is almost rigid, but, although it has no patience with lolling cocoanut manners, on the dykes it is often forced by over-crowding in early youth to dip away from its fellows, straightening upwards when the pressure of the neighbouring great heads is removed.

At the foot of the hill is a little golf course where the tiny group of Westerners take their exercise.

It was in the hot weather that I visited Petchaburi, and most of the small company of American Presbyterian Missionaries in charge of the hospital, schools and church, were away at the sea. Of other occidentals there is at least one British railway inspector. Although I did not have the pleasure of meeting him, it is impossible to forget the delightful tale of how the unfortunate man had been singled out by a couple of elderly adventuresses. They were surely unique of their kind, for they arrived in Siam with red flannel nightdresses which buttoned to the neck ! I had already heard of them at Bangkok, on which they had descended with letters from a church dignitary—small blame to him for speeding them from his diocese—and quartered themselves on their victims, appropriating house, clothes and worried selves. The nightdresses were the only truly picturesque and redeeming touch. The way they swooped on the railway man at Petchaburi had almost passed into legend. In spite of protests they had taken absolute possession of his bungalow, ousting its owner, and were too comfortable to move when invited to go elsewhere. Memory fails me as to how long it took them to exhaust the interests of Petchaburi, but, as it will surely gratify them to know should they chance to read this true tale, they made history wherever they touched—a monument to commanding personality.

On the way back to the little town, at the foot of the hill and beyond the golf links, we crossed an avenue of fine mahogany trees. As white blossom crowned the hill above so here below was Poinciana round all the houses, flaming scarlet or crimson, and the most beautiful tree of all was in the Mission grounds. Its shape was the perfect dome, twigs falling from its summit in a thick rain, laden with gorgeous blossom and upheld by giant limbs. The group of Mission houses stood on the turning river's bank, so that the clustered town dwellings, bridge and boats upstream, were a constant entertainment. The doctor's house at which I was guest had the distinction of being the only one in Petchaburi 'screened' against mosquitoes. Unfortunately the floors were not so insect proof as doors and windows ! In that dry season the river was far below down steep banks, but after rains there are sometimes floods, and they are glad to be raised on piles.

Though Petchaburi is an ancient city it is pleasantly provincial, and in some respects primitive ; no electricity, for instance, so that evening lights meant evening roasting. It is conveniently easy there to pass from street into country lane or path through the paddy fields, all bone-dry just then, and there are several short excursions to be made in the neighbourhood. To the south-west in jungly fields some interesting Cambodian fragments are scattered, and in a low hill to the north-east are some celebrated caves.

These were probably the goal of my Pegu friend, for they are dedicated to the Holy One and are full of his statues. The caves in themselves are beautiful. Huge chambers in the limestone rock, they are hung with great stalactites which have combined in places with their stalagmite counterparts, and together make great pillars. The formations are of lighter colour than the parent rock, and variously tinted with streaks of pale red and green. The greatest of the caverns is lighted in the centre by Nature with a big round eye open to the sky, and lashed with overhanging trees. The sun, where it strikes the floor, turns the red tiles to scarlet, which reflect warm life into dark corners, turn by turn. Trying as I was to sketch, it moves with most disconcerting rapidity, its blinding finger pushing me further and further from my subject.

Hundreds of still figures enhance the cave's natural mystery ; they range in size from the colossal image, many times larger than life, that dominates the temple, to tiny models set in some stalagmite cavelet. The Great Buddha has his attendant rows of smaller replicas all meditating with him, but many and many an individual image preaches and meditates in the caves beside them. A famous statue is of Gautama's mother showing the Cesarian birth miraculous, more wonderful than beautiful. The figure that pleased me most was a Buddha in stone, seated, and at his feet the monkey and elephant of the sacred story, one offering

ELEPHANT AND MONKEY, PETCHABURI CAVES.

a honeycomb on a stick, and the other water in a gourd. One of the Jataka stories, they are full of instances of the recognition of holiness by the animals.

It was midday when we left the caves and wandered down through the trees to where our exceedingly ramshackle gharry and sad little horse waited. Roads are not many, nor indeed meant for anything much better hung than paddy carts. The only vehicles for hire in Petchaburi were gharries too bad for Bangkok, where they are being fast superseded by motor-cars. I saw no rickshas.

My hostess, who assisted her husband in his medical work, told me of some of the abuses they were struggling to overcome. She welcomed many a little Siamese into this sorrowful world, increasingly often as the courageous pioneers who first gave themselves into the foreigners' hands on such occasions reported the treatment they had received, and showed a quick recovery. To escape the roasting considered necessary in Siamese midwifery, for the newly-delivered mother —the unfortunate woman stretched on a plank and shut into a small room with a big fire—is in itself an alleviation, and rich and poor alike are glad to avail themselves of the missionaries' services.

The little hospital attracts the sick from far and wide. Besides the curing of bodies, Missionary enthusiasm, when disappointed of converts to the Christian faith, can at least look upon it as a seed-bed for the spirit of Christianity.

As all the world knows, in the American Presbyterian Church there is room for great differences in belief between the Fundamentalists, to whom the literal interpretation of the Bible is essential, and the Modernists, to whom it is precious to be able to reconcile the Word with scientific discovery. I stayed at Missions in various parts of Siam, and was struck with the fact that it was not always those with a scientific training who were the Modernists as to Bible teaching. In at least one centre I know that the Pastor was a Modernist, while the Doctor—a man of considerable scientific attainment—was a Fundamentalist.

Endless playing of Siamese *Mouvement perpétuel* airs on the circular instrument set with a series of small horizontal gongs of high pitch, called *Klong Lek*, was one of the intriguing things to be heard from the Petchaburi Mission. Happily, for they never seemed to cease, the sweet dropping sounds were very pleasant in the distance across the river. I came to the conclusion that it must be a master with pupils, but, if so, they were nearly as expert as he.

The little city is worth a wander. Wat Prakar, an ambitious beginning in an earlier reign, dominates the town, though it was never finished. One building in the temple group has the aspect of a great red-brick tower—a landmark above the clustered houses. At the time of my visit some sort of festival was toward, lending animation within, as did the market, interesting here as everywhere, without the temple grounds. The red tower can be seen from the Mission, and on the preceding evening, my sketching done, I had strolled towards it alone, but did not reach it. The road became less obvious, as one drew nearer, and it had been discouraging to see a man resting on his heels in front of his house, seize some stones and hurl them behind me just in time to check two big dogs making silently and swiftly for me. The ferocity of some of the South country dogs is notorious, but I had only encountered the type hideously noisy but easily driven off, which are much more startling though less dangerous.

The most unbelievable sunset I ever witnessed was at Petchaburi, and until an astronomer at home, when he saw its portrait, said : 'Oh ! a nacreous sky,' I had been glad that three missionary witnesses had been present, and could attest to the phenomenon.

We saw it above King Mongkut's hill. The sun was sinking behind thunder-clouds like piled rocks. In the upper sky were fantastically-shaped cloudlets, scattered broadcast—tatters of a badly torn rainbow they seemed by their colours, and across them the thunder-clouds spread great wings of shadow. I watched it from the raised centre of the fine old bridge in the middle of the little town, and noted the queer shapes. Later, on the Irrawaddy, I was to see hints of such rainbow clouds but never again so dramatic a display. The explanation is that the cloudlets, floating at a great height, are composed of particles of ice—hence the prismatic colours.

Plenty of entertainment for the wanderer in Petchaburi streets. In one weavers, both Chinese and Siamese, were at work within their shops, and without were stretching the newly-dressed, brightly-coloured cloths along the roadside to dry. There was a road in Bangkok where the same sight always pleased me, but here the houses, with steep roofs of thatch, were far more picturesque. The street had lately lost its chief beauty, fine trees, all cut down on account of the many robberies which took place with the help of their overhanging branches. One fine tamarind and a banyan were left. The banyan, a sacred tree, would in any case have been spared; as to the tamarind, I have heard, and heard it contradicted, that thieves fear the Phi whose home it is.

The Petchaburi visit was all too short. I found endless subjects to sketch, much friendliness in the Mission, and with its help much more possibility of getting glimpses of Siam at home than in my busy Bangkok days. I hold in admiring recollection the old artist I met at Petchaburi, whose works are mentioned in an earlier chapter.

My last days in Siam were spent at Trang, a beautiful corner of the extreme south, its charm enhanced by remoteness. When leaving the main line at 5.30 a.m., before the faintest streak of dawn, was one of the few occasions on which I found it a drawback to travel servantless. Not a coolie in sight, and so far as I have ever heard in no place but England can hand packages be left to take care of themselves. An American friend was immensely struck by our touching faith in the national honesty as shown on railway platforms, where unregistered luggage stands for the owner to pick out.

There are few places where it is unreasonable to look for an Englishman, and one was there who befriended and found me a coolie, and I was left free to present my letter to the station-master.

By the courtesy of a Siamese acquaintance in the railway department at Bangkok special arrangements had been made to deliver me from the tyranny of my luggage—that bane of travel. From Trang I was going by road across the famous Chong Pass to rejoin the main line at Patalung. The toy railway to Trang meanders from village to village, pleasantly close to the country. All around was the luscious growth only to be seen in the seasonless tropics and in hilly country. where the monsoons mean merely a slight increase in rains more or less constant. No dry weather here, and although further north by the first week in September the flowering season was long past, here, leaning over us, were great bushes of a kind of tree mallow (if memory serves) in full bloom, and in the grass groups of graceful ground orchid.

Tall hedges of a kind of tea were a feature of the Trang Mission, and among the many varieties of trees in that green land is nutmeg, great orchards of the handsome trees fruit-laden. The nutmeg we know is its kernel, and wears the mace of commerce stretched over it in a kind of lacework, bright red over dark, displayed when the fruit bursts open. The cream flesh is edible but the texture is rather unpleasant, and has the same strong taste as the mace and kernel.

Dark blue-green bushy trees, roughly pyramidal, hung with fruit ranging through greens to yellow often reddened, and often, too, slit open on to red and cream, recall some rich tapestry.

My invitation to Trang was from the headmistress of the girls' school, one young American lady alone in charge of the large school, with Siamese teachers to help her. True, the hospital, with the doctor and his family, were only a stone's-throw away, but she was alone in the house, and on one occasion disturbed a burglar at work. To keep her in mind of their possible depredations the gaol gongs sound every quarter of an hour, rung from sentry to sentry all round the enclosure on the hill above. Trang is the chief town of its province. The Governor's house overlooks the gaol on the hillside, and below, in the little city, is a large covered market. A great cotton weaving centre, the cloths have a different character to those seen further north. Men's fashions in shawl-sashes—for either use according to the weather, as shown on the various stalls—are very pleasing. I liked best the minute checks enriched with dots in several colours—red and yellow with purple dots or black, or else orange and yellow and many other variants, but red was generally the predominant colour.

There were gorgeous handkerchiefs, bright dark-blue on brilliant yellow is a favourite combination. The Siamese equivalent of 'Hurrah' repeated many times gives a good effect; there is an excellent *Krut* pattern and many others, but just now there is an unfortunate vogue for mercerised cottons which takes from the character of the cotton weaving. Matting is made of cocoanut leaf in coloured patterns, and there are a variety of attractive things, fruits and nuts well seasoned, as elsewhere, with a large sprinkling of European and American goods. There seem few corners of the globe to which their commerce does not penetrate.

Of three households in the Trang Mission only one had a motor-car. With true American hospitality its owners showed me the beautiful country round the town. The progressive Governor, certain that so attractive a place is destined to grow, has secured a pretty lake and the grounds around it as a public park, a rather surprising possession for a small Eastern town.

The finest excursion in the neighbourhood is to Chong, where a good road leads over the pass to Patalung—the road by which I was to leave Siam. The beauties of the pass are so well recognised that, at its foot, there is a group of little houses built in the lavish Eastern fashion for a royal visitor and his retinue. Paths had been made for the occasion and little bridges over the numberless streamlets that feed the main torrent. Now lesser people can sometimes get the loan of a house, and all who pass that way, and care to step off the main road, may use what remain of the bridges and paths. A motor-car can go as far as the lower fall, or could when I was there, though a corduroy bridge gave us some anxiety even then, and there is a *salà* where one may rest fascinated by the churning water.

We climbed up the remains of royal paths and circumvented decayed bridges to a point just below the great upper fall. I have seen finer waterfalls, but nowhere vegetation more exuberant, from the Lycopodium-like growth, Prussian-blue in the shadow at our feet, to the straight boles of the sun-seeking trees. It was a botanists' paradise, I was told, and easily believed it, with its innumerable ferns, besides hundreds of other specimens. There was no rain to spoil a perfect day.

My last farewell to Siam was from that lovely place when, two days later, after leaving Trang in the chill of earliest morning, at 4.30, by bright moonlight, we breakfasted at daybreak at the entrance to the pass. Then up through the gorgeous forest, and down again to Patalung, where, save from the train windows, my last sight of Siam was the huge limestone hill for which it is known.

Now that my face was set definitely homeward, regret at the prospect of so soon leaving the East took the upper hand against a weariness of great distances, which, for the past year, had been gaining on me.

Well ! there was still the Irrawaddy.

CHAPTER XX

BURMA

UNFORTUNATELY, although I cannot forbear a postscript about Burma, that engaging country is summed up for me in the Shway Dagohn and the changeful Irrawaddy.

I was in Rangoon at a moment of great difficulty for the Irrawaddy Flotilla Company, just then in the grip of a general strike. The whole river was in it, but as the Company had no rivals it could manage things in its own way, a plucky way. Whatever the rights and wrongs then at issue, its employees are said to be well treated. Dislocation was complete, but in spite of it the Company organised a makeshift service, and kept boats running until the strike was broken.

So, much against my will, I was held up at Rangoon for about a fortnight, and unluckily had neither friends nor introductions. My quarters at the Y.W.C.A. hostel were excellent, but to one who hates towns the neighbourhood was depressing. From the point of view of the girls for whom it exists, and their occupations, the situation is perfect, and for those who love to be among their fellow-creatures, there is endless interest in all that comes and goes in the narrow street. From my window I had glimpses of very varied life in the houses opposite, and there were sounds of their denizens of many nationalities at work, play and prayer. The last, Hindu I think, began in the very early hours !

THE SHWAY DAGOHN PAYAH. RANGOON.

To face page 274.

Fellow-women travelling alone, and anxious to avoid expensive hotels, may be glad to hear that it is also possible to get rooms at the G.F.S. on the hill outside the town. I stayed there happily on my return to Rangoon, but although air was fresher mosquitoes were much worse than in the town.

My first pilgrimage was to the Shway Dagohn Payah. It dominates the landscape as its prestige pervades all Buddhism, and small wonder. So sacred and beautiful a shrine in so perfect a position is arresting. Hours before landing I had been thrilled to see its golden gleam. It is easy to imagine the emotion of the millions of pilgrims who, since 1564, have brought offerings and prayers to the Payah as we see it to-day, and for long ages before to even earlier pagodas. Shwe Yoe in the *Burman* says:

'Buddhists fix the date of the erection of the Shway Dagohn Payah at 588 B.C., but the site must have been sacred for cycles before, since the relics of the three preceding Buddhas were found interred when the two Talaing brothers Poo (dove) and Tapaw (plenty) came, with their precious eight hairs to the Tehngoottara Hill.'

The Payah of 588 B.C. is said to have been only twenty-seven feet high, but was repeatedly encased until it reached its present magnificence and height of about 370 feet.

Modern history as well as legend circles round the Payah. One of the last events in connection with it was the struggle of King Mindoon Min to present the new Hti (honorific umbrella which crowns the spire), all gold and jewels and worth a fabulous sum, as his own personal gift. The British Government, well knowing that to allow the gift would be tacit recognition of his suzerainty, insisted that the offering must be national.

To-day, under its sheltering sanctity, subversive politics are said to flourish, protected by us, inasmuch as we do not interfere with the rules made by the monks for their sacred places.

The irony of the order 'Footwearing prohibited' (terse if not very English !), which is exhibited at every gate of every pagoda which Europeans might be expected to visit throughout Burma, lies in the fact that it was suggested by one of our own agitators, and is altogether foreign to the tolerance of the Buddhist spirit, and peculiar to modern Burma. Elsewhere the offer to remove one's shoes is sometimes accepted as an act of courtesy, never demanded as a right.

In the face of this attitude dignity deprived me of the sight of the interior grounds and wonderful courtyards and secondary shrines surrounding the Payah.

Hygiene reinforced dignity, for it was said that the *Hpungyi* (monks) insisted that stockings as well as shoes should be taken off, and that was not to be contemplated.

Gleaming gold and soaring lines made it imperative to add one more to the 1000 attempted sketches of the pagoda. The choice of a point of view was governed by wet afternoons and a desire to avoid including the elaborately over-ornamented and fretwork-ridden approaches to the shrine. Eventually the sketch was made from the east side, sitting on the floor of a second-class Tikka gharry with my feet on the step. Absurd boxes on wheels these gharries, with the driver more remote from his fare than a Hansom cabby, and without the communicating trapdoor. Although not a method to recommend, it had the merit of combining shade and isolation. There was an intriguing element of chance too in the uncertainty as to where the next jerk from the pony would take my point. I made the driver stand and kill what flies he could, but still the pony kicked.

That sketch finished I was impatient to be off and could not settle to work, indeed for some days I felt the Zoo to be my only refuge in a friendless world !

The lake of the sacred fish was another favourite spot, and as most people think it lugubrious they will gauge the depths of my depression ! Certainly the sight of the sacred fish hurling themselves by the hundred in squirming heaps upon the food that is thrown them, though amusing, is disgusting. But the little lake set with gorgeous diptocarps, under whose shade the monks' cells were a background to graceful growths fringing the water, made a sketch not to be missed.

It was only on my return to Rangoon, on my way to India, that the rather sophisticated beauty of the Royal Lakes prompted a sketch from the Boat-Club. Nowhere have I seen a Club to approach it in beauty of setting, but it is a type of beauty to suggest drop scenes of twenty years ago.

At long last a boat was announced to sail for Mandalay, and I rushed to book on it. It was early in the season, but it was reasonable to expect that because of the difficult service it might be crowded. Going on board overnight for an early morning start I felt faintly surprised at a certain lack of expectancy, and more so the next morning to find myself the only first class passenger. However, I reflected that the lower reaches of the river were not popular in these days of rushed travel, and that most travellers for Mandalay join the boat only at Prome.

There were delays at starting and we did not make anything like our scheduled run for the day, so that at dusk, instead of tying up for the night at a picturesque port as I had been led to expect, the Captain came up to navigate the ship by searchlight. Except for the boy who served me he was the first soul I had seen all day. Happy to be in the open again, the river interested me, and I had books and work, and did not mind solitude.

It was two or three days before any officer appeared at meals. When they came at last I learnt what a crew they had to shepherd, teach and direct, the rag-tag and bobtail of Rangoon. Not a single thing could be done as a matter of routine by men who, in every-day life, were gharry drivers, porters or any other kind who could be pressed into the service in the emergency. Virtually it was the officers, of whom only three, the Captain, First Officer and Engineer, were of pure British blood, who were doing the whole work of the ship. No time to entertain a passenger !

We were towing a flat of merchandise, or rather it was lashed alongside of us, a complication to landings already made difficult by constantly shifting sandbanks. The river's capricious changes are circumvented by carrying a pilot for very short distances, in relays. Each goes up and down the same stretch of water every few hours that he may note any change, as it occurs.

Big spaces are my chief recollection of the lower river. Near Rangoon great deltaic expanses and a tall golden pagoda. We circled round and round it for hours, though it seemed as though it were moving rather than we. Finally before we reached the Irrawaddy, it disappeared, and now the spaces were of water instead of green alluvial meadow. The meadows were there, but screened from us by a belt of fine trees. In those windswept lower reaches it was difficult to recognise any of them with certainty, storm-blasts had cut them into strange shapes. That same wind carried my pet drawing overboard, but on the other hand piled the sky with great columns of cloud, last remnants of the retiring monsoon. Theirs all the glory and importance of the world. Great tropic trees were dwarfed to insignificance by them. We stopped at ports and *Hpungyi Kyaungs* (monasteries), and golden pagodas were most wonderfully many, shining gold by day and circled with silver at night, for all those of any importance were ringed with electric lights.

Our first night on the river was towards the end of the Buddhist autumn festival at which the faithful present their robes to the priests. Illuminations form part of the celebrations, and the daintiest flotilla of glowing lanterns brought us news of the festival in mid-stream. First seen in the searchlight's long rays it seemed a flock of little water birds, and when the light moved away it was turned by the magic of the dark to shining lotus flowers, each with a lamp at its heart. They recalled those seen at Peking on the canal outside the Dung Pien Men at the Festival of Chung Yuang Chieh, the Chinese All Souls.

The various stops were characteristic and entertaining, though, as in all travel, we seemed deliberately to miss out that which was specially fascinating, for commercial interest controlled our stops. The wonderfully sculptured face of the cliff known as Gaudama Hill, for instance, is seen only from mid-stream and through field-glasses. Rows and rows of carved figures of all sizes, each in his niche is visible, and each of the size or in the attitude fancied by the Merit-Maker of olden days.

For four days without incident I had the saloon and deck to myself, then at Prome came an influx of seven men, four of them the roughest of American drillers bound for the oil fields, and farewell to quiet !

Rain and no time at Prome ; instead of the scheduled stop we had to press on, and I saw little besides the fascinating banks. Flat country was left behind, and the charm was now of wooded hills, pagoda-topped, sloping to the river. Often flights of white steps guarded at their base by fantastic monsters of the Lion-dog description, led upwards with smaller pagodas or rest-houses, or lesser shrines to break them, to that which crowned the hill.

After Prome almost every place we touched was full of pictures, if only there had been time for more than the quickest sketch. The first real opportunity came at Magwe. There a line of the characteristic Irrawaddy paddy boats with splendidly carved and coloured high prowlike sterns had settled themselves for my benefit !

Fine in line I never saw them really alive as boats only are under sail, for the winds had dropped. At anchor they looked like beautiful toys, and like rather cumbersome toys when rowed or poled along. In common with many boats in Further India they are of the gondola family, built to present the slightest possible resistance to a quickly flowing stream. It is curious that a build of boat peculiar to the still waters of the lagoons in Europe should be so frequently met

PADDY BOATS. MAGWE.

To face page 280.

with on the rapid rivers of the East—rivers subject, too, to sudden and violent storm.

As a friend was to meet me at Mandalay, and our boat with its ridiculous crew was late, I had considered landing at Mingyan and taking the train, but when I saw the place I was glad to have decided against that plan. In the then state of the river there was a long crossing by ferry boats which, for no special reason save that they were unique and fantastic, recalled Charon's. They were being poled from the bows, and the rather high stern was a pair of butterfly wings with a seat between—doubtless the steersman sat there when a sail was used. I have never anywhere seen such terrible ophthalmia as on that sandbank of fishermen's huts. It seemed as if one in every three of the people had lost an eye. Wisdom's provision seemingly, that dwellers on the banks of Styx should have the single eye.

There are many miles of winding river between Styx and Magwe, and after Magwe the first stop of importance had been Yenan Yaung. It is a landscape killed by earth's riches, the headquarters of the great petroleum industry in Burma. Instead of trees the hills are covered by a forest of derricks. They have a curious fascination, rather evil, as of the thorny flank of some unimaginable monster. Stern utilitarianism in complete physical contrast to the stupas crowning smiling hills a few miles away! Looking deeper, perhaps things made solely for merit are not absolutely free from commercial taint—if only tentative.

Splendour of the past and lasting beauty at Pagan. Sad to say the place of all on the river that left the deepest single impression remained perforce unvisited. Its numberless pagodas and the extraordinary diversity of their shapes, as I saw them on my upward journey, decided me to stop there on my way down. But difficulties remained too great. There is a rest-house where people with camping kit and servants, or at any rate a knowledge of Burmese, may stay. And, above all, they must have time. And time is money, and money occasionally lacking !

The Director-General of Archaeology in India, Mr. J. H. Marshall, in a note quoted by Scott O'Connor in *Mandalay* says :

. . . Pagan was the capital of the Burmese Empire when it reached the zenith of its power ; it is to Pagan that the religion of the people owes its greatest debt ; here that their art achieved its highest triumph ; and here that age has imparted to their monuments a beauty unequalled at any other site in Burmah. . . .

' For, by a fortunate coincidence, this city rose to eminence at the time when the sun of Buddhism was setting in India, and she absorbed much of the vitality of the religion that was sapped from the older country.'

Its end was tragic. Coming down the river from the north Kublai Khan's hosts vanquished the fair city and made it feudatory to the Chinese Empire. Yet, even to the sight of a traveller passing on a river boat, enough remains to show the wonderfully cosmopolitan character of its architecture, betokening the sanctuary given by Anawarata, the Asoka of Burma, to persecuted Buddhists from afar.

By some of us Pagan is remembered because, at its nearest stopping-place, Nyoungu, ' We bought those nice bits of gold lacquer. Wonderfully cheaper than in the Mandalay market.'

The best lacquer of Burma is made there, and the

MINGYAN, CHARON'S FERRY.

To face page 282.

women crowd on board with it to find buyers. Poor things, on that occasion I alone represented the whole genus!

Great expectation of beauty lies in the very name of Mandalay. Though its name is not enticing, Sagaing's pretty hills, pagoda-topped, seemed intended to prepare a fitting approach. Disillusion followed. From the river nothing of Mandalay is visible. There is a mud bank at the landing, and on the top of it trams. Possibly the mud that Mandalay chose to show us may be pleasanter than the dust for which it is famous.

Not till we reached the Fort did we begin to recognise the Mandalay of our imaginings. The long moat surrounds a wall four-square. It is supposedly for defence, but suggests an invitation to interior delights rather than the exclusion of enemies. Four-square and one and a quarter miles each way, it has four gates connecting it with the outer world by white bridges across the water. Minor gates open on the strip of land dividing the wall from the moat.

But that which distinguishes it from all else are the airy pavilions which rise above the gateways and between them, breaking the top line of the wall with their cheerful, many crotcheted roofs. The pavilions are dark red, each diminishing in a series of roofs to a sharp point. It must be their gaiety in contrast to the long solid line of a wall twenty-six feet high and nearly twenty-four feet thick that gives the Fort that enticing air of invitation.

The main supply of the town-people's drinking water is, we were told, the Lotus-filled moat. Under British municipal rule it had been kept clear, but the Burmese Municipal Council, then recently established as a first experiment in self-government, gave the lovely Lotus the freedom of the moat, a most beguiling sign of other lapses from the path of hygiene.

Within the Fort all was British regularity. The order was pleasant but withal a poor substitute for royal grandeur. Military quarters with neatly arranged gardens were utterly out of place, and the British Club was hardly in the same category as the late Queen's Palace. The comfortable Club was built on its present site when evacuated from the suite it had appropriated to its use in the Palace itself. Lord Curzon decreed its departure in response to a request from the Burmese, and the Palace is now, rightly, considered a national monument.

A wonderful setting for drama that Palace, and curiously difficult to reconcile with European ideas of a dwelling-place. The principal entrance faces east, over-topped by a many-staged spire, dark red roof above roof diminishing to a finial gemmed with flashing mirror. The roofs and their peaked corners and sham gables with the help of paint still make a brave show, although the teak shingles have been superseded by that same corrugated iron that 'entered into the soul of Burmah.'

Within, the magnificent teak columns overlaid with gold still stand, and the famous throne room is there, though desolate.

The cumulative effect of certain decorative details that in another setting might seem tawdry is harmonious. Green glass supports to a balustrade is an instance, I remember, which in the fierce heat of the dry zone must help towards a precious illusion of freshness.

As with some European fashions of times not very

far past, the Court dresses in the Museum are hard to picture filled with living and moving human beings, but it is easy enough to see the little Burmese ladies wandering in their water garden, a maze of shady islets.

The Palace is kept in repair, but apparently it was not worth while to re-roof the nearby *Kyaung* even with corrugated iron, and the attractive wooden buildings are slipping sideways in melancholy collapse; a picturesque decay in its quiet parklike surroundings, decked with graceful trees. It is happily easy to discount the various buildings standing all too close around it, but not visibly related to the central pile.

He who does not mind rough ground should walk on the Fort's enclosing wall, its gay pavilions and the moat below a foreground for the view of distant hills, the hills where are Maymyo and Gokteik. A terrific storm (out of season !) upset our plan of a night at Gokteik, to see the gorge and wonderful railway bridge, and we had only a glimpse of Maymyo on our return from Bhamo. Its cultivated charm, balm to those who come up from the heat of plain or forest, lacks the local character that would endear it to the traveller.

On Mandalay Hill it was amusing to move in just such a landscape as we had admired on our way upstream; numberless stairways broken by terraced shrines so arranged as to combine pleasure in the landscape and the line of winding river with opportunity for offering and worship. Immediately at our feet were the famed 450 pagodas. The Arakan Pagoda and the Queen's Kyaung are of great repute, but 'Footwearing Prohibited' forbids that I should speak of either.

As Mandalay became better known its charm grew, and I could have stayed on long, happy and busy, but the river called and in the upper reaches the strike was over.

We chose a cargo boat for our sail to Bhamo that we might stop as often as possible. It was very much smaller than the boat which had brought me so far, and the first class was nearly full for the first day's run. The saloon was large, but deck space very limited.

Stalls of cotton and silk were on the main boat's upper deck, the Bond Street, so to speak, as compared to the flats lashed to us on either side, one a Covent Garden and the other a New Oxford Street of a delightfully picturesque description. At every stop there was an invasion of villagers, as we were their travelling market.

Often there was time to land and walk about. The villages were generally attractive, and cleanly kept, and the vividly coloured groups of people were in bright contrast to the primitive dwellings. It was as interesting to view the river from the village, as the village from the river, and a colourful foreground made the water look even more fascinating from its banks.

A party left the boat at Thabeitkyin to visit the ruby mines at Mogok—one of the excursions we had to forgo for lack of camping kit and servants. We were nearing the edge of the tropics by then. Nights were cold and early morning mists delayed us. Time had to be made up by running after dark, and we were disappointed of our promised afternoons and evenings on shore. In compensation the searchlight gave us brilliant scenes of village gaiety. At one place the people pretended to be on the stage—all Burmans love a theatre—and danced in the ray's round eye.

As mists came clouds vanished, and the great after-

THE LAST OF THE MONSOON CLOUDS.

To face page 286.

monsoon cloudscapes of the lower river were no more, but night still came up as a visible wall of opaque blue growing quickly over the sky.

In the river sketch is one of the last of the great clouds with its vivid counterpart in the depths of the giant stream whose surface hurried by busy with swirls and unreflecting. The seeming island half-way to shore is a great raft of teak logs, and on it cabins for the men who have charge of its fortunes for the weeks and months of its journey downstream. When the raft gets stranded, as may happen, on a sandbank, it must await the next year's rise to continue its voyage. We passed several such wrecks on sandbanks alive with water birds of many kinds. Grotesque individually, pelicans are wonderful in flight or flotilla. There were rafts or raftlets waiting for a sufficiently great assembly at Shwegu, and on them we were entertained to see the people catching fish with their hands. A shoal had apparently become involved among the rafts, and leapt to clear the logs, but many of them landed on them instead, to their doom.

Possibly Shwegu is the most delightful of all the upper river townlets; it is a great centre for pottery, and better still for the sightseer, is wonderfully placed on a bend of the river and high on a steep bank. Beyond the pretty village there are shrines and pagodas and *Hpungyi Kyaung* approached through a grove of fine ficus of some upreaching variety, and from the pagodas a lovely view up and down the shining river.

The first defile, insignificant at that season, was already passed. The second above Shwegu is far grander, its characteristic feature one great perpendicular cliff rising sheer 800 feet out of the water (some authorities give 600 feet, but it is a pity to understate !). Many legends gather round it, but I believe that, as a matter of history, it was long a place of execution. Inducements were many to prisoners to go over the edge, and nature took charge of the rest. At its base is a pinnacle topped by a tiny pagoda. It looks a toy at the foot of the mighty cliff, but the climb up to it is said to be stiff, and great trees embower it.

As in other places where they grow huge diptocarps stand head and shoulders above the crowd of lesser greatness. Then they waved bare arms, for it was late October, the time of their wintering, and we had crossed the tropic of Cancer on the fourth day's sail from Mandalay. Midday was hot and sunny, but morning and evening we were glad of every wrap we possessed, especially when mist-bound. Not very long after the second defile Bhamo the elusive came into view full two hours before we reached it.

Its importance as southern gateway of the Middle Kingdom is not proclaimed in its aspect, and except for one street of Chinese shops its amenities are British.

A few miles behind the town rises the fine mountain barrier between Burma and China, and over it a track goes winding by which, for countless ages, mule caravans have passed backwards and forwards bringing tea and silver, and who knows what besides from far Cathay. The caravans assemble under spreading trees on a sandy camping ground by the river, and there the patient beasts have their burdens removed and piled after the arduous journey.

Is it possible that those people who see a rejuvenated Nationalist China in the near future foresee among its activities a crusade for the prevention of cruelty to

DAWN, LOADING WOOD ON THE UPPER IRRAWADDY.

To face page 288.

animals? The raw backs of caravan mules cry to Heaven.

At that spot the blue of China dominates, elsewhere Shans and Kachins, and of course Burmans abound. A small Brahmin temple was close by the camping ground—what did the Hindu there?

One of the sights of Bhamo is the small Chinese temple known as the Joss House. It serves as club, theatre, school, Place of Worship, and, last but far from least, storehouse for the Chinaman's coffin.

It is a place delightful to the eye from the circular entrance arch to the fantastic roofs as seen from the upper gallery of the inner court, which is the priests' garden—precious, indeed, but without the overdone artificiality often found in such places.

And from Bhamo, though we went no further towards China, there was a picnic by the frontier stream. As far as the driving road has gone, to the seventeenth mile, by car, and then walking to the swing bridge over rapids which are almost a waterfall. In the woods autumn was proclaimed by the bamboos about to winter, sheaves of pure gold like mounting fireworks against a vivid sky. It was easy to welcome autumn here on the eve of a return to the seasonless tropics.

Another delightful excursion was upstream to the Bombay-Burma Co.'s Camp for Sick Elephants, but, alas! the first defile still remains a land of heart's desire—one of the many, both East and West, so, after two days of the hospitality from residents which is showered on wayfarers in the far corners of the earth, and during which we learned all that we were missing by not staying longer at Bhamo, downstream again, and less than another three days ended our river-trip at Mandalay.

On the way back we stopped at Mingun to see the huge bell, said to be the biggest in the world, and the enormous foundations of the pagoda that was to have been the world's largest. King Bodawpya began it in 1795, but fear conquered pride. It was prophesied that at its completion the King would die, and the King, who loved life and would see good days, ceased to build. In his reign the great bell of eighty tons, twelve feet high and over sixteen feet across the lip was cast. The monster hangs in a small pavilion, not much more than clear of the ground. Round it sits a guard of ancient Buddhist nuns, to receive the alms of those who come to strike the bell.

The bell's tone is sweet and sonorous. It sounded our reluctant farewell to the great river, and shortly to Burma too, for the curse of travellers was upon us, and we must go.

GLOSSARY

APSARAS : Dancers of the Hindu Heavens.

GEOMANCERS : Diviners through Earth's lines.

HPUNGYI : Monks.

KYAUṄG : Monasteries.

HUTUNG : Lane.

KINORN : Birdmen.

KLONG : Canal.

KRUT : Garuda.

LINGAM : Symbol of Siva's creative power.

MEH : Miss.

NAI : Mr.

NORASING : Dog-lion.

NAGA : Serpent King in Hinduism.

PANUNG : Length of material twisted into seeming knickers, worn by both sexes in Further India.

PASIN : Short length of material worn folded skirtwise round the person by women.

PHI : Ghosts, spirits.

PRACHEDI : Stupa, Buddhist reliquary.

PRAPRANG : Hindu form of spire as opposed to Buddhist.

SALÀ : Shelter. Roof supported on columns.

SATANG : 100th part of a Tical.

STUPA : Buddhist reliquary, generally bell-shaped.

TEWADAS : Angels of the Hindu Heavens.

TICAL : Siamese dollar, roughly 2s.

T'INGZE : Roof supported on columns.

WAI : To revere with hands pressed palm to palm.

WAT : Monastery.

YAK : Giants.

INDEX

INDEX

INDEX

INDEX